CREATING THE CULTURE OF PEACE

May 24, 2024

Ambassador Anwarul K. Chowdhury has been a career diplomat and his responsibilities have included Permanent Representative of Bangladesh to the United Nations, UN Under-Secretary-General, President of UN Security Council, President of UNICEF Executive Board, and Senior Special Advisor to UN General Assembly President. He has received Honorary Doctorates and prestigious awards for his inspiring work on the culture of peace and women's equality including the U Thant Peace Award, UNESCO Gandhi Gold Medal for Culture of Peace, Spirit of the UN Award, University of Massachusetts Boston Chancellor's Medal for Global Leadership for Peace and 2018 Global Women's Peace Award. He is the Founder of New York-based NGO coalition, Global Movement for The Culture of Peace (GMCoP).

Daisaku Ikeda is President of Soka Gakkai International, a Buddhist organization with some twelve million adherents in 192 countries and regions throughout the world. A prolific author, poet, peace activist and educator, he is the author of numerous books on Buddhism, humanism and ethics, and received the United Nations Peace Award in 1983. His work to restore Chinese-Japanese relations as well as his contributions to the promotion of world peace, cultural exchange and education have been widely recognized. The world's academic community has awarded him more than 350 academic degrees.

CREATING THE CULTURE OF PEACE

A Clarion Call for Individual and Collective Transformation

ANWARUL K. CHOWDHURY
and
DAISAKU IKEDA

I.B.TAURIS
LONDON • NEW YORK • OXFORD • NEW DELHI • SYDNEY

Co-author Ambassador Chowdhury expresses special thanks to
Anando Chowdhury for the cover page support
and to Vicki Mokuria, Mikiko Otani and Hiro Sakurai for the
editorial/research assistance.

I.B. TAURIS
Bloomsbury Publishing Plc
50 Bedford Square, London, WC1B 3DP, UK
1385 Broadway, New York, NY 10018, USA

BLOOMSBURY, I.B. TAURIS and the I.B. Tauris logo are trademarks of Bloomsbury Publishing Plc

First published in Great Britain 2020

A catalogue record for this book is available from the British Library.

A catalog record for this book is available from the Library of Congress

IISBN: HB: 978-1-78831-326-1
       PB: 978-1-78831-327-8
       ePDF: 978-1-78673-570-6
       eBook: 978-1-78672-570-7

Typeset by Initial Typesetting Services, Edinburgh
Printed and bound in Great Britain

To find out more about our authors and books visit www.bloomsbury.com and sign up for our newsletters.

Contents

This publication commemorates
the 20th anniversary of the UN General Assembly's
pioneering resolution on the culture of Peace in 2019
and the 20th anniversary of the groundbreaking
UN Security Council Resolution 1325 on
Women and Peace and Security in 2020

ONE
Bangladesh Beginnings

────────

Ikeda: Ambassador Chowdhury, for many years at the United Nations, as a great leader of peace and humanity, and as a courageous, compassionate diplomat, you have worked tirelessly to create the culture of peace. I consider it a great honour to participate in a dialogue with a person who has devoted his noble life to global peace and the people's welfare. We first met in Tokyo at graduation ceremonies for Soka University and Soka Women's College on 19 March 2003, just one day before the Iraq War broke out. Because we were both pressed for time then, I am especially glad to have this chance to engage in a thorough discussion with you now.

Chowdhury: Those graduation ceremonies remain a wonderful memory for me. My wife and I would like to take this opportunity to thank you and Mrs Ikeda again for the inspiring experience, which we still cherish. Our frank and unpretentious exchanges were especially remarkable in helping me realize fully why you are so beloved and respected by so many around the world and why you have devoted your life to the cause of peace and human happiness.

On that occasion, you spoke in clear, simple, and candid terms. We struck a rapport very quickly and exchanged our experiences from the various stages of our lives. Because you are an individual with deep inner enlightenment, I always learn a very great deal from interactions, exchanges and discussions with you.

Ikeda: You are most kind to say so. I deeply appreciate your numerous invitations for me to visit the United Nations. When we met again in August 2006, you kindly urged me once more to visit.

I made my first visit to the UN Headquarters in New York in October 1960. Since then, I have formed friendly relations with secretaries-general and other leaders of the organization. We of the SGI have consistently considered the United Nations of central importance.

Chowdhury: I have repeatedly urged you to come back to the United Nations because the people of the world can learn so much from you as a man of peace and a consistent, long-time supporter of the world body. What you say and write are even more important today than nearly 50 years ago, when you last visited the United Nations. For instance, the annual peace proposals that you began issuing each January 26, starting in 1983, continue to intensify in value. In them, you have regularly stressed the importance and relevance of the United Nations and global cooperation. I know of no one who has done this both consistently and substantively for such a long time. Full of enriching thoughts, wonderful ideas and valuable suggestions, your peace proposals alone entitle you to a truly welcoming forum at the United Nations, where representatives of Member States, the Secretariat, civil society and the media can learn first-hand the essence of your message of peace and human development, which has inspired millions around the globe.

Ikeda: You are too generous in your praise. I am grateful to have a deeply understanding friend like you, and I hope to discuss the United Nations, the parliament of humanity, in great depth as we proceed. Given your many years of diligent struggle working with the United Nations for peace, the opportunity to discuss the nature and meaning of your work there in detail is in itself an important treasure for humanity.

Chowdhury: Thank you. The dialogue format that you have employed with leaders in various fields is a wonderful contribution to understanding you both as a man of peace and as a leader of humanity facing global issues crucially relevant to humankind. I believe whatever fire I have inside me to continue to work for humanity, to promote the culture of peace, to ensure women's rights, to guarantee children's rights, and to make the United Nations a better and more effective organization can find a place for expression, elaboration, and – I hope – action through my dialogue with you.

I am very touched by your enthusiasm in bringing together this tête-à-tête between us in such a thoughtful manner. The dialogue format is a wonderful way both for me personally to benefit from your thoughts and for us to share our views on the crucial issues facing humanity with a wider readership and audience.

Literary Fathers

Ikeda: I hope that in this dialogue, while examining your life and invaluable experiences, we can cover a wide range of issues, including the poetic spirit and culture, development and human rights, women in relation to peace and security, and youth and education in the twenty-first century. Let me start by asking about your background and childhood memories of Bangladesh.

You were born in the midst of World War II, on 5 February 1943, in Dhaka, now the capital of Bangladesh. At the time, your nation was still under British rule. In 1947, India and Pakistan won their independence from Britain, and at that point you lived in what was known as East Pakistan, which, together with West Pakistan, 1,100 miles away on the other side of India, made up the nation of Pakistan. The present name of your country, Bangladesh, means 'Country of Bengal/Land of Bengal'. Within the Bengal region on the Indian subcontinent, the eastern portion is Bangladesh, and the western portion is the Indian state of West Bengal.

When the two parts of Pakistan split [in 1971], your family decided to remain in Dhaka. What were your mother and father like? What kind of family life did you experience as a child?

Chowdhury: First, I want to thank you for asking about this part of my life, because it gives me a chance to recall many fond memories connected with my parents and my dear 'Golden Bengal'. I was their first child. I have one sister. The two of us received our parents' most careful attention but, thankfully, were never indulged.

As was traditional in Bangladesh at the time, many people – relatives, friends, even acquaintances – would come to stay for different durations at our house in a kind of big, extended family. My father's friends' children from our village or outlying areas would stay with us to pursue higher education or job opportunities. Since it was convenient in many ways, they would generally put up in our compound. My father considered it a natural obligation for us to look after them in place of their guardians. Though I have only one sibling, all these people, plus many, many cousins and distant relatives were like older brothers and sisters who exposed me to what college life and education were like. Early in childhood, my sister and I learned to interact with people in ways that greatly enhanced our learning on a variety of subjects, sharpened our communication skills, and developed empathy and compassion in us. We were very lucky to have parents who were open to others and who encouraged us to benefit from the diversity of other people's backgrounds. My mother in particular treated everyone as part of our family.

What was your family like?

Ikeda: I come from a large family of eight children. In those days, large families were common. We lived in Tokyo and were in the edible-seaweed business. I was the fifth child. When I was in fourth grade, my oldest brother – 12 years my senior – went to war.

Eventually, all four of my older brothers went, too. At the time, Japan was pursuing the foolish path of militarism.

My oldest brother, who I really looked up to, was discharged and then called up again. Before leaving for his second tour of duty, he told me: 'It's up to you now. Look after our parents and the younger kids.' Then he added, 'Daisaku, there's nothing noble about war'. This comment made a deep impression on me, especially at a time when so many people were glorifying war.

This brother died in battle. We only learned of his fate a year and nine months after the war ended. I shall always remember how grief-stricken my mother looked when she received word of his death. These experiences with war mark one of the starting points of my pacifist activities.

I understand that, in addition to being a government employee, your father was a prolific writer. What kind of interaction did he have with the students and other lodgers staying in your house?

Chowdhury: He would advise them, guide them, and tell them about the challenges of life and the importance of education. If somebody made a mistake or did something wrong, he would reprimand or discipline the person. But, more important, he would explain how error and wrongdoing could be avoided in the future. He always advised them to learn from mistakes. Observing him doing this had an educational effect on me, too. It was like living lessons.

Living among many people made me mature more quickly and take interest in things that ordinarily do not interest children. For example, though I did not understand much about them, I leafed through older students' serious books, magazines and journals. In this way, I became not only a passionate reader but also interested in a wide range of subjects.

In this context, my father had a great influence on me. He was a literary person par excellence. He was an avid reader with a taste for essays, poetry, fiction, nonfiction, historical books and auto-biographies. Though their content was mostly unintelligible to me, I enjoyed having full access to them. On special occasions, he would bring me children's books. These were eagerly awaited treats. Sometimes he surprised me by bringing home from his travels books that I least expected. Even in his old age, he kept this tradition for my children also. Now I do the same for my own grandchildren. Books are priceless in expanding the horizons of your mind, soul and intellect.

Ikeda: I also used to give my sons books as presents. On their birthdays, I would take them to a bookshop and tell them to select a number of books as their gift. In my own youth, I was a voracious reader, finding tremendous inspiration and spiritual nourishment in books. Japan's defeat in war had undermined our previous beliefs and called our value system into question, and we young people were hungry for new ideas. I still recall the happiness I derived from spending my hard-earned savings on books I wanted from the second-hand bookstores in the Kanda district of Tokyo.

Later, my mentor, Josei Toda, second Soka Gakkai president, lectured me on such classics of East and West as the Chinese novel *The Water Margin*, Alexandre Dumas' *The Count of Monte Cristo*, and Hall Caine's *The Eternal City*, as well as university-level texts in a variety of subjects. He always advised young people to set aside time for reading and thinking, and would rigorously query me on a daily basis about my reading. It is to this instruction by my mentor that I owe everything I am today. He would thunder against wasting time on cheap magazines and other worthless writing, warning that it would turn us into third- or fourth-rate human beings. He told us to read serious works and the classics, insisting that this was the way to develop character and become true leaders.

In recent years in Japan, young people have been reading much less and are missing out on the character formation and intellectual stimulation provided by good books. Many in Japan decry the ongoing decline in the culture of the written word.[1]

Chowdhury: I believe reading has a profound impact on building an individual's personality. Nothing can replace the special world that you create around you when you immerse yourself in a book in a quiet corner. Of course, modern technology has made it possible to have quick access to knowledge and printed matter. In today's fast paced life, such accessibility is very practical. My concern is that speed and access are depriving today's young people of the time and opportunity to absorb the serious matters of head and heart that influence the totality of the persona – they are, as you say, 'missing out on the character formation and intellectual stimulation'. I agree fully with your analysis of this very significant issue, and I would add that this unfortunate trend is emerging not only in Japan but also in other parts of the world.

Ikeda: This is why I have stressed that we revive the culture of the printed word as an essential way to bring depth of character and spiritual development to education today. But please continue your recollections of your parents.

Chowdhury: Among things that our parents taught my sister and me, one far-reaching lesson was how to treat other people. We always had domestic help to clean and cook, and our parents treated them all like members of the family. In addressing my sister and me, our helpers used Bangla words for *brother* and *sister*. Treating everybody equally therefore became very natural to us. Growing up in an environment of plurality and diversity had a profound impact in my life.

Children First

Ikeda: You have acknowledged the role your parents played in fostering in you at an early age the sympathy for the underprivileged, to whom you have referred as siblings living in all parts of the world. In keeping with these wonderful words, you have devoted your entire life to the neediest and most underprivileged. As Under-Secretary-General and High Representative for the Least Developed Countries, Landlocked Developing Countries and Small Island Developing States at the United Nations, you have won unsparing praise from all quarters for your noble, selfless efforts. Describing your commitment, you have said that you wake up every morning 'to see what needs to be done for the poorest nations of the world'.[2] The way you have put these words into dedicated, sincere action impresses me deeply.

What memories of your father are deeply engraved in you?

Chowdhury: Of many instances of his sense of solidarity with fellow beings, one especially vivid memory is connected with his efforts to bring some happiness into the lives of impoverished children. Once, when he was the administrative head of a sub-district in Bangladesh, he created a children's toy park and asked us all – my sister and me and our friends – to contribute some of our own toys. He said, 'You'll just throw them away after you've played with them for a while, but many poor children never even have the opportunity of touching playthings like these'. He put our used toys, plus some new ones he bought, in the toy park where anybody could play with them. For local poor families and their children, the park was a dream come true. I still remember being thrilled by going there with my father to watch the children playing – all smiles – in a place full of their joyful giggles.

When I started college, my father gave me the idea of donating all my childhood books – numbering hundreds – to create a children's reading corner at a public library. I am so happy that many children are enjoying the same books that kept me engaged for hours when I was young.

Ikeda: As president of the UNICEF Executive Board[3] and in numerous other capacities, you have worked tirelessly for children's happiness. I am moved to learn that one of your starting points was this joint effort with your father for the happiness of less privileged children when you were still a boy.

I proposed holding a World Children's Toys exhibition to delight and stimulate the imaginations of children around the globe. SGI members in many different countries contributed toys, and in September 1990, an exhibition was held in Tokyo. Since then, the exhibition has been held in 160 cities both in Japan and abroad, and more than 2.1 million people have viewed it. Featuring 1,000 toys from around the world, the exhibition has been enormously popular. I am grateful to UNICEF and to people in many regions for their cooperation in and support of this project.

Article 31 of the Convention on the Rights of the Child, adopted by the UN General Assembly in 1989, clearly cites the right of the child to play.[4] Adults need to summon the will and ingenuity to find ways to enable children to spread their creative wings and grow and develop through play.

To return to our discussion of your family, you once told me, 'From my mother, I inherited a commitment to work for others, to engage in dialogue with others, and a spirit of being open to other cultures'. Clearly, she treated all people the same and cared for them in a profoundly compassionate way.

Chowdhury: My sister and I had a very affectionate mother who was wholeheartedly attached to us. I think I was more attached to her than my sister was. But my mother could be very strict. My father rarely disciplined us, while, throughout our growing-up, Mother regularly told us what we could and should do and what we could and should *not* do. Still she was very, very caring and showed or told us about the need for compassion, for dealing with other people with understanding, and for being part of a bigger family, in which members must share things.

In her late years, after my sister and I became adults, Mother converted our garage into a kind of private school, where she taught reading and writing to homeless children from nearby streets and slums. This was one of the many things that she did to help others throughout her married life.

Religion that Elevates

Ikeda: She nobly exemplified the spirit of service to others. Coming from a Muslim family, what role did faith play in your youth?

Chowdhury: Faith was something that came naturally — to have faith in something, to believe in the Supreme Being, to believe in the Universe, to believe in faith itself as having a profound effect on our lives. The ability to believe in something much bigger than your existence creates confidence. If you believe in something — you may call it God, Allah, or Buddha — it creates an enormous confidence in you. That is significant. Most important, for me, my faith in humanity, in the goodness of humankind, is empowering and meaningful.

Ikeda: Religion should guide human beings in the direction of goodness and happiness. In a dialogue he and I conducted, the British historian Arnold J. Toynbee said,

> A future religion that is to bring into being, and to keep in being, a new civilization will have to be one that will enable mankind to contend with, and to overcome, the evils that are serious present threats to human survival.[5]

Religion exists to enable human beings to live in a humane way. It should enable us to uplift ourselves, so that we can overcome egoism and develop an expansive spirit of altruism. At no other time has there been a more urgent need for a religion and philosophy that can empower us to transform and elevate ourselves, so that we can strive for the happiness of ourselves and others alike.

Chowdhury: I agree generally with your contention. I believe strongly that all religions ask their believers to be better human beings – no religions want their followers to be bad or dishonest. I also believe all religions need to encourage their adherents to work for the good of humanity as a whole. It is unfortunate that religions have been and continue to be used and abused by society for selfish and vested interests. That is another dimension of the challenge the world of religion needs to address in addition to the impact of science and technology on human life.

Ikeda: While working against the kinds of social abuses of religion to which you refer, we of the SGI strive for a religion for the sake of human happiness. At a later stage in our dialogue, I hope we can discuss the role and significance of religion at greater length.

But at this point, let's return to your childhood. What kinds of games did you play? What was your sister, Anar Kali Yusuf, like?

Chowdhury: My sister and I got along well. We were supportive and protective of each other. She is more open in dealing with people and has a delightful personality. She was so well known in our neighbourhood that visitors looking for directions to our house had only to mention her name to a passer-by to find the way.

Although I played only soccer, or football as we call it, she played all sorts of games. Because I was generally more interested in books than in games, my cousins sometimes teased me and called me a bookworm. They were right – I would rather read indoors than play outside.

Ikeda: I can understand. Do you have other memorable recollections of your childhood?

Chowdhury: Well, when we were growing up, moving often from place to place was a reality in our family. As a government civil servant, my father was transferred to different posts and places at regular intervals. He would remain in one place for a year or two, then move on to another. Each time we moved, I changed schools – on one occasion, twice in one year – and had to make new friends.

But I was prepared to adjust and be comfortable with new places, new situations, new atmospheres, new surroundings and new friends. This habit of being constantly on the move persisted in my life as a diplomat travelling from place to place, country to country. The difference is that my movements involved more distant places. In my recent jobs, too, I have had to travel a great deal, either speaking up for my country or advocating for the most vulnerable countries of the world. Movement in pursuing new challenges has been part of my life, very much part of my personal culture.

Golden Bengal

Ikeda: The great Bengali poet Rabindranath Tagore praised your homeland of Bangladesh as 'My Golden Bengal' (Amar Shonar Bangla).[6] In your youth, in addition to the rich spiritual nourishment you received from books, the lush natural setting of Bangladesh must have exerted a powerful influence on you.

Chowdhury: Yes, it did. The nature of my motherland influenced me and my personality in a big way. They say that in every Bangla-speaking person abides a poet. This poetic spirit is bred in us by nature and the changes of the seasons. Nature is bountiful in my Shonar Bangla, or Golden Bengal in my language. Any seed tossed on the ground sprouts and grows. Although cyclones and floods can be destructive, the bounties of nature have given us soil so rich and fertile that Bangladesh was once known as the granary of the region.

Nature conditioned my mind. I loved the incessant downpours during the monsoon and the flowers that bloomed in the changed air of autumn. Summer brought us bounteous food, including mangoes and the jackfruit – a huge durian-like fruit in which the flesh-covered seeds constitute a kind of fruit within a fruit.

Ikeda: Most of our readers are probably not familiar with the jackfruit. I have read that it is the largest fruit in the world, not infrequently reaching lengths of more than 20 inches. Perhaps because of its size, in Japanese it is called *haramitsu*, the Sino-Japanese rendering of the Sanskrit *paramita*, meaning 'supreme'. The mango, on the other hand, is of course well known.

Chowdhury: For us, eating mangoes was a festive occasion. My father would bring home a basket full of different kinds of mangoes, and we would peel and devour them. Our hands and faces got messy, but, after a wash in a bowl of water, we would start eating again, losing count of how many. I still remember those fun-filled and stomach-filling experiences with my cousins and friends from my childhood.

Ikeda: That must have been a great treat for the children. What kinds of fruits did you enjoy in winter?

Chowdhury: The special winter treat was date palm juice. You nick the bark of the tree and insert a tube through which the sweet juice drips and is caught in an earthen bowl suspended on a rope. A molasses-like syrup can be made from that juice. Like my fellow villagers, I loved drinking it sweet, cold and refreshing on a winter morning. On autumn mornings, I used to take my father's advice and walk barefoot over the dew-laden dark green grass, enjoying the special sensation it produced on my feet.

Ikeda: It sounds delightful. My mentor, a great educator, used to say that children should be allowed to go into the countryside and walk barefoot on the earth. Lack of direct contact with the earth, he believed, made children frail and weakened their connection to life. A connection with the richness of nature is essential to forging an outstanding character and to fostering our full humanity. This is one reason why, instead of locating them in urban centres, I selected sites with fine natural surroundings for our Soka schools and Soka universities.[7]

As a child, I grew up playing in the sea and the fields, surrounded by the blessings of nature. I still vividly remember the magical sight of fireflies dancing in the night sky in summer and the dragonflies flitting about on autumn evenings. Such interactions with nature are formative experiences and invaluable lessons on the beauty and preciousness of life.

Chowdhury: I understand what you mean. For me, too, the splendours and variety of nature have taught me much, not all of which has been pleasant: for instance, the enforced inactivity during the Bangladesh monsoon season, when it can rain unabated for a number of days. Accepting nature was a part of our life, and the beauty and fury of nature have helped me appreciate much more beauty in general. It has affected my mind, heart and intellect, making me more compassionate, poetic, loving, creative, empathetic and imaginative.

Ikeda: I can understand why this would make you a great lover of poetry. The richness and beauty of nature in Bangladesh's natural environment are indeed so powerful as to make everyone living there a poet. Yours is a country of remarkable natural features, including the world's largest mangrove forest. I am reminded of the lovely scene described in Tagore's poem 'My Golden Bengal', adopted as the national anthem of Bangladesh:

My Bengal of Gold,
I love you.
Forever your skies,
Your air set my heart in tune
As if it were a flute.
In spring, O mother mine,
The fragrance from your mango groves
Makes me wild with joy,

Ah, what a thrill!
In autumn, O mother mine,
In the full blossomed paddy fields
I have seen spread all over sweet smiles.[8]

In November 1995, travelling from Nepal to Singapore, I stopped off in Bangladesh. The rainy season had just ended, and the dry season was setting in. I vividly remember taking a picture from the plane of the beautiful scene of water and greenery below as we set down at Hazrat Shahjalal International Airport in Dhaka.

Chowdhury: In 2006, at the Makiguchi Memorial Hall in Tokyo, I saw a beautiful photograph you had taken of my country's vast, natural expanse.

Ikeda: Unfortunately, global warming is raising sea levels, increasing hurricane intensity and causing huge stretches of land to be inundated, thus threatening the beautiful natural environment of Bangladesh and inflicting great harm on the population. As one who loves your country deeply, I am greatly pained by these developments. In addition, the twentieth century was a time of great turbulence and trials for your nation's people.

As a young man, motivated by love of your country, you decided to become a diplomat, and you played an important part in its struggle for independence.

In the succeeding conversations, I hope we can touch on your experiences and troubles during that struggle and modern Bangladesh's history and culture, and the outlook for its future.

TWO
The Struggle for Independence

Ikeda: A life of connecting with young people keeps one youthful, and a life dedicated to encouraging young people is sublimely admirable. In February 2008, you delivered a wonderful commemorative address on the occasion of the opening of the exhibition *Building a Culture of Peace for the Children of the World* at the SGI-USA Chicago Culture Center. Many of our young members have expressed to me their joy at having had the opportunity to speak with you informally following your address.

It is becoming increasingly important to build the culture of peace to serve as the foundation for the creation of a new global society. I thank you again for your warm understanding and support of the SGI in promoting the culture of peace.

Chowdhury: In my speech at Chicago, as you have done so often, I said emphatically that building the culture of peace is the most significant effort we need to make at this juncture of human history. Though the United Nations has been using the expression 'a culture of peace' in its resolutions and in its Declaration and Programme of Action on a Culture of Peace,[1] I believe the time has come to start referring to the initiative as *the* culture of peace – the reason being that the concept of the culture of peace articulated by the United

Nations and all its Member States and adopted by consensus at the General Assembly is the only such document that is accepted by all nations and their peoples. In view of this and to avoid any doubt about what I am advocating, I have been referring to it as *the* culture of peace.

As you know, the Chicago Culture Center is also the home of the Chicago Culture of Peace Resource Center, the fourth such centre in the United States.[2] The others are in New York, Los Angeles, and Honolulu. These centres are providing SGI members and the general public with wonderful opportunities to inculcate in themselves the essence of the culture of peace. SGI young people are the primary beneficiaries of these institutions. I thank you most wholeheart-edly for encouraging their establishment. I am always impressed by knowing first-hand the spirit and enthusiasm with which each young SGI member is being transformed into an agent of peace and non-violence, and a concerned global citizen. You have given them a mission that not only makes them capable persons but also contrib-utes to a better world.

Diplomatic Aspirations

Ikeda: Young people must be the focal point of the age. Knowing that we have no option but to entrust the future to them, I have dedi-cated myself to fostering youth and establishing a global network of youth. With youth, I hope to lead the way in making our world a better place in this new century. This is the perspective from which I intend to carry on our dialogue.

The twentieth century was an era of war and upheaval. Your homeland of Bangladesh achieved its cherished goal of independ-ence in December 1971 but only after a long series of tribulations. I understand that before Bangladeshi independence, you were a Pakistani diplomat. What prompted you to enter the diplomatic service?

Chowdhury: I received my master's in contemporary history from the University of Dhaka in 1964. In Pakistan at the time, countrywide examinations were held for recruitment into the civil service, the foreign service and various other government services like the police, accounting and so on. Candidates who placed at the top of the list got into the civil and foreign services. Foreign Service was my own preference, though my well-wishers wanted me to join the civil service because it commanded greater power and authority. But I was drawn toward the foreign service because of its greater opportunities for exposure to the world and for representing my country.

Ikeda: Where were you in 1971, when internal fighting broke out?[3]

Chowdhury: I was in India working as a diplomat. In 1969, I had been sent by the Pakistan government to India to work as a political officer at its mission in Kolkata (Calcutta), the capital city of the West Bengal state. The place was my preference, as I wanted to be close to Dhaka, where my parents lived. My diplomatic colleagues were surprised when I went so far as to plead with the senior officer to receive a Kolkata assignment. Unsuccessful at first, I finally arranged to swap my assignment to Vienna with a colleague who was being sent to Kolkata. People were amazed at my action, because Vienna was a much more comfortable and pleasant assignment than Kolkata, a provincial city of India. I made this decision for the sake of my parents.

Ikeda: I am touched by the great concern you demonstrated for your parents. I always urge young people to express sincere respect for their parents at every opportunity. Buddhism, too, teaches the importance of recompensing parents for the care they give us:

> Mount Sumeru is paltry in comparison to the towering debt you owe your father; the great ocean is shallow compared to the profoundness of the debt you owe your mother. You must bear in mind these debts you owe to your father and mother.[4]

It is the fundamental human way to take care of the parents who endure hardships to bring us up. No one who fails to be grateful and to repay benevolence can hope to help others. Indeed the creation of the culture of peace must start with a grateful attitude and good deeds in one's personal life.

Chowdhury: Going back to the struggle for the independence of Bangladesh, it started in March 1971, as I was completing two years on assignment in Kolkata. Though I was a diplomat working for the Pakistan government, I was deeply outraged by the Pakistani army's crackdown on the innocent people of East Pakistan, the territory that finally became the independent nation of Bangladesh.

With a distinct history, culture, and ethnicity, Bangladeshis constituted the majority of Pakistan's population. Though they had been at the forefront of Pakistan's own independence movement in 1947, the Bengalis were exploited in many ways and treated like second-class citizens. The senseless military crackdown on 25 March 1971 was the straw that broke the camel's back. On the next day, in a brave act of defiance, the people of Bangladesh responded by declaring independence.

Because their cause was just, and as an expression of my solidarity with the freedom fighters, I decided to join the liberation war of Bangladesh as a son of the soil. Since I was a diplomat, my efforts focused on mobilizing international support in favour of independence. I played a key role in the 'diplomatic struggle' that we waged throughout the world to muster the support of the international community in support of an independent Bangladesh.

The people of Bangladesh demanded independence because, notwithstanding their majority status, they lacked commensurate political power, economic progress, or representation in the public services. They came to consider themselves both marginalized and exploited.

The serious rift resulting from the need to select a state language for Pakistan hastened the process leading to independence. Urdu, the language of the western part of Pakistan, was imposed as the official language of Pakistan with no regard for the majority of the people living in the eastern part of Pakistan who spoke Bangla (Bengali). Students in Bangladesh protested vehemently, young lives were sacrificed for the cause of the mother language, and the seeds of Bangladesh's independence were sown.

Ikeda: You refer to the famous Bengali Language Movement (Bhasha Andolon). Language is the essential symbol of ethnic and cultural identity. In March 1948, Muhammad Ali Jinnah, first governor-general of Pakistan, and in January 1952, Khawaja Nazimuddin, prime minister, proclaimed Urdu as the country's sole national language. Against this unilateral decision, as you said, a resistance movement arose throughout East Pakistan, where Bengali was the predominant language.[5] Those were times of upheaval in Asia and the world. The Korean Peninsula was split into North and South Korea, and Berlin was divided into east and west sectors.

Risking Everything

Chowdhury: On 21 February 1952, students mainly from the University of Dhaka and neighbouring educational institutions took a central role in leading a mass protest march. This initiated full-scale separation from the Pakistan authorities. The Monument of Martyrs (Shaheed Minar), erected overnight by students to commemorate the victims of the Bhasha Andolon, later became a symbol of Bangladesh's yearning for freedom and self-assertion.

Ikeda: Every year, on 21 February, people gather by the thousands at the foot of the Shaheed Minar and recite poems on the theme of *ekushey* (21). Most famous of them is *Amar Bhaiyer Rokte Rangano Ekushey February* (My Brothers Blood Spattered 21 February) – adapted as the Language Movement's song – by the well-known writer Abdul Gaffar Choudhury. I find it deeply moving, but I am sure in Bangla it is even more powerful. In English, it begins:

Can I forget the twenty-first of February
incarnadined by the blood of my brother?
The twenty-first of February, built by the tears
of a hundred mothers robbed of their sons,
Can I ever forget it?[6]

Chowdhury: Every time I listen, the lyrics' intense emotionality overwhelms me. Gaffar Choudhury, whom I know and respect, has made a unique contribution to the liberation of Bangladesh with this patriotic song. I am delighted that you perceive the real essence of the poem. Though sad in its expressions, the song contributed tremendously to the people's resolve for independence. Inspired by the determination of the people of Bangladesh who, weary of long years of neglect and exploitation, had the courage to sacrifice their lives to preserve the identity and sanctity of their mother tongue, UNESCO and its Member States designated 21 February as International Mother Language Day,[7] which is celebrated in many countries as well as at the United Nations Headquarters in New York and UNESCO Headquarters in Paris.

Ikeda: That deeply significant memorial day demands renewed acknowledgement of the importance of mother tongues, for which people have been willing to lay down their lives.

Historical sources attest to the widening economic gap between East and West Pakistan. Whereas they started at about the same GDP (gross domestic product) level in 1947, by 1970, just before independence, West Pakistan was 60 per cent richer than East Pakistan. This gap, among other factors, contributed to growing dissatisfaction among the people that finally emerged as the struggle toward independence.

Chowdhury: As said earlier, the Bengalis in East Pakistan felt that they were being exploited by design, without any concern for their wellbeing and development prospects. Consequently, feelings of being discriminated against kept simmering in their hearts. A commonly mentioned instance of exploitation was the production and export of jute bags from East Pakistan – one of the two largest producers of jute in the world – which were used for sandbags in constructing bunkers for the troops during the Korean War. Big sales of these bags resulted in something of an export boom. The foreign exchange earned thereby, however, was spent in West Pakistan, while East Pakistan remained as impoverished and underdeveloped as ever.

Ikeda: From your position in Kolkata, you were able to know hour by hour the way the Bangladesh independence movement was progressing.

Chowdhury: Yes, I could get first-hand, up-to-date information and listen to numerous harrowing tales of escapees from the atrocities of the occupation forces on a daily basis. On 25 March 1971, the military's ruthless, unprovoked crackdown had an unexpected effect on the otherwise gentle-natured, poetry- and music-loving Bengalis. They rose in revolt as one nation, and the independence of Bangladesh was declared the next day, 26 March. Thousands joined the ranks of the *muktijoddah*, the Bangla word for *freedom fighters*, further fanning the fires of patriotism for the liberation of their motherland.

Our struggle for independence was much more than an internal conflict, a civil strife. It was a full-fledged war of liberation for Bangladesh against occupation forces. As a diplomat working at the Pakistan mission in Kolkata, which was close to the scene of the action, I saw hundreds of fleeing refugees and listened to their stories of atrocities. Soon after the 25 March crackdown, a friend came across the border from Dhaka to Kolkata and related to me in graphic details what had actually happened. After listening to him, I told myself that I could no longer represent the Pakistan government, which was cracking down on my people, on my nation. That decision changed everything, turning my life from the comfortable one of a diplomat to that of a protestor, a freedom fighter, who, instead of selling the 'positive image' of the Pakistan government, would be accusing it of committing genocide against our people. That was how it all started.

On 17 April 1971, Bangladesh liberation forces formed a government. The swearing-in ceremony took place inside the territory of Bangladesh at a village that came to be known as Mujibnagar after the name of the Father of the Nation, Sheikh Mujibur Rahman,[8] who is lovingly, affectionately and respectfully revered as Bangabandhu (Friend of Bengal). Once the government was officially formed, almost all of us Bengalis working in the Pakistan mission felt encouraged to express allegiance to it and to work openly and actively for the independence of our country.

Ikeda: From that time on, young as you were, and paying no heed to the personal risk involved, you gave up your diplomatic position and, establishing connections with comrades in many parts of the world, worked diligently to arouse international public opinion.

Chowdhury: I was responsible for the day-to-day running of the nucleus of the foreign ministry of the new government as well as engaged in convincing Bangladeshi diplomats from Pakistani missions in the United States, Japan, Europe, Asia and the Middle East to leave their positions and declare allegiance to the independent government of our own country. One by one, many of the Bengali diplomats joined in what was called Operation D ('defection' from Pakistani missions) coordinated by me during 1971. Month after month, Bengali diplomats openly announced their support for the liberation war and allegiance to the newly formed government of independent Bangladesh. Their actions had a very powerful public awareness impact and generated wide-ranging support bases in various parts of the world in favour of Bangladesh's sovereignty.

The rationale behind Operation D, which I operationalized, was that diplomats tend to be accustomed to a comfortable life and the avoidance of confrontation. There must be something fundamentally wrong to make them willingly give up their easy lifestyle. So when they did exactly that, their actions generated worldwide public opinion against the cruelty and inhumanity perpetrated on the people of Bangladesh and in favour of their right of self-determination.

Family United

Ikeda: You said that your parents were still in Dhaka at the time. How did they fare?

Chowdhury: After they learned of my intentions, they maintained as low a profile as possible in the neighbourhood and within the community. Once their whereabouts were known to Pakistani intelligence and their local collaborators, my parents were pressured to make me return to Dhaka. The intention was clear – once I returned, the Pakistani authorities would deal with me as a seditious, anti-government diplomat. Meanwhile the Pakistan government charged me with treason and branded me as a traitor. As a diplomat, I was said to have betrayed the country and its laws. In absentia, the authorities sentenced me to a very harsh punishment. This sentence, however, could not be carried out because I was out of their reach.

Even though they were under pressure, my parents knew full well that for me, under a court-imposed charge of treason, returning would be suicidal. I still have a copy of the Pakistani newspaper announcing the decision against me.

Collaborators of the Pakistani forces attacked and looted our home in Dhaka. Fortunately, forewarned by a friend, my parents had moved out a few days earlier. I felt sad that they had to suffer for my action. But they wholeheartedly respected my decision. I am very proud of them and what they endured for me.

Ikeda: A very moving story. Were you able to communicate with your parents? What words passed between you?

Chowdhury: I received no direct messages from them. In addition to being a public servant, my father the late Abdul Karim Chowdhury, was a distinguished literary person and a prolific writer on the British colonial period and on the historical dimensions of Indian and Pakistani independence as he perceived them. He also wrote about the role young people should play, asserting their linguistic, cultural and ethnic identity. Influenced by his powerful thinking, I developed strong support for the independent identity of the Bengalis, who were politically part of Pakistan, and for their desire to determine their own destiny. My mother, Anwara Karim Chowdhury (my first name was derived from hers) was a very kind, loving and compassionate person, shaping my personality in my early years. It was my parents' genes which keep working in me. Their lives continue to encourage my own immensely.

My parents' great forbearance supported me and encouraged me in my decision. I learned from friends that they fervently supported my work for the Bangladesh government in exile and prayed daily for my safety and for our success. They were concerned about the uncertain future that I embraced but not afraid for me. They felt that what I was doing was for a greater cause and were very, very supportive. I always felt that they were with me, inspiring me all the way.

Ikeda: For you, the fight for independence was also a kind of family triumph, because it was waged in unison with your parents. I understand that during the independence struggle, a broad-ranging movement among young people, especially students, arose.

Chowdhury: Yes. My most inspiring moments were when I saw young men and women dedicating themselves to the preservation of the identity, freedom and sovereignty of their motherland. Some of them took up arms to become freedom fighters; some of them engaged in other creative ways of encouraging and enhancing Bangladesh's independence movement.

Some of my friends formed a musical choir to boost the morale and strengthen the patriotic fervour of freedom fighters and the suffering people in general by performing all along the border areas. I would always eagerly await news from the freedom fighters brought to me by young people working as intermediaries between the war front and the government in exile. The glow of pride at serving their country that I saw in their eyes remains bright in my mind and always gives me reason to hope for a better future for Bangladesh.

Independence Achieved

Ikeda: Inspiring songs often play a part in movements that change history. The French national anthem *La Marseillaise* is a good example. My mentor often said that wherever people flourished, there has been song. The development of the Soka Gakkai, he added, would also be accompanied by the appearance of many new, inspiring songs. From the early stage of our development, songs have been an important part of our movement. I often joined other young people to sing for Mr Toda. Many of our songs were written by the members themselves. I myself, with my comrades in mind, have tried my hand at writing both the lyrics and melodies for some of our songs. Singing our songs fills us with the courage to press on in our struggle and unites us in our common cause. It has been a powerful shared experience for us.

I understand that, in addition to songs, theatre (known as *natok*) exerted a significant influence on the Bangladeshi independence movement – in particular, street theatre (*patha natok*) performances, held by the roadside without any formal stage. Travelling from town to town, freely created by the people themselves, these performances conveyed the significance of independence to the masses.

Spreading like wildfire, the movement arrived at a historic turning point in December 1971.

Chowdhury: We were expecting it at any time. On 3 December 1971, I joined a huge public gathering to hear Mrs Indira Gandhi, who was the prime minister of India at that time, present an elaborate rationale for India's support of Bangladesh's independence, detailing her talks with world leaders for a peaceful solution to the problem. That very night, a combination of Indian and Bangladeshi forces made a counterattack against Pakistan forces in what was Bangladesh territory. On the same day, Bhutan was the first country to establish diplomatic relations with Bangladesh as a sovereign state. India was the second nation to formally recognize Bangladesh, three days later.

Ikeda: This marked the outbreak of the third India–Pakistan war. Speaking of Indira Gandhi reminds me of my meeting with Prime Minister Rajiv Gandhi, her son, at the state guesthouse in Tokyo in November 1985, a year after Indira Gandhi fell to an assassin's bullet. I found him an imposing, intelligent young leader. He himself was assassinated by a terrorist in May 1991. I was shocked and saddened to hear of his death, and I remain on close terms with the family. The loss of a young leader with such a brilliant future ahead of him was truly regrettable.

Terrorism has become a despicable force for destruction around the globe, creating a constant stream of tragedies. The shocking assassination of Pakistani leader Benazir Bhutto in December 2007, for example, still remains fresh in our memories. We must break this cycle of hatred and violence, and build, through dialogue, a world in which peace and harmonious coexistence prevail. To accomplish this, world leaders must return to the fundamental point – the dignity of life – and work together in unity. I hope to discuss this point with you subsequently.

To return to Bangladesh, the day of the nation's independence finally arrived.

Chowdhury: Thirteen days later, on 16 December 1971, the Pakistani army surrendered publicly in Dhaka to the combined forces of Bangladesh and India. Bangladesh became a fully independent nation in an emotional and historic juncture for all Bangladeshis. It was a great inspiration for many of us to have an independent country for which to work and build its image as an emerging progressive nation.

I was delighted with the prospect of having a great opportunity to represent and serve my own independent country. Exhilarated by the liberation of our motherland, we were all determined to work hard to make our sovereign nation economically, politically and diplomatically viable and vibrant.

Upon his release from prison in Pakistan, the Father of the Nation returned to Bangladesh via London on 10 January 1972. I was one of the tens of thousands of people waiting to welcome him home as he returned to his free nation as a free man – a dream come true.

Ikeda: Bangladesh's poet laureate Shamsur Rahman gave voice to the joy of the event in a famous poem titled 'Freedom, You', which begins:

> *Freedom, you're*
> *the farmer amidst his fields, beaming face.*
> *Freedom, you're*
> *the village lass's lightsome swim in mid-day pond.*
> *Freedom, you're*
> *the sinewy muscles on a skilled workman's sun-bronzed arms.*[9]

The ardent hope for independence had finally been realized. But the glorious victory and the birth of the People's Republic of Bangladesh are said to have claimed about three million victims. You yourself have lamented that such great loss of life might have been avoided if the problem had been resolved through peaceful means. Was not this experience the starting point of your development as an advocate for the culture of peace and a champion of peace and humaneness?

Passion for Peace

Chowdhury: I am happy that you brought up this important aspect of the Bangladesh war of liberation. The human cost of our independence was enormous. A British journalist commented that if the price of freedom is blood, then Bangladesh paid more than enough. I was seriously moved and traumatized by what I saw and what I heard from fleeing refugees. Yes, it had a long-lasting impact on my future emphasis on multilateral cooperation for development.

My passion for and faith in the culture of peace has its foundation in three main elements – first, my parents, their values instilled in me, and my upbringing; second, the nature of Bangladesh with both its gentle and fiery faces; and, third, the liberation war of Bangladesh in all its dimensions.

The opportunity I had to work at the United Nations from the early days of Bangladesh's independence enabled me to understand that the culture of peace must be promoted on a global basis because all countries – big or small, rich or poor, new or old – stand to benefit from this absolutely essential human endeavour at the onset of the twenty-first century and the realization of this concept to ensure a peaceful and secure future for us all.

Ikeda: As we look at our world, we see that misery and unhappiness still exist in many places. I feel I can understand at least in part the degree of effort you have exerted in your profound dedication to promoting the culture of peace.

After independence, you began your work as a diplomat for your new nation.

Chowdhury: In June 1972, soon after celebrating the first anniversary of our independence, I completed my assignment in Kolkata. Soon after the United States recognized Bangladesh, I was sent to Washington, DC, to bolster our first embassy there. As I made the changeover from the life of a rebel diplomat to that of a regular one representing a new country, the driving spirit remained the same – promoting the case of an independent, impoverished Bangladesh to the world's richest and most powerful nation.

In August 1972, I arrived in New York with the special assignment to work for securing UN membership for Bangladesh. That was the beginning of my long 'love affair' with the United Nations. From that time till 2007, when I completed my last stint with the United Nations – for nearly four decades – I was immersed deeply in multi-lateral diplomacy either on behalf of my country or representing the world body.

Ikeda: I can envision the pride with which you made your brilliant start as a diplomat for your homeland. The opening of the Rahman poem I mentioned contains the line, 'Freedom, you're / Tagore's timeless poetry and everlasting lyrics'.[10] I certainly can understand the great pride the Bangladeshi people took in Bengali poet Rabindranath Tagore at the moment of their independence. The people sang Tagore's song 'My Golden Bengal' during the independence struggle and chose it as their national anthem.

Bangladesh was admitted to the United Nations in 1974. Your work to obtain the approval of the Security Council for Bangladesh's admission demonstrated your outstanding diplomatic abilities. With the United Nations as your stage, you dramatically embodied the importance of peaceful diplomacy.

Tagore, a great poet whom we both respect and love, and who exemplifies the Bengali soul, has encouraged and inspired you time and time again. In our next conversation, let's discuss Tagore and his works, with which you have been familiar since your youth.

THREE

Rabindranath Tagore, Poet of Humanity

Ikeda: Since my youth, I have loved reading the works of the great Rabindranath Tagore, which I have turned to over and over. I fondly remember opening his collected poems and reading passages aloud, so often that I memorized them.

> *With the storm as my friend, I do not fear his dreadful face.*
> *Let us go. Let us go now.*
> *I shall go, living and enduring winds and rains.*[1]

The stirring cry of Tagore's soul inspired my young heart, opening my eyes to new, profound worlds, providing me with tremendous courage and spiritual nourishment.

Chowdhury: I am absolutely moved by what you just said. It speaks so eloquently about the power of Tagore's writings and about your sensitivity. The ability of even translations of his poems to inspire a person from a faraway place, as you described, is a testament to his poetic genius. Although Tagore reached great heights in all literary genres, he was first and foremost a poet. As a mark of respect, we refer to him as Kobiguru, which in Bangla means poet-mentor. I would add here that his last name is in fact spelled Thakur, and we pronounce it that way. *Tagore* is an Anglicized version of Thakur.

When you and I met in August 2006, we had a most lively discussion – though not to our hearts' content – on Tagore's poetic spirit. I was delighted to learn that Tagore and his writing connect us as friends of the heart and soul.

Ikeda: Our discussion of Tagore was both enjoyable and meaningful. Soka University of Japan is graced with a statue of the great poet. Three metres tall, it is the work of celebrated Kolkata sculptors Gautam Pal and his father, K. C. Pal, and was given to Soka University by the Indian Council for Cultural Relations. On a visit to Soka University, Niranjan Desai, ICCR director, said the statue was presented to our university as a symbol of the Asian spirit.

Chowdhury: As Asians, we should be proud of Tagore's accomplishments and for the honour we feel in his having won the Nobel Prize in literature in 1913. His excellence sparkled in every field that he touched – music, drama, art, and, most impressively, in the area of educational reform. His spiritual message for humanity has eternal and universal appeal.

Poetry of Fearlessness

Ikeda: Tagore lifted his voice in a hymn of praise to existence and humanity. Far transcending any particular ideology or parochial nationalism, it is filled with a burgeoning compassion for all living beings. This is the very spirituality our present time needs most.

A discussion of Tagore is a discussion of his universal humanism and love for humanity. It is also, I have come to believe, a discussion of the culture of peace that is absolutely indispensable to our global society in the twenty-first century.

What aspects of his poetry do you find most appealing? Can you cite examples of his poetry that have deeply impressed you?

Chowdhury: One of his spiritual poems that has had an enduring impact on me is the following:

> *Where the mind is without fear and the head is held high;*
> *Where knowledge is free;*
> *Where the world has not been broken up*
> *into fragments by narrow domestic walls;*
> *Where words come out from the depth of truth;*
> *Where tireless striving stretches its arms towards perfection;*
> *Where the clear stream of reason*
> *has not lost its way into the dreary desert sand of dead habit;*
> *Where the mind is led forward by thee into ever-widening thought*
> *and action—*
> *Into that heaven of freedom, my Father, let my country awake.*[2]

Ikeda: These are famous lines from the collection *Gitanjali* (Song Offerings), and these are favourites of mine, too. I have quoted them in my speeches.

Chowdhury: This particular poem is of special significance for me because it deals with character and human spirit, with universalism and openness of mind. In 1983, Prime Minister Indira Gandhi of India came to the UN Headquarters in New York to receive the first-ever United Nations Population Award, which she jointly shared with Qian Xinzhong, the Chinese minister for health and family planning. At that time, I was the chairman of the intergovernmental committee that selected the laureates. Before the awards ceremony, we met and, realizing that I am from Bangladesh, Mrs Gandhi started talking about Tagore's poetry and her visits to Shantiniketan (Abode of Peace). She told me how fortunate I was in being able to read Tagore's works in his own language. In the course of our conversation, she also told me that, if she had had her way, India's national anthem would have been the poem I just quoted to you as my favourite. It was such a revelation to me, and I believe it would be to many.

Ikeda: Prime Minister Indira Gandhi studied at Tagore's school, Patha Bhavana, at Shantiniketan. No doubt she was deeply drawn to Tagore's poetry.

Many of the Indian leaders I have met – including former prime ministers Inder Kumar Gujral and Atal Bihari Vajpayee – love poetry and write it themselves. Unfortunately, there are not many Japanese politicians who share this trait.

The lines 'Where the world has not been broken up / into fragments by narrow domestic walls',[3] Tagore's heartfelt call for the harmony and peaceful coexistence of humanity, represent a sentiment that the leaders of today's world would do well to take deeply to heart.

Nature and Action

Chowdhury: I believe so, too. I think they should.

I read this poem first when I was still in primary school but only came to understand its full meaning and inner significance much later. From my student days to the present, whenever I read it, I am deeply inspired by its profound and spirit-uplifting thoughts.

Of course, his philosophical poems had a lasting impact on us. But we also loved his unique poems about nature, his poems about the seasons, his poems describing things like rivulets in rural Bengal, and his poems expressing love with intense delicacy and sensitivity. As a Bengali, I am always amazed at the way this man seemed to know and describe my own innermost feelings about love and spirituality. I think all Bengalis feel the same way. He was the quintessential Bengali writer about love as an emotion amongst his fellow Bangla speakers.

Ikeda: He is a treasure of whom you can be proud before the whole world. Tagore was born, the last of 14 children, in Kolkata on 7 May 1861. I visited India for the first time in February 1961, the centennial year of his birth. Travelling to Kolkata on that occasion, I was powerfully moved to see places associated with the great poet whose works had so deeply impressed me during my youth.

In February 1979, I visited Rabindra Bharati University, established on the centennial of Tagore's birth, on a mission of educational exchange. The home in which Tagore was born is located on the university campus. I received the strong impression that both the university's faculty and students loved Tagore's poetry and were committed to keeping his philosophy alive.

Three rivers flow through Bangladesh from their sources in the Himalayas. Tagore wrote of one of them, the Padma, a tributary of the Ganges, recalling his memories of visiting it as a child:

O Padma, my love,
We have met so often!

. . .

Sitting on your banks
So many times I have thought —
If I am born again in some far away land
And sailing on a boat along your wild currents
If I come to this place once more
Passing these villages, their meadows and trees
These sandy beaches, the crumbling banks
Won't they rekindle in my mind past memories
Lying deeply dormant in my consciousness?[4]

Tagore set his nature poems to music, and eventually these songs spread and became popular among the people of Bengal — including farmers, fishermen, the children. They are known as 'Tagore songs', and you can hear these songs everywhere in Bengal, from street corners to farmers' fields. What do you think is the principal reason for the continued popularity of Tagore's poetry among the Bangladeshis?

Chowdhury: First of course is the language. Tagore wrote in Bangla, the national language of Bangladesh, which has been recognized all over the world as the language of Tagore's writing and of the independence of the nation that spoke it.

Second, many of his best-known works were written in the territory of Bangladesh, where his family owned extensive landed property. He would travel around for days in large houseboats. He sat on the deck observing nature in all its splendour and writing many of his most loved poems.

Under the British Raj, we were all part of the same empire; the linguistic association and our pride in a man who was – and remains – the greatest, best-known, most prolific writer in Bengali make it natural for us to identify with him. Our shared sentiments, feelings, emotions and thoughts appear with such intensity in his poems, in his writings.

Ikeda: We Japanese, too, feel great pride in Tagore. The Japanese people were delighted in 1913, when he became the first Asian to win a Nobel Prize in literature for *Gitanjali*. In his five visits to Japan, he got to know the local people and travelled to the famous mountain resort of Karuizawa in Nagano Prefecture, where many go in the summer for a cool retreat. I have introduced Tagore's life and achievements to our young people on many occasions in my speeches and essays. Great poets and a rich spiritual culture are treasures of humanity that we must pass on to the future.

Chowdhury: In addition to the lines from *Gitanjali* that I shared earlier, many of his other poems strengthened my determination to speak out, to stand up for my principles, and to not allow my thoughts to be drowned in conventionalities. I always wanted to do things a little bit differently, a little bit proactively, a little bit passionately; in that sense, his poetry encouraged me, inspired me immensely.

Ikeda: These are indeed the sentiments of a man of action like you. During the struggle of your homeland for its independence, Tagore's poetry offered the people inspiration and support. For the people of Bangladesh, Tagore's work was like the morning light illuminating the spirit, the pealing of a bell of encouragement, and a rousing drum of courageous advancement in the quest for freedom.

Chowdhury: We champions of Bangladesh's independence especially derived great strength and encouragement from 'My Golden Bengal', which became our national anthem. During the war for independence, and even before it, whenever we heard this song, we all felt an inner patriotism for our country, for our people, for our culture and natural environment. That is why we always find it uplifting both emotionally and in terms of our spirit.

Restoring the Poetic Spirit

Ikeda: What is real glory for a nation? In the past, political, economic and military affairs have often been overemphasized. But, as the American poet Henry Wadsworth Longfellow said, the true glory of a nation is the scope of its spiritual strength; its intellectual dignity; and the 'height, depth, and purity' of its morality.[5] In the twenty-first century, a fundamental shift in emphasis to the qualities Longfellow lists is absolutely essential.

A beautiful poetic spirit indeed shines in your country. What does poetry mean for the people of Bangladesh?

Chowdhury: Bengalis are a sentimental, emotional and romantic people. Poetry is an expression of their emotions. Poetry gives meaning to our lives. At the same time, poems have aroused in us the spirit to fight against injustice and for our freedom and independence.

Poems set to music become songs, which provide us with an enormous emotional outlet. That is why poetry is very important in our lives, both as a nation and as individuals. Even farmers in the fields or boatmen plying their boats have songs or poems for encourage-ment, communication, and enjoyment. Poems and songs are very much part of our life.

Ikeda: A way of life constantly resounding with poetry is in itself an epic, a masterpiece.

One thing that has impressed me in my encounters with Tagore's poetry is that many of his poems are addressed to the people and to children. Because of his profound love for humanity, his poetry tran-scends religious and ethnic differences, time and space, and is loved by all. His great soul brings East and West together in a tightly forged bond.

Chowdhury: Tagore was also unique in creatively responding to the traditions of the West. He opened the doors for an intermingling of the best in the East and the West, thereby enriching not only cultur-ally, but also intellectually and spiritually.

Ikeda: While eloquently praising the beauty of nature and the seasons, Tagore, with a richly poetic spirit, stirringly extolled the great, eter-nal being at the foundation of all phenomena:

> The same stream of life that runs through my veins night and day runs through the world and dances in rhythmic meas-ures. It is the same life that shoots in joy through the dust of the earth in numberless blades of grass and breaks into tumultuous waves of leaves and flowers.[6]

The universal perception of life that pulses in Tagore's spirit, a kind of cosmic humanism, can be seen as a profoundly sympathetic, all-encompassing poetic spirit.

I have long advocated the need to revive such a poetic spirit in modern society. This perception of the eternal, subtle rhythm that permeates the self, the world and the entire universe has existed in the hearts of all true poets from time immemorial – and indeed, pulses in the depths of all human beings. It is frequently pointed out that our contemporary society faces a crisis of alienation, in which the powerful underlying connections between the self and the world, the individual and nature, and the individual and society, are in danger of being severed. Undeniably, this loss of a sense of oneness with nature and the universe is causing major social upheaval. This is why there is a powerful need to rouse a new global awareness and vigorously revive an abundant poetic spirit that will forge strong bonds reconnecting human beings with one another and with all things in the cosmos.

Chowdhury: Poetry and music have important roles in life as expressions of both our softer sentiments and our stronger emotions and determination. Mired in its complexity, modern life has somehow lost the love of poetry and these expressions of beauty. The restoration of poetic inspiration in modern society is necessary. We are all much too engaged in the rat race of material pursuits.

First we need to bring out our gentler, inner emotions through a restoration of poetic inspiration. Second we must realize that poetry makes everyone a vastly better human being. Poetry, I believe, evokes the finest in each of us. The ability to express emotion is a very powerful way of eliminating the negative nature of our personalities. Only poetry can achieve this. That is why there is a serious need for restoring poetry to its rightful place in our lives. I think that the poetic spirit and poetic inspiration affect society in an unmistakably positive way.

Ikeda: As a poet myself, I concur entirely. William Wordsworth, whom Rabindranath Tagore loved and respected, called the poet the 'rock of defence for human nature; an upholder and preserver'.[7] He also wrote, 'The Poet binds together by passion and knowledge the vast empire of human society, as it is spread over the whole earth, and over all times'.[8] A humanistic poet upholds human nature, forges ties binding human beings to one another, and articulates the underlying truth permeating humanity and the cosmos, sublimating it to the guiding spirit of the age. Such a poet also engages in the struggle for humanity and justice to triumph.

Chowdhury: Before we ever met, reading your poetry awakened my interest in you. I found a collection of your verses immensely appealing, and your beautiful nature photographs intensified my interest. I was further attracted by a series of your written works on philosophy, Soka education and the Soka Gakkai. I was encouraged especially by your annual peace proposals (see Conversation One). In other words, a good impression triggered by your poetry and photographs was strengthened by a close look into your philosophical writings and your peace proposals. I entered your world first by way of your poems, then by way of your beautiful photographic expressions. I was certain that only a truly remarkable and wonderful person would be capable of expressing things so beautifully, inspiring us and encouraging us.

Ikeda: I am humbled by your praise. Since my youth, it has always been my wish that as many people as possible be filled with hope for the future and successfully overcome life's trials. I especially want young people, as the leaders of the future, to triumph over their difficulties and hardships and grow into outstanding individuals. Based on this wish, I regularly present them with poetry I compose in both traditional Japanese styles such as *waka* and longer forms.

You have visited our Soka schools in Tokyo. The students themselves wrote the first four stanzas of their school song. I composed the fifth:

Oh, we can see Mount Fuji
from here, the Musashino Plain,
where flow mountain streams
as pure and fresh as we,
the phoenix fledglings.

For what purpose do we strive for peace?
To open up a brilliant way
for our beloved friends.
Let us spread our wings into the future,
both you and I.

I wrote this hoping that young people would reflect on their purpose in life and develop into persons of justice, doing their utmost for the happiness of others and world peace, and cultivating enduring friendships with a rich empathy for and appreciation of life. I am happy to say that they have exceeded my expectations, and a steady stream of capable individuals active in every arena has come from the Soka schools.

Some are diplomats, like you, active on the international stage, while others are scholars, educators, economists and political leaders. In these areas and many others, they have won the trust of their fellow citizens and are excelling in their chosen fields. I am absolutely overjoyed to witness their success.

Chowdhury: Your words of encouragement to young people are truly worthy of our wholehearted appreciation. Your spirited poems are a blessing for your young members.

I am disappointed that today's children are no longer required to memorize poems as we were in childhood. I believe that poetry should be part of our education, not just in schools, but also at colleges and universities. Poetry reading and comprehension should be universally recognized as part of our societal institutions. These days we arrange musical events, concerts; why not poetry readings? Poetry reading is becoming a dying art. Once poetry recitations and competitions were big events in which children participated with great enthusiasm. I believe that exposing young children to poems is an important way to ignite their creativity and inspire their imagination.

Tagore's Awakening

Ikeda: Familiarity with first-class poetry and cultivating an appreciation for poetry from a young age are extremely important in forging character and building a sound foundation for life.

At the age of 17, Tagore went to England to study English literature and music. During his stay – from 1878 to 1880 – he observed Western society in considerable depth and breadth, and he visited the British Parliament, where he heard Prime Minister William Gladstone speak. A short while after returning home, he published a poetic anthology titled *Sandhya Songeet* (Evening Songs), which was received with high praise. Though beautiful, a mood of melancholy and suffering dominates his verses of this period. Then, one morning in October 1882, as he stood looking out from his veranda, he reached a turning point. He expressed the joy he felt in the famous poem 'Nirjharer Swapnabhanga' (Awakening of the Waterfall).

My life has awakened from its sleep;
And the waters surge and swell.
Oh the desire of life and its urge
I cannot hold back. . . .
When life rouses itself with an unself-conscious joy
Neither darkness nor mighty boulders can block its path.[9]

Chowdhury: That was the moment in which Tagore, the great poet of the world, was born. At that particular moment, as the sun was rising, he suddenly experienced an inner awakening that made him feel that the world, nature, and humankind had been flooded by a universal wave of joy. A poet of humanity-at-large emerged.

You, too, have written a poem on the theme of a waterfall. A musical setting of your 'Verses of the Waterfall' was sung by a chorus at the Sounds of Joy concert held in late December 2007 in New York to celebrate your eightieth birthday. My children and I had the pleasure of attending and wishing you many happy returns of the day.

Ikeda: I am delighted that you mention it, and I thank you for the sincere, friendly greetings you made on that occasion. Actually, the poem was inspired by a cascading, clear, cold mountain fall I saw when I visited Oirase, Aomori Prefecture, in the northeastern part of Japan, in June 1971.

Like the waterfall, fierce,
like the waterfall, unflagging,
like the waterfall, unfearing,
like the waterfall, merrily,
like the waterfall, proudly,
a man should have the bearing of a king.[10]

Later, Soka Gakkai members set it to music, and it has been performed from time to time. I shall always remember how, in a speech nominating me to an honorary professorship at the University of Glasgow, in June 1994, the clerk of the university senate, J. Forbes Munro, concluded his remarks by reading that poem aloud.

But to return to our discussion, what aspects of Tagore's youth make an especially strong impression on you?

Chowdhury: His early poems were basically nature-related. His wonderful descriptions of nature are reminiscent of the feelings of many Bengalis. Whenever I went to my village home during holidays or on special occasions, it reminded me of many of his poems about the rural life and scenery. His trip to England, which you mentioned, widened his intellectual horizon in a big way. His musical settings for his own Bengali songs, a number of which are based on English folk tunes, are a wonderful blend of his association with England and his writings for us Bengalis. This gave him the freedom to create a new form. He once said, 'Only the weak are afraid to borrow because they knew that they never will be able to repay their debt in their own currency'.[11]

I think the greatest significance of his trip was the intellectual internationalization of his political beliefs and expressions. His experiences in England transformed him from a poet to an intellectual leader devoted to individual emancipation and to the emancipation of India from British colonial rule. We all benefited greatly from his reflections on his experience in his writings and songs.

Ikeda: As Tagore insisted, the more we deepen our knowledge, the better we can overcome obstacles that appear in our path and move forward. Refining his intellect and exchanging ideas with people from a different culture helped him break out of his shell and expand his horizons.

In addition to his encounters with Western civilization, his move to the Bangladesh village of Shilaidaha must be taken into account in discussing Tagore the poet. In 1891, at the age of 30, entrusted by his father with overseeing the family farming lands, he moved there. During his years there, sharing the villagers' lives, he developed greatly both as a poet and as a human being. In 1891, he wrote

A sudden longing came upon me . . . with a poet's song on my lips to float about the world on the crest of the rising tide, to sing it to men and subdue their hearts. . . . to burst forth through the world in life and youth like the eager rushing breezes.[12]

The Shilaidaha years were a highly productive period, during which Tagore wrote many works of prose, poetry and drama, including *Sonar Tari* (The Golden Boat, 1894); *Chitra* (a drama in verse, 1896); *Chaitali* (a collection of poems, 1896); *Galpoguchha* (a collection of short stories, 1900); *Kalpana* (Imagination: a collection of short stories, 1900); and *Kshanika* (The Fleeting One: a collection of poems, 1900).

As you say, this was the time when, with Bangladesh as his stage, Tagore's creative powers came into full bloom. Shilaidaha was also the place of refuge where, when he encountered life's sufferings, he could return for consolation and renew his sense of fulfilment in life.

Starting with the death from illness of his beloved wife in 1902, at the age of 41, Tagore lost several family members over the next five years. But, as is well known, he overcame his cruel trials to write such gemlike collections as *Gitanjali*.

Chowdhury: The loss of people close to him caused him great suffering and created a void in his life. The early deaths of his wife and two children were emotional traumas that he overcame through writing to express his emotions. The characters in his writing were derived from his personal experiences and reflected the intensity of his feelings. Perhaps this kind of exposition gave him a release and helped him overcome his challenges.

Ikeda: Confronting the greatest of sufferings – the loss of dearly loved ones – deepened Tagore's insight into the nature of life. Toynbee told me he was especially fond of Dante because, by creating great art, he converted his personal unhappiness into the good fortune of many people all over the world. Dante experienced the double misfortune of the premature death of his loved one and banishment from his native city, yet he overcame his sorrow, soaring to great heights and casting a great spiritual light illuminating humanity.

Sympathy for the Suffering

Chowdhury: Managing his father's estates, Tagore toured various parts of Bangladesh. The people and the landscape of Shilaidaha are closely linked to the poetry he wrote then. While travelling for days by boat on the mighty river Padma, he was able to view the river, its sandbanks, flora and fauna, sunrises and sunsets, the poverty and simplicity of the people who lived by the banks, and the passions that swayed them. All of these find their way into his writings, which till that time were basically created out of his own mind and his imagination. But now he had the opportunity to come close to the ordinary people and observe the life of the impoverished and their sufferings from close quarters. It was as if Kobiguru had descended from the world of the imagination to the real world.

Ikeda: Getting to understand the sufferings and misery of ordinary people, as you point out, opened his eyes to political, economic and social problems, and motivated him to become involved in trying to ameliorate them. Tagore did not indulge in romantic fantasies divorced from the people's lives; the poet's soul was tempered in the midst of the harsh realities of village life. He urged other poets to join him: 'Rise, O poet, and give voice to these dumb and stupefied faces, bring hope to these tired, emptied and broken hearts. Tell them to raise high their heads and stand united.'[13]

Later Tagore established an experimental agriculture development centre for the reform of village life. He also established a school and advanced the cause of educational reform. By speaking out against a variety of social injustices, he became active in broader social reform.

Chowdhury: The feudal system in agricultural Bangladesh was oppressive and inhumane. Most of the feudal lords were ruthless and totally indifferent to the poverty of the peasants. When Tagore observed their suffering, he understood and strongly sympathized. Some people claim that he himself was a part of the feudal system because his family had been big local landowners. Although born and raised in a feudal family, he felt closer to the suffering peasants. The main thrust of his prose pieces was to rectify oneself through principles derived from a humanistic outlook, to be self-reliant, and to do without the alms offered by the colonial rulers.

Ikeda: His youthful experiences in Bangladesh were of immense significance to him. Anger at and profound empathy with ordinary people's sufferings eventually empowered him to serve as a spiritual mainstay in the campaign for Indian independence.

In the next conversation, let's discuss Tagore's views — on education, the culture of peace, and religion for the sake of the people — which served as the foundation for his struggle as a reformer of his times.

FOUR
Education of the Whole Person

Ikeda: Tagore's heart was always with the young, and he felt tremendous gratitude for the fresh hope they continuously impart to humanity. This was his motivation for establishing a school at Shantiniketan and dedicating himself to education.

Visva-Bharati University is the successor to Tagore's school. In May 2006, we welcomed the university's vice chancellor, Sujit Kumar Basu, and his colleagues to Tokyo, and I enjoyed a friendly discussion with them. Though Soka University of Japan and Soka University of America do not have the long history and tradition of Visva-Bharati University, Vice Chancellor Basu said that our shared commitment to Tagore's educational ideals and the hope of fulfilling the dream of world peace gave him a strong sense of the link among three institutions.

Chowdhury: That is a wonderful way of recognizing the close intellectual affinity among these educational institutions. I have visited both Soka University of Japan and Soka University of America. I am amazed to note how close the Soka University of America campus is to Santa Barbara, California, the place where, in 1916, Tagore conceptualized the total-personality educational principles he was to apply at his own Visva-Bharati. The name of his university means the communion of the world (*visva*) with India (*bharati*) and symbolizes his hope of connecting India to the whole planet. The institution chose for its motto the Vedic text '*Yatra visvam bhavatieka nidam*' (where the whole world makes a home in a single nest).

A key objective of Visva-Bharati University is to 'study the mind of man in its realization of different aspects of truth from diverse points of view'. It also seeks to

> realize in a common fellowship of study the meeting of the East and the West and thus ultimately to strengthen the fundamental conditions of world peace through the free communication of ideas between the two hemispheres.[1]

I find this connection fascinating.

Ikeda: Tagore's visit to Santa Barbara followed his first trip to Japan. It was a time when imperialism was sweeping the world, and World War I had just broken out two years before, in 1914. With the sound of soldiers' marching feet echoing throughout the world, Tagore addressed the wrongs of imperialism and courageously expounded the path humanity ought to follow. It was during this journey that he arrived at his new ideas about education.

Chowdhury: It was in this part of the United States that Tagore conceived the idea that the study of humanities – or learning in general – should be based on knowing about humanity and intended for humanity. I see a close similarity between his ideas on humanity and humanism and your own philosophy and that of the value-creating education of the Soka school system. I am deeply impressed by Tagore's insistence that education must transcend national and regional boundaries. In today's world, we must realize that the object of education must not be limited to domestic or even regional concerns only.

Ikeda: In the early twentieth century, when Tagore was highly active, the first president of the Soka Gakkai and father of Soka (value-creating) education, Tsunesaburo Makiguchi, was advocating a humanistic, educational philosophy for peace and sound moral values. I can't help but feel that some wondrous connection has led to the friendship that has now been established, roughly a century later, between Soka University of Japan and Visva-Bharati University.

Investing his own money in the project, Tagore founded his school in the shal and mango groves of Shantiniketan in 1901, the first year of the twentieth century. A journey of a thousand miles begins with a single step – it was at first a modest undertaking, with just five teachers, including Tagore himself, and five pupils. People who could not understand what he was doing criticized the school as the poet's caprice. When the school experienced financial difficulties, Tagore sold some of his property and his book collection; his wife sacrificed her jewellery to help.

From this beginning, Visva-Bharati University developed. I find the history of hardship that Tagore faced in establishing the school deeply moving. Shantiniketan, I understand, is just a two-hour train ride from Kolkata, where you served as a diplomat.

Chowdhury: Shantiniketan is located in a rural setting about 100 miles by road from Kolkata, where I served as a diplomat. It was my first diplomatic assignment abroad, after joining the foreign service in 1967.

In 1921, two decades after the start of Shantiniketan, Tagore set up in a nearby village the Institute for Rural Reconstruction, which he later renamed Shriniketan (Abode of Wealth). That institute and Shantiniketan constitute the two campuses of the Visva-Bharati University, which I visited in 1971. The serenity and tranquillity of the place are striking. Many classes there are conducted outdoors in the shade of big banyan trees, encouraging a harmonious relationship between humans and nature. Some students study music, drama and other performing arts. Others specialize in painting or sculpture. My visit there was spiritually uplifting for me and had a long-lasting impact.

I would like to underscore one point here. Tagore's innovative and far-sighted educational concept has been overshadowed by his global recognition as a poet, as a man of literature. He was truly a pioneer in the field of education. He was one of the earliest thinkers to conceptualize for himself and put in practice principles of education that have now been accepted as a worthwhile educational theory, though not yet fully in practice. I believe that our future generations would be better equipped to face the challenges of an increasingly globalized world if we could understand the significance of his principles and reflect them in all levels of educational reform efforts.

What Tagore has contributed in the field of education is sufficient to rank him as one of the great nation-builders of South Asia. It is said that Mahatma Gandhi adopted the scheme of teaching through crafts many years after Tagore had worked it out at Shantiniketan.

Ikeda: Tagore looked to education as a source of light to dispel the darkness of his times. His vision is firmly upheld today in the educational values of Visva-Bharati University: education of the whole human being; education in harmony with nature; fusion of learning and art; open relations with the local community; an India-wide and international outlook; fusion of Eastern and Western cultures; and the quest for a universal religion for all humanity that transcends sectarianism.

In the spring of 2008, a group of Soka University of Japan students travelling to India on a language-study programme visited Visva-Bharati University. They all spoke with appreciation of the warm welcome they received and the wonderful learning environment there.

Tagore wrote, 'The main object of teaching is not to give explanations but to knock at the doors of the mind'.[2] By its very nature, education should develop human beings' limitless potential and draw out their creative powers.

The education to which Tagore was subjected in his youth, however, sought to force the pupil into a standard mould, and Tagore rejected it. As is well known, he stopped attending school altogether at the age of 14. Tagore's educational philosophy, which originated in his negative schooling experiences and subsequent desire to create a school of his own, has much to offer us today.

Nature as Teacher

Chowdhury: When you make that point, I think of your own remarkable words: 'Education deals with the essence of what it means to be human. No undertaking is more valuable, more sacred.'[3]

For Tagore, the development of the whole personality, not the acquisition of information, graduation, or an academic degree, was the most important goal of education. His philosophy lays special stress on this point. He also emphasized the importance of closeness to nature, from which we can learn much about human strength, weakness, courage and endurance.

He used his own distinctive teaching methods, which to a considerable extent are carried out in the Soka education system, too. A few examples come to mind. The first is that both teaching methods concern themselves with helping students gain a vast global perspective. The second is that both teaching methods encourage students to develop their inner creativity and also provide students with a much broader education than a traditional educational system does.

By the way, I am sure that, during their trip, the students from Soka University enjoyed visiting Shantiniketan's Nippon-Bhavana (Japan House), which helps Visva-Bharati enrich its international character and strengthen the cultural bond between Japan and India.

We must realize that learning through activity and practical understanding is more real than learning through the written word. Education is much more than academic knowledge. It has been rightly said that wholesome education consists in training all the senses along with the mind, not in cramming the brain with memorized knowledge. In Tagore's own words, 'The tendency in modern civilization is to make the world uniform. . . . Let the mind be universal. The individual should not be sacrificed.'[4]

I believe all of us, particularly those dealing with our education systems, need to internalize the thoughts that you expressed at the Rajiv Gandhi Institute for Contemporary Studies in New Delhi in 1997:

> Education makes us free. . . . It is through education that we are liberated from powerlessness, from the burden of mistrust directed against ourselves. . . . The individual who has been liberated from self-doubt, who has learned to trust in him- or herself, is naturally able to believe in the latent capacities of others. . . . Education enables us to look beyond superficial difference to perceive the great earth, the great sea of life that sustains us all.[5]

Ikeda: I am grateful for your warm understanding. As you say, nature is the supreme life-teacher. In his great work *A Geography of Human Life*, Tsunesaburo Makiguchi offered a pioneering ecological vision and examined the influence of nature on character formation from many different angles.[6] This is, as I said before, one of our reasons for choosing wooded, suburban sites for the Soka schools, Soka University and Soka University of America.

Soka education consistently strives for the all-round development of individuals, fostering their ability to contribute to humanity and create value conducive to peace. The humanistic education to which we subscribe is an attempt to redress the unbalanced emphasis on mere information unmediated by wisdom, prevent the unfettered expansion of egotism, and halt the runaway advancement of science that has lost sight of its moral compass and its true purpose of contributing to human welfare.

Chowdhury: You are absolutely right in your rationale for Soka education. Tagore strove to cultivate the whole human being and proposed basing teaching methods more on practical activities than on written words alone. His schools were a conscious repudiation of the system introduced into India by the British colonialists. Simplicity was a cardinal principle for him. Through it, he wanted to enable each student to live a fulfilling life. Opportunities were made available for stimulating and sustaining the myriad potentials and faculties of the human personality.

Forever for Justice

Ikeda: In 1916, speaking of the school he had founded, Tagore wrote, 'The victory-banner of the universal man will be unfurled here'.[7] Just as he prophesied, young people gathered from all over the world, and many outstanding figures were educated there, among them Dr G. Ramachandran, Mahatma Gandhi's senior disciple; Dr B. N. Pande, former vice chairperson of the Gandhi Memorial Hall; Prime Minister Indira Gandhi; and Amartya Sen, Nobel Prize laureate in economics.

Dr Sen is famous around the world as an economist attempting to combat poverty. Tagore gave him the first name *Amartya*, which means 'eternal'. Dr Sen's maternal grandfather, Kshiti Mohan Sen, was a close associate of Rabindranath Tagore and accompanied Tagore on his visit to Japan in 1924.

Dr Sen has said with great emphasis that Tagore believed leaving injustice uncorrected is in itself unjust. In a similar vein, President Makiguchi proclaimed that those who see evil but pretend not to, thus refusing to combat it, are complicit in the evil. As Japan pursued a headlong course into militarism, he consistently spoke out for justice and ultimately died in prison for doing so. His courageous spiritual struggle and unbending fidelity to his convictions are the eternal starting point of our SGI activities. I constantly insist that young people in particular must have the fighting spirit and commitment to justice to combat evil.

Chowdhury: Developing the resolve to combat injustice is the first step toward a just and fair world. We must work to oppose and correct injustice wherever it occurs because allowing it to slide by amounts to violating justice.

Tagore insisted that truth cannot be forbearing in the face of evil. I agree with both him and you. You believe and emphatically say that education must train heroes not of war but of peace. Your belief connects you and Tagore. His philosophy was that the power of the strong lies in the protection of the weak. I, too, firmly believe that protecting the weak, vulnerable and defenceless is a true manifestation of strength in nations and in individuals alike.

The reverse is not true: bullies are decidedly not strong. Bullying of any kind or type reveals weakness, not strength. Tagore's pedagogy laid great emphasis on fostering caring and compassionate attitudes, which education must reflect.

Ikeda: The late Dr B. N. Pande, whom I mentioned earlier and with whom I had several warm conversations, took pride in having studied at Shantiniketan. To him, Tagore was a great man of universality and abundant humanity. Whenever Tagore was at the school, Dr Pande said he would sit at the great poet's feet and receive his direct instruction, which cultivated his insight and broadened his intellectual horizons immeasurably.[8] Dr Pande's voice as he recounted this rang with pride in having lived out a life of great struggles in accord with Tagore's teachings.

Tagore firmly believed that life's ultimate truth, as well as academic learning, can only be conveyed through the mentor–disciple relationship; establishing this relationship between teachers and pupils was his prime objective for founding the university.[9] Dr Pande's recollections vividly communicated the beautiful mentor–disciple method of learning.

Chowdhury: Tagore believed deeply that the mentor–disciple relation is extremely important to character formation, as well as to both learning and teaching. People learn from other people, particularly from mentors. In the olden days, teaching about life and the skills involved in living was conducted on a one-to-one basis between a teacher and a disciple. Tagore wanted to recreate that time-tested tradition. To him, the teacher was the source of all learning, not only of formal education but also of life philosophy, emotional expression, and the ability to face life's challenges. He felt that the teacher has much more to give than merely advising on reading materials and formal education. At Visva-Bharati, teachers and students shared a single integral socio-cultural life, as they do now at the Soka Universities.

To Continually Learn

Ikeda: Speaking of the teacher, in an expression of his famous pedagogic philosophy, Tagore wrote: 'A teacher can never truly teach unless he is still learning himself. A lamp can never light another lamp unless it continues to burn its own flame.'[10] 'He (a teacher) will do himself credit only if he can put life into his pupils with his own life, light their lamps with his own learning, and make them happy with his affection.'[11] Educators today should bear these thoughts in mind always. Education must never involve compulsion or coercion. The true spirit of teaching is learning together with one's students, drawing out each one's inherent powers, and striving tirelessly to enable the student to surpass the teacher.

Chowdhury: Many of Tagore's philosophical writings and religious thoughts are connected with the Hindu scriptures, a very important part of which is the Vedic teaching. The concluding part of the Veda, called the Vedanta, discusses life, spirituality, the nature of god and the nature of belief. The same content appears in the Upanishads, the title of which means 'sitting down beside somebody'. This is actually the manifestation of the mentor–disciple relationship; the disciple sits at the feet of the mentor and learns from him. Many of Tagore's writings are related to the Upanishads, from which he derived philosophical inspiration.

The hectic and complex modern world, however, has neither the energy nor the leisure for the time-honoured mentor–disciple relationship, which Tagore nonetheless wanted to revive, as it was critically important in developing personality. That is why I think he would have been horrified if he had known about computer learning or the long-distance learning now often used. Maybe modern social and societal needs are pushing us in this direction.

Ikeda: Obviously teaching methods and forms may change with the times. But the quintessence of education, which Tagore strove to revive through the mentor–disciple relationship, does not – indeed, must not – change.

Religion of Man

Chowdhury: Another significant point deserves our attention. In my understanding, religion did influence Tagore in a positive and wonderful way.

Ikeda: Tagore's views on religion are very instructive. He called his religion a 'religion of man'. He sought a religion that proclaims human dignity, and he opposed discrimination of any kind, under any circumstances. What kind of religion do you think Tagore meant by the words *religion of man*?

Chowdhury: It means service for humanity. That is the essence. I think that to contribute to humanity, to be of service to humanity in general and individuals in particular, should be the objective of every human being – man and woman. It is not the ritualistic demonstration of one's faith, it is one's conviction that he or she is here in this world to serve humanity, because we are all an integral component of it. If we can contribute to humanity in whatever way we can – small or big, then the purpose of our life is fulfilled. That is the value of our life. Born as a human being, each of us bears a responsibility to our fellow human beings, to our planet. That is how I explain the phrase *religion of man*.

Ikeda: Though born and raised in the Hindu tradition, Tagore's religious views were extremely open-minded. As he often said, he held Shakyamuni in high regard. In a passage that deeply impressed me as a young man, Tagore wrote:

> Shakyamuni made man a great being. . . . Shakyamuni revealed man's innate strength and tried to bring about blessings and happiness from within man rather than seeking them in Heaven. With deep respect and affection for humanity, Shakyamuni praised wisdom, power, zeal, and other qualities inherent in man. In this way, he proclaimed that man is not a trifle, a miserable being buffeted by destiny.[12]

Chowdhury: Well, to be more specific, Tagore's father was a leader of the Brahmo Samaj, which was a new religious sect in nineteenth-century Bengal relating deeply with the Upanishads. Tagore grew up as a Brahmo, educated at home, in a much more open, non-traditional setting.

The statement you quoted expresses an extremely important aspect of what Tagore wrote of Shakyamuni and about the connection between the two of them. Religion, including Hinduism, Buddhism and Islam, had an effect on Tagore's writing, philosophy and spiritual growth. In his treatise *The Religion of Man*, he describes his Bengali family as the product of 'a confluence of three cultures: Hindu, Mohammedan, and British'.[13] Many find this intriguing, but to me, the most meaningful point is that he assumed a very broad and open attitude toward religion.

Ikeda: I understand what you mean. Whenever I hear the words *religion of man*, I am reminded of a famous incident in the life of Shakyamuni. Once a sick man lay suffering and abandoned by all. Observing him, Shakyamuni relieved his pain by stroking his soiled body with his own hands. He then changed the mat on which the man lay, washed him, and clothed him in fresh garments. When people asked why he had done so much, Shakyamuni replied, 'If you would serve the Buddha, care for the sick'.[14] To me, this is the distillation of Shakyamuni's view of religion.

Chowdhury: There is a similar well-known incident concerning Mahatma Gandhi.

Ikeda: Yes, to a visiting missionary who asked him what his faith was, Gandhi pointed to two sick people in the room and said, 'To serve is my religion. I do not worry about the future.'[15] Tagore, too, taught that we must serve the ill, the poor and the suffering.

Though Gandhi and Tagore had many differences of opinion, they were in deep agreement, transcending all their disagreements, on dedication to the happiness of all human beings.

Chowdhury: Tagore gave precedence to universalism over the goals of individual nations. Consequently, he and Gandhi did not see eye to eye on several issues like Gandhi's nationalism and the Purna Swaraj movement for Indian independence.[16] Nonetheless, Tagore always had great respect for Gandhi's philosophy and for his struggle for Indian freedom. It was in fact Tagore who gave Gandhi the title *mahatma*, or 'great soul', which is now applied to him the world over. The two of them were fundamentally connected on the wider plane of life view and the desire to serve and contribute to the wellbeing of humanity. In addition, both of them sensed the immense value of education.

Ikeda: Gandhi showed great respect for Tagore by calling him *gurudev*, or 'holy master'.

What contributions do you think religion should make to society in the future; what actions should it undertake?

Chowdhury: All religions must adopt as a fundamental doctrine the realization of their mission to serve humanity as a whole. Such a mission should be apparent in all aspects of life and work. Religions must teach how to live in ways that are useful to others even in such apparently minor ways as helping the blind or disabled to cross streets. The world would be a far better place of mutual support if we all strove to be of use to one another.

Unfortunately, religion today seems to be losing its essential spirituality. I find this very disappointing and disturbing. The fundamental spirit of religion should be to contribute to the building of the culture of peace. The mutual understanding, tolerance, and respect for diversity that are part of the culture of peace can be attained only when serving humanity in its true sense is the goal of all religions and their followers.

Ikeda: I have conducted dialogues with numerous world leaders and intellectuals of many faiths, including Christianity, Islam, Hinduism and Judaism. Though they may express it in differing ways, I believe that most of the world's religions seek the attainment of world peace and human happiness. In the East, in particular, it has traditionally been believed that the discovery of the sacred within each of us reinforces this spirit of service to humanity. Tagore keenly observed, 'Human beings can rely on their own power only if they realize that the universal law is inherent in themselves'.[17] This resonates deeply with the Buddhist teaching that an unsurpassed, supremely respect-worthy and noble light shines within each of us, in the depths of our being.

One of the special features of Buddhism is its revelation of the eternal, universal Law that pulses vibrantly within all life. Dr Toynbee also expressed a keen interest in this. All individuals, through their faith and practice, can transform their self, their family, their society, and eventually the entire world, reorienting everything in a positive direction. This is the principle of human revolution that is our guideline in the SGI.

As you point out, today most religions have become fossilized, lost their vitality, and are unable to carry out their true mission. We of the SGI are, as I noted earlier (see Conversation One), engaged in a grassroots people's movement based on a return to the starting point of Buddhism – as a religion for the sake of human beings.

Chowdhury: Human revolution is extremely critical for the progress of humankind and should be the goal of all religions. Their role and responsibility are to enable and empower each individual to develop in a positive way. If they fail to fulfil that, they lose the essential meaning and basic purpose of religion. Religion is not a ritual – it is a way of life. It is the quest for vitality, humanism, self-reform and self-empowerment.

All kinds of inner senses – positive, profound and negative, evil ones as well – go into the making of a human personality. The human being must be empowered to manifest positive impulses and to control negative instincts. While suppressing evil aspects, we must evoke good ones.

Greater Inclusiveness

Ikeda: Religion must exist for the sake of human beings, not the established powers or authorities. We of the SGI know only too well from actual experience the extent to which a self-righteous clergy can deviate from its proper role, twisting religion for their own authoritarian agenda and producing devastating results.[18]

Mahatma Gandhi always emphasized 'reform from within'.[19] The role of religion should be to strengthen and encourage people, enabling them to create value in life and society. Gandhi said that 'my politics and all other activities of mine are derived from my religion'.[20] Tagore proclaimed that all our enduring achievements in this life are the products of our inner religious and moral impulses. President Makiguchi asked, 'What social raison d'être could a religion possibly have apart from leading people and society toward enlightenment?'[21] Humanity must return to what ought to be our real starting point: religion exists for the sake of human beings.

Chowdhury: I also think that religion ought to be more humanity-oriented. Religious practice should not be limited to routine, mundane customs and rituals. Instead it must reflect the way people live every day. We must look upon integrity, honesty, love for one another, caring for other people, devotion to duty and work, and a sense of responsibility to society as integral to religion.

Ikeda: In 1993, I spoke at Harvard University for the second time, delivering a speech titled 'Mahayana Buddhism and Twenty-first-century Civilization'. I stressed the importance of adopting a criterion transcending any sectarian differences for evaluating religion: whether following a particular religion makes a person stronger or weaker, better or worse, wiser or more ignorant.

In addition, I discussed the importance of the religious spirit and its connection with human nature.[22] In *A Common Faith*, the American educator and philosopher John Dewey wrote

There is at least enough impulse toward justice, kindliness, and order so that if it were mobilized for action, not expecting abrupt and complete transformation to occur, the disorder, cruelty, and oppression that exist would be reduced.[23]

Religion's fundamental mission is to help us rouse and develop the power of good we have within ourselves.

Chowdhury: Tagore was not bound by ritualism or narrow religious views. Religion only broadened his outlook. I believe that religion must never be exclusivist, discriminatory, prejudiced, or obsessed with rituals and ceremonies. Religion must instead be all-embracing and inclusive. To be meaningful, religion should exist in a social context, not solely in a devotional context.

As Tagore would have said, inclusivity is the key element in any religion. Discrimination and exclusivism generate tension and hinder the attainment of the basic objective of a religion to bring good to society and its members. Extremely important to any religion, this inclusivity is the soil in which the culture of peace can be nurtured.

I believe all religions want to improve society and humanity – they want each of us to be a good person. They must shun the destructive, negative thought that one's own religion is better than others. The heart of a religion – its spirit – is more important than superficial ritual. This is why I believe that religion is best taught in a broader social context, more in-depth than is now the case.

Ikeda: Education is absolutely essential if religion is to serve as the soil in which the culture of peace can grow. Helping religion maintain its inclusive, accepting nature, without lapsing into exclusivist, self-righteous attitudes, requires the strength of intelligence informed by conscience. At the same time, education that overstresses knowledge and ignores ethics and spirituality presents the danger of seriously distorting our humanity.

Religion and education need to work together in tandem, like the two wheels of a cart, for society to develop in a healthy way and to enable us to build the culture of peace. This is the reason we of the SGI are developing our peace, culture, and education movement on the basis of Buddhist humanism.

FIVE
Children's Rights

Ikeda: On a daily basis, the women of Japan create, discuss, study and strive to expand the culture of peace that you have consistently advocated and advanced. The exhibition *Children and a Culture of Peace*[1] (sponsored by the Soka Gakkai Women's Peace Committee) has received an enthusiastic reception all over Japan. In support of the United Nations' International Decade for a Culture of Peace and Non-violence for the Children of the World (2001–2010), it strives both to inform the world of the plight of children suffering from poverty and war, and to extensively promote the spirit behind the United Nations Convention on the Rights of the Child (see Conversation One). Since the exhibition's initiation in 2006, it has been to more than 90 cities worldwide and been visited by roughly 700,000 people.

Chowdhury: I am very much aware of this wonderful project. Since the time it was conceived, I was privileged to be kept regularly informed about its progress. The leaders of the Women's Peace Committee briefed me extensively about it when I met with them in Tokyo in 2005. As I have been an ardent advocate of the culture of peace at the United Nations and formally took the initiative to propose that the General Assembly include a self-standing agenda item on this issue in 1997, I feel very proud and encouraged that this project was taken up by the SGI Women's Committee so earnestly. It is truly encouraging to know that many people in many cities visited the exhibition. I am profoundly honoured that you have strongly championed this remarkable concept in your annual peace proposals, in your speeches, and in your messages addressed to humanity on various occasions.

Ikeda: As you kindly say, it is encouraging that the exhibition has been viewed by so many. Building the culture of peace is an absolutely indispensable foundation for the happiness of humanity and the stability of society.

Chowdhury: Awareness of this indispensability is steadily deepening. I would also add emphasis to what you said by asserting that the global spreading and personal internalization of the culture of peace is indispensable for the safety, security and development of our world. I was humbled by the privilege of chairing the nine-month-long negotiations to draft the UN Declaration and Programme of Action on a Culture of Peace, which was adopted unanimously by the General Assembly of the United Nations on 13 September 1999. I had the honour of introducing the resolution (A/Res/53/243) proposing adoption of the Declaration and Programme of Action by the Assembly on that day on behalf of all Member States.

In the preceding years, the United Nations undertook two other major initiatives with regard to the culture of peace – both proposed by me as the Bangladesh ambassador to the organization. In 1997, the General Assembly declared 2000, the first year of the new millennium, as the International Year for the Culture of Peace. In 1998, the General Assembly declared the period from 2001 to 2010 as the International Decade for a Culture of Peace and Non-violence for the Children of the World.

I consider the last three years of the twentieth century to be significant and meaningful in terms of UN decisions integral to building the culture of peace in the world, both individually and collectively. As the world was coming out of the Cold War and possibilities of global tension, conflict and war were diminishing, we felt that a new mindset, a new approach, was needed to ensure a sustainable peace. I felt very strongly that the United Nations should take the lead in articulating that new direction and proposed in the final years of the century all three initiatives on the culture of peace as the central focus of building a peaceful and secure environment for all nations and their peoples. I was inspired by the work done by UNESCO under the leadership of my dear friend Federico Mayor in this regard.

Treasuring the Future

Ikeda: Your contributions to the culture of peace are eternal and indelible. Building such a culture illuminates the irreplaceable brilliance of life itself and shines a light on children, on whom the future depends.

Many visitors to the *Children and a Culture of Peace* exhibition have responded with emotion and sympathy. Its theme of promoting children's happiness is a fundamental principle of Soka education. Over the years, we have strived through various forums to heighten popular awareness of children's issues at the grassroots level.

As I recall, it was on the occasion of the exhibition *World's Children and UNICEF*, organized by the Soka Gakkai Women's Peace Committee and held in Hiroshima in July 1990, that you and I first came into contact.

Chowdhury: Yes, I remember it vividly with joyful nostalgia. It was the first official event in which I participated as the new UNICEF director for Japan, Australia and New Zealand. With my base in Tokyo, I used to travel extensively in these three countries advocating, building coalitions of support and fundraising for children in need.

Within three days of assuming my responsibility in Tokyo, I travelled to Hiroshima to inaugurate this heart-warming, mind-absorbing exhibition. That was my initial introduction to the SGI and its most praiseworthy work for the welfare and wellbeing of humanity. Thus from the outset, my relations with the SGI and its members centred on children. I consider it a great honour and the gateway to a larger, more profound and sustainably long lasting relationship with you and the SGI entities.

I was moved to observe that the exhibition highlighted the UN Convention on the Rights of the Child, an issue that in Japan at that time was not among the public priorities. Nonetheless, SGI members had the foresight to create an exhibition that focused on children's rights, thus helping persuade Japan to join the Convention and inviting all concerned to engage in its implementation. In my view, that was the correct course to follow.

To my great satisfaction, this first contact has flowered into extensive collaboration with the SGI in many areas in recent years, mostly focusing on the culture of peace and women's empowerment. I am particularly pleased that the contact that commenced more than two decades ago has led to the opportunity to engage in this soul-enriching dialogue with you.

Here I would like to recall with deep gratitude the whole-hearted support and sincere assistance that I received from Chisako Kobayashi, at that time the chairperson of the Women's Peace Committee, and Nagayo Sawa, my colleague and UNICEF information officer in Tokyo, in establishing and consolidating my relations with the SGI over the years, commencing with Hiroshima. I will always remain grateful to them for adding this wonderful dimension to my life's mission.

Ikeda: We are deeply grateful both to you for your long years of continuous support and to Nagayo Sawa and the other people at UNICEF for the numerous occasions on which they have helped the Women's Peace Committee with public lectures and exhibitions. The SGI started touring the exhibition on children's rights in 1991, the year after the UN-organized World Summit for Children. You attended the opening of its inaugural showing in Kobe.

Chowdhury: Yes. With the cooperation of Soka Gakkai members, I travelled all over Japan – from Hokkaido to Okinawa – with the objective of deepening society's interest in and understanding of child-related issues, including their rights and the UN Convention that put all those rights together for global application. That was a wonderful experience, and I was impressed by the extensive outreach and partnership that the members had at local levels. While advocating for child rights, I was also able to sensitize the mayors of many cities – big and small – whom I met through the courtesy also of Soka Gakkai members on another global initiative known as 'Mayors for Children', intended to channel local energy and resources for the benefit of children at the municipal level.

After my transfer to New York in 1993, I had the pleasure of continuing exchanges with SGI members in support of children at the UNICEF headquarters. This relationship further blossomed when I became the Bangladesh ambassador to the United Nations in 1996 and since 2002, when I became Under-Secretary-General and High Representative of the United Nations for the most vulnerable countries of the world.

I was invited to attend the SGI exhibition *Treasuring the Future: Children's Rights and Realities*,[2] held just outside New York City in May 1998. Unfortunately, owing to an end-of-the-day traffic jam in one of the city's tunnels, I did not arrive until the event was over, and the audience was beginning to disperse. Nonetheless, the organizers urged me to speak, as I had been scheduled to do. While I spoke, everyone listened attentively, and later on many asserted to me their determination to advance children's rights in their families and communities.

In a number of events organized by the SGI to highlight the cause of children and their rights in which I spoke, I was delighted to notice that the SGI organizers always took special care and were very mindful to adjust the contents of these events to suit local conditions, thereby making them more appealing to local people. That was very thoughtful and smart too.

Women's Voices

Ikeda: As long as people remain indifferent to events occurring far away, nothing will change for the better. But when people realize the connections linking themselves and their immediate communities to the rest of the world, their interest is sparked, and they become forces for action. This is why I believe it is important to employ lots of photographic panels and graphics in our exhibits, to make a strong visual appeal. Exhibitions for children demand special inventiveness. Many people praise our exhibitions for the way they inspire pleasant, positive parent–child discussions.

The interest and concern of adults are critical factors in ensuring the happiness of children. As the nineteenth-century American philosopher Ralph Waldo Emerson wrote:

> Our modes of Education aim to expedite, to save labor; to do for the masses what cannot be done for masses, what must be done reverently, one by one: say rather, the whole world is needed for the tuition of each pupil.[3]

Chowdhury: This is why I find the forward-looking work of the Soka Gakkai women's division for the wellbeing of children deeply impressive. As they raise awareness, the members themselves master the issues before explaining them to their associates. This approach is vital to any kind of advocacy work, any kind of wide-ranging networking, any kind of broad-based movement for the good of humanity. In the case of religion for example – as in the case of any substantive human endeavour – people cannot be true believers unless they internalize and thoroughly understand the true meanings of the doctrines of their faith.

Ikeda: A movement's participants are only self-motivated and take initiative when they have a full grasp of and conviction in the movement's true significance. This is also crucial for building an enduring movement. These are the keys to the success of any popular movement, and this is why the SGI especially stresses each member taking initiative. Nothing is as strong as inner motivation generated by a spiritual awakening. The starting point of the SGI movement for peace, culture and education is to create a global network through one-on-one dialogue. One of the aims of the SGI's humanistic movement is to create the culture of peace in a way that transforms society through the empowerment of the individual.

Chowdhury: In my numerous interactions with them, I have found members of the Soka Gakkai women's division very perceptive, sincerely motivated and highly intelligent. In cooperation with the youth division, they make remarkable efforts for the good and benefit of humanity. Engaging in frequent exchanges with them, I have found members of the youth division also to be impressively enthusiastic and eager to learn. At lecture meetings, I am impressed by audience questions, especially those from women who are impassioned to reach out to the people from other parts of the world and who seem to feel a sense of duty and responsibility to contribute to the betterment of the world. I believe that this spirit is created in them through your leadership and inspirational guidance. Women and youth feel especially empowered by your continuing words of appreciation and encouragement. In addition, they seem to believe that the issue of the world's children is a perfect bridge connecting them and the rest of the globe, particularly with the developing nations.

Ikeda: There is truth in the voices of good women, and they are a steadfast force that can direct the world toward peace and society toward happiness. I have constantly insisted that humanity's advancement hangs upon whether we heed them. This is a crucial axiom for all groups and organizations.

Chowdhury: I am very encouraged to hear you articulate this reality in such a simple and at the same time comprehensive manner. A society that fails to involve its women as equal partners in all its endeavours fails altogether. There can be no mistake more serious than ignoring or neglecting 50 per cent of humanity.

In my work at the United Nations for the most vulnerable countries, I have observed again and again that a country that values the involvement and empowerment of women progresses confidently on the road to peace and development. Particularly in countries engaged in post-conflict nation building, women's participation in decision-making ensures longer-term and sustainable development because women invariably want to ensure that their society, their community, is a place where their children and grandchildren can grow up and live in peace and stability. For men, it is always power-grabbing and position-seeking that influences their actions in a post-conflict situation.

Your strong emphasis on the need for the true participation of women has given the SGI a meaningful mission. Your visionary role in this regard surely deserves global recognition. Personally I have observed its positive results in women's leadership at all levels in as many SGI chapters as I have been privileged to visit in various parts of the world.

Ambassadors of Peace

Ikeda: Women's powers are great.

The SGI has held significant exhibitions at the UN Headquarters in New York, including *Nuclear Arms: Threat to Our World*, in 1982, and *War and Peace*, in 1989. Then, in 2004, with your support and that of others at the United Nations, we were one of the cosponsors of the exhibition *Building a Culture of Peace for the Children of the World*.

At the opening, Nobel Peace laureate Betty Williams delivered a splendid speech. She is a courageous mother and moral champion who, to protect children from the violent conflict in Northern Ireland, rose up and demanded that the world leaders hear the cries of mothers and children. She quoted a passage from the Universal

Declaration of Rights for Children, which her group and others are promoting: 'We, the Children of the World, must live with justice, with peace and freedom, but above all, with the dignity we deserve.'[4]

Chowdhury: Yes, Betty's speech made a deep impression on us all. The opening of the exhibition took place on 4 February 2004. It is worth mentioning that four UN ambassadors from four regions of the world cooperated with us as cosponsors. Such broad-based joint sponsorship of a peace event at the United Nations does not happen often. The exhibition was sponsored by my office[5] at the UN Headquarters, the SGI, and the Permanent Missions to the United Nations of the Bahamas, Laos, Mozambique and Tuvalu. During its nearly one-month duration, it probably attracted more visitors than any other exhibition the United Nations had ever held before.

After years of preliminary discussion, all preparations were completed by early 2004. The time was right. The carefully planned installation was situated in the conspicuous UN Headquarters visitors lobby. The world-renowned jazz pianist and great promoter of the culture of peace Herbie Hancock, well-known tenor-saxophonist Wayne Shorter, and accomplished flutist Nestor Torres – all activists belonging to the International Committee of Artists for Peace (ICAP) – celebrated the occasion with splendid performances and enthralled the UN and New York City invitees, in particular many teachers from city schools.

Ikeda: In the press release announcing the exhibition, Kofi Annan, then UN Secretary-General, wrote that

> [I]t is not enough to dispatch peace-keeping forces to separate warring parties; it is not enough to engage in peaceful rebuilding after conflict has destroyed society. We require above all a culture of peace.[6]

The cessation of fighting is not the equivalent of peace. To

win and sustain firm, lasting peace, we must build the culture of peace and leave it for posterity.

Chowdhury: As the initiator and chief sponsor, I was especially pleased
by the large number of young people visiting the exhibition. At the
opening ceremony, I suggested that teachers bring their students as
part of their schoolwork. Older students formed groups to explain
the exhibition to the very young ones. At a later date, in recognition
of their special role, I presented to these senior students from various
parts of New York City the Peace Ambassador Award. A number of
the awards went to students from the Renaissance Charter School,
with encouraging support from its principal, Monte Joffee.

Ikeda: That's wonderful! I was told that a chorus of middle-school students from the UN International School sang a selection of folksongs
from different countries. I am sure the students who received the
Peace Ambassador Awards regarded them as a great honour. Having
the opportunity to take part in a peace- and child-centred UN
programme like this exhibition contributing to the International
Decade for a Culture of Peace and Non-violence for the Children of
the World must have been deeply significant for these young people.

Chowdhury: Yes, the children's chorus from the United Nations
International School enlivened the opening event.

In 2010, the UN-proclaimed Decade ended, but we need to continue striving to realize our objective to build the culture of peace
as envisaged in the UN Declaration and Programme of Action on
a Culture of Peace. At the same time, I am encouraged that more
than 1,000 civil society organizations presented a report to the UN
Secretary-General and the 192 Member States of the United Nations
in October 2010, recording their activities during the Decade,
advancing its objectives. This is a truly remarkable achievement
commensurate with the role assigned to civil society in Article 6 of
the Declaration.

Bearing in mind the potential of civil society's commitment and grassroots outreach, we must redouble our efforts and keep bringing the message of the culture of peace to humanity. We have an excellent opportunity to raise our voices and our level of activity to bolster the global efforts for sustainable peace. In November 2010, the UN General Assembly called upon 'all concerned that renewed attention be given' to the 'objective of the effective implementation of the Programme of Action on a Culture of Peace aimed at strengthening further the global movement for the culture of peace following the observance of the International Decade'. I intend to devote my time and energy to that end and hope that SGI members in 192 countries and territories, covering all regions of the world, will further intensify their efforts to the same end.

The international community greatly appreciates your continuing advocacy and inspiration for the culture of peace. Your advice, leadership and encouragement will be extremely important both to individuals and to the burgeoning movement for the culture of peace as a whole.

Children in War

Ikeda: Both the SGI and I are determined to continue our efforts in this area, and we are eager to cooperate with others around the world who share our commitment to peace. The predicament of children today grows increasingly grave throughout the world. Your words from an earlier meeting remain ever-present in my mind:

> There are many, many children in the world today who don't even have clean water to drink or cannot go to school. While some children in wealthy nations can buy athletic shoes that cost $200 a pair, many people elsewhere must live on less than a dollar a day. With $200, one could buy 100 pairs of shoes for children in a developing country. Approximately 80 percent of the world's population is suffering from deprivation

and poverty. It is especially important for those of the younger generation to be aware of this.[7]

Of the 2.2 billion children under the age of 18, 1.9 billion live in developing countries. According to a UNICEF white paper issued in 2005, one in three children in impoverished regions lacks adequate housing, and one in five has no safe water to drink. The distressing conditions of many children today are symbolized by the problem of child soldiers.

Chowdhury: It is an evil manifestation of the scourge of wars and conflicts. Nothing could be more immoral and inhuman than using innocent children as tools of war. In introducing its Global Report for 2008, the coalition Child Soldiers International reported:

> Child soldiers continue to be used in armed conflicts by some governments. Governments also use captured children for intelligence gathering, or detain them rather than supporting their rehabilitation and reintegration. A wide array of armed groups – with diverse aims, methods and constituencies – continue to use children as soldiers and they have proved resistant to pressure or persuasion to stop the practice.[8]

According to the NGO Human Rights Watch in 2007:

> Denied a childhood and often subjected to horrific violence, an estimated 200,000 to 300,000 children are serving as soldiers for both rebel groups and government forces in current armed conflicts.[9]

At this time, some counts estimate the number of child soldiers in the world as a whole at nearly 500,000. In 2007, Africa had the largest number of child soldiers, reaching 100,000.[10] However, it is impossible to get a correct number, as most are deployed in armed rebel groups.

Ikeda: The Optional Protocol to the Convention on the Rights of the Child on the Involvement of Children in Armed Conflict specifies that forcing children to take part in war activities is a grave infringement of human rights.[11] It sows seeds of hatred in future generations and threatens to make war a permanent state of affairs. As long as society breeds this cycle of hatred and desire for revenge, eliminating the root causes of war will never be possible. For this very reason, through my annual peace proposals, I have repeatedly urged nations to ratify the Optional Protocol to the Convention on the Rights of the Child.

Chowdhury: As you brought up this unique human rights treaty, it is with great pride that I recall how I was directly involved in getting UNICEF engaged in the drafting process of the Convention on the Rights of the Child and played a crucial role as the chairman of its executive board in 1986. I also recall with deep gratitude the tremendous support that I received from the SGI and other civil society organizations during 1990 to 1993 as chief of the UNICEF office in Tokyo for Japan's ratification of the Convention. I am delighted to say that we were successful in our efforts, though certain strong forces worked tirelessly to frustrate our efforts.

Going back to child soldiers, let me underscore that children, ignorant of what is happening, enticed by promises of food and money, are kidnapped from their homes and families. Tortured, coerced into obedience, and compelled in various ways to take up arms, they are physically and mentally driven to exhaustion and transformed beyond all recognition. They become like trained animals incapable of thinking or feeling independently.

Ikeda: Transforming children into weapons of war exceeds the bounds of cruelty and horror. The immorality of adults who rob children of their potential and future, and stain their minds with hatred and violence is completely unforgivable.

Chowdhury: Several factors help explain why the practice of using child soldiers has reached its present scope. First of all, children cost less to keep than adults. Second, they are easier to manage. Third, they can be useful longer because they remain cruel beasts into adulthood. Indeed, with more than a decade's experience, albeit traumatizing, behind them, they may even make more ruthless adult soldiers. This is the most revolting aspect of the practice.

It is heartening to note that, during the last few years, as a result of heightened global interest in eliminating the use of child soldiers, a number of mandatory international decisions have bolstered the Convention on the Rights of the Child in this matter. In 2002, the Optional Protocol on the involvement of children in armed conflict came into force, further obligating states to take all feasible measures, including legal steps, necessary to prohibit and criminalize the use of child soldiers. Also, in the Statute of the International Criminal Court, which came into force the same year, using child soldiers was recognized as a war crime. In 2005, a unanimous resolution of the UN Security Council (1612) established the first comprehensive monitoring and reporting system for enforcing compliance by groups using child soldiers in armed conflict. Also the International Labour Organization's 1999 document *Worst Forms of Child Labour Convention* defined recruitment of children for use in armed conflict as one of the worst forms of child labour.[12]

Recently a strong international movement has emerged to put an end to this evil practice. Since 2002, Red Hand Day[13] is observed every year on 12 February (the day the Optional Protocol came into force) to draw public attention to the practice of using children as soldiers in wars and armed conflicts.

Sword in the Heart

Ikeda: A Buddhist scripture teaches the pricelessness of children: 'Surely, there is no treasure greater than a child!'[14] Indeed, children are our supreme gem. A society that sacrifices them has no future.

We must strive to halt the practice of using child soldiers. Of course, we also need to provide proper care to children whose minds the practice has already scarred.

Chowdhury: In October 2000, as the Permanent Representative of Bangladesh to the United Nations and as chairman of the Sierra Leone Sanctions Committee of the United Nations Security Council, I visited Sierra Leone, where many children had been forced to become soldiers, terrorized by the rebels in the internecine fighting. I observed personally the traumatic aftershocks experienced by these young girls and boys, and the efforts that rehabilitation centres were making to help them overcome their pasts.

I was particularly distressed to find the most inconsiderate treatment that the girls were receiving. My experience has been explicitly reflected in the words of Child Soldiers International:

> Girls in particular continue to be excluded from official programs – whether by design or default – despite well-documented information of their involvement in armed conflict and their need for DDR [disarmament, demobilization, and reintegration] programs which respond to their particular needs. Programs to support the sustainable reintegration of former child soldiers have been inadequate and many returning children have received no support; and funding has been lacking in many cases.[15]

This is absolutely unacceptable.

Ikeda: You are absolutely correct. *The State of the World's Children*, published in 2002 by UNICEF, reports that in Liberia, during the violent fighting that took place between 1989 and 1997, 150,000 people died, 1,000,000 became internal refugees, and 666,000 were driven from the country. During that time, 15,000 children became soldiers.

The report reveals how former child soldiers desperately tried to reintegrate into society by driving from their minds the horrible things that had happened to them. When asked about their hopes for the future, it was heartbreaking that many replied they just wanted to be allowed back in school and to be a normal kid or reborn as a different child.

Chowdhury: Very sad and moving. In this context, it is noteworthy that, in Sierra Leone, some people wanted to have child soldiers tried and punished. A number of them who had reached adulthood were actually put on trial. Some members of the Security Council, myself included, felt that the traumas they had suffered constituted sufficient punishment, especially since they had not acted under their own volition. Feeling that they had suffered enough from being forced to take up arms, we could see no purpose in re-punishing them as war criminals.

Ikeda: Obviously the people most deserving of prosecution are the ones who compelled the children to become soldiers. World leaders must unflinchingly face this hard truth and work together to break the vicious cycle of hatred. It is essential that we effect a fundamental transformation, eradicating the culture of war, which employs violence to resolve issues, and building the culture of peace conducive to the wellbeing and happiness of children.

A story about Shakyamuni ably illustrates this point. When a man was about to attack him with a sword, Shakyamuni told him to throw away his weapon. Thinking this was an invitation to hand-to-hand combat, the man did as he was told. But Shakyamuni repeated, 'Put down your sword'.

Enraged, the would-be attacker cried out: 'I've already put it down. Why are you telling me to do it again?'

'The sword in your hand means nothing. You still have a sword in your heart.'

Regaining control of himself, the man reflected and then converted to Buddhism.[16]

Until each person puts down the sword in his or her heart, there can be no end to the cycle of evil and its tragedies. We must start ridding ourselves of inner weapons by reforming not children but adults.

Alpha and Omega of Human Folly

Chowdhury: That is why, instead of putting them on trial, I feel we should rehabilitate and reintegrate former child soldiers. Trials may be acceptable for young people when there is clear proof they acted intentionally and culpably. But it is wrong to imprison and subject to further trauma those children whom adults compelled to commit inhuman acts of barbarity.

At the UN Security Council in 2000, when I was representing Bangladesh, I proposed that various regions and nations of the world should declare 'child-soldier-free zones'. As in the case of nuclear-weapon-free zones, nations would declare individually or as groups that their territories were off limits to the use, recruitment, training, arming and financing of child soldiers. Making such declarations would encourage other nations to join, until the use of child soldiers was eliminated throughout the world. This seems to me the best and the most effective way to get rid of this scourge.

Ikeda: Childhood should be a time for playing with friends, studying for the future, enjoying parental affection, and making golden memories to last a lifetime. Converting it into a time for armed killing is tragic beyond words. Destroying children's spirits destroys the future: It is the alpha and omega of human folly and tragedy.

When I was young, I worked for Josei Toda as editor-in-chief of children's magazines like *Boken Shonen* (Adventure Boy) and *Shonen Nippon* (Boys' Japan). The postwar period was still a confused, desperate time, when hope was hard to come by. I fondly recall how, with the idea of supplying young minds with dreams and hope for the future, I worked until late at night, taking everything upon myself – commissioning articles, writing, laying out pages and proofreading. I requested inspiring, hope-giving stories from some of the leading writers of the day, including the famous novelist Sohachi Yamaoka, the father of Japanese science fiction Unno Juza [pen name of Sano Shoichi], and the mystery writer Rampo Edogawa. I believe the reason that all the authors complied with my request was because of their deep sympathy with my ideas.

Chowdhury: I am delighted to know this aspect of your working life. It shows that you were aware of the positive role popular journals and books can play in shaping the characters of children.

I would like to raise here my concern about the negative impact of popular modern media on today's children. In the United States, by the time a child is 18 years old (the Convention on the Rights of the Child considers a person a child up to that age), he or she will have witnessed on television (based on the average viewing time) 200,000 acts of violence, including 40,000 murders. A 2005 study established that children ages eight to 18 spend more time (44.5 hours per week, 6.5 hours daily) in front of a computer, a television or a game screen than they do in any other activity except sleeping.

Since the 1950s, countless studies have been done on the effects of violence in television and movies. The majority of these studies conclude that children who watch significant amounts of television and movie violence are more likely to exhibit aggressive behaviour, attitudes and values. Violent video games can cause people to have more aggressive thoughts, feelings and behaviours, and decrease empathetic, helpful behaviours with peers.[17]

I strongly believe that there is an urgent need for a global convention to restrict or ban violence in the media and electronic gadgets, keeping in mind the best interests of children as envisaged in the Convention on the Rights of the Child.

Ikeda: I agree. In this respect, too, we must admit that children's environments are deteriorating. Parents of all political and economic convictions and of all races and ethnic groups pray for their children's happiness. We must make giving children's happiness supreme precedence a shared standard for all humanity. The Convention on the Rights of the Child is a result of this spirit at work. We will go into it in greater detail in the next chapter.

SIX
A Constant Renewal of Strength

Ikeda: In one of my favourite poems by Rabindranath Tagore, he wrote:

> On the seashore of endless worlds the children meet with shouts and dances.

> They build their houses with sand and they play with empty shells. With withered leaves they weave their boats and smilingly float them on the vast deep. Children have their play on the seashore of worlds.[1]

In this poem, we can hear the bright, laughing voices of children – the hope of the future. True peace exists in a society where children can grow up freely and without worry.

Chowdhury: You have quoted from one of my own favourite Tagore poems. As a matter of fact, it is loved by many. In a similar vein, you emphasized the link between peace in society and the wellbeing of children. I also strongly believe that a nation's credibility rests on how well it takes care of its children.

Though the international community has to do much more, it can be proud of the special attention given during the last two decades to enhancing the best interests of the child, first by adopting the United Nations Convention on the Rights of the Child in 1989, and second by holding the World Summit for Children at the United Nations in New York in 1990. This summit was the brain child of UNICEF Executive Director James P. Grant, who occupies a very special place in my heart as a person of the highest calibre and one of the greatest humanitarians the world has known. We do not see such a saintly person in the UN system anymore. These are two very significant, purposeful and forward-looking multilateral endeavours in favour of the world's children. It has been a privilege for me to be closely associated with both.

Ikeda: It is also a great accomplishment. Thinking of children's laughing voices reminds me of something that happened during the opening of our exhibition *Nuclear Arms: Threat to Humanity* in Costa Rica in June 1996. The exhibition was held in San José in the Costa Rican Center of Science and Culture, a building that once housed a prison. Repainted bright yellow, it had then become a children's museum. I am reminded of the remark attributed to Victor Hugo that 'he who opens a school door, closes a prison'.

José María Figueres Olsen, president at the time, and Óscar Arias Sánchez, president from 2006 to 2010, attended the solemn ceremonies. Only a partition that stopped well short of the ceiling separated our space from that of the adjacent museum. The constant laughter and noise from next door upset some of the people responsible for the arrangements, but I began my remarks by saying:

> The lively and spirited voices of children playing in the center's Children's Museum next door can be heard even here in this hall. The sight and sound of these youngsters, boisterous and full of vitality, are the very image of peace. It is here that we can find the power to stem the tide of atomic bombs. It is here we can find hope.[2]

The brilliance of children's smiles and their lively laughter are the truest measures of a nation's wealth.

Chowdhury: Working for the United Nations and as Bangladesh's envoy, I have had many unforgettable encounters with children in many parts of the world. Being with children and interacting with them – wherever they are – have always been energizing and reassuring for me. Their innocence, their frankness, their radiance always renew my trust in humanity and strengthens my optimism. The most moving experience for me, of course, has been the daily struggle that is being waged for the survival, protection and development of children by the poorest and weakest segment of humanity.

Ikeda: One of the greatest issues confronting the world today is the protection of people suffering in poverty, especially children.

Chowdhury: While during the last two decades visible progress has been made, the Least Developed Countries[3] of the world are facing not only an uphill task in improving their infant, under-five and maternal mortality rates but also newer challenges that are surfacing.

Millions of orphans, abandoned children, street children, children caught in conflict, children in detention and trafficked children are growing up without the loving care and protection of a family environment. An estimated 143 million children in the developing world – one in every 13 – have suffered the death of at least one parent. Globally, tens of millions of children spend a large portion of their lives on the streets, where they are exposed to all forms of abuse and exploitation. Worse, these children are often not treated as children at all.[4]

I am deeply saddened to see that armed conflict, trafficking, sexual exploitation, HIV/AIDS, abusive practices of child soldiers and child labour – compounded by intolerance, discrimination and deprivation – have had a very negative impact on the welfare and wellbeing of the world's children. It is most inspiring, however, to find that despite all the problems they experience daily, children everywhere have unbounded enthusiasm about life. A nation's real progress is measured by the width of a child's smile.

Convention on the Rights of the Child

Ikeda: Children have limitless potential. Their eyes glow with the light of hope for a better future. We adults must do nothing to dim that light. My mentor always said: 'Children are the treasures of the future. Think of them as emissaries from the future, and take the best care of them.'[5]

It is sad that, in the world today, many children are exploited. Their human rights are violated, and they are compelled to lead miserable lives. Again, in 1989, with the objective of rectifying this situation, the UN General Assembly adopted the Convention on the Rights of the Child. I know that, as the chairman of the Executive Board of UNICEF, you played an important part in drafting and promoting the Convention.

Chowdhury: Consisting of 54 articles, this exceptional and profoundly forward-looking international treaty has tremendous potential for humankind. For the first time in the history of the global treaty regime, all human rights – political, civil, economic, social, and cultural – are addressed to ensure these rights for children in a comprehensive manner.

Ikeda: It is indeed a pioneering achievement among human rights treaties.

Chowdhury: And that is why it should be a top policy document. Leadership – every head of state and head of government – must give it top priority and say so publicly. Such a public commitment to implement the Convention fully and effectively is the best way to protect children. By ensuring that our children enjoy the rights enshrined in the Convention, we can greatly improve, by extension, the observance of all human rights in our societies as a whole.

Ikeda: I am reminded of your statement in a speech to the UN General Assembly:

> It is said that poverty has a feminine face. We say it has the face of the children as well. When the mother is struggling with poverty, children are the definite victims. In addition, being the most vulnerable section of society, children remain at the receiving end of every kind of poverty onslaught. Therefore, any efforts directed at improving the condition of children have a societal dimension that needs to be appreciated properly.[6]

I am in total agreement with your belief that true peace is found in the happiness of children and their mothers. In your attitude, I sense the strong influence of your mother, who welcomed underprivileged children into your home and taught them to read and write.

Returning to the Convention on the Rights of the Child, how were you connected with its preparation and promotion?

Chowdhury: As a Bangladesh delegate to the United Nations and a member of the UNICEF Executive Board, I was closely involved in the Convention on the Rights of the Child, not so much in the actual drafting process but in its intergovernmental adoption process and its promotion throughout the international community. We highlighted two main points: first was the basic philosophy that children have rights that the adult world must recognize. Second was the vital importance of consulting children about adult actions that may have an immediate or future impact on them. Child participation is a significant element in this context. In addition, we emphasized the need to establish appropriate institutions and mechanisms in individual nations to address child-rights issues.

It is worthwhile to recall that the Polish government initiated the idea of a convention on children's rights. I am speaking of socialist Poland, not today's Poland, which has made its own remarkable contributions demonstrating concern for children.

Janusz Korczak

Ikeda: During the Holocaust, the Nazis destroyed two million Polish Jewish children. Joseph Rotblat, the British physicist active as the president and subsequently president emeritus of the Pugwash Conferences on Science and World Affairs, was Polish by birth. He was a lifelong opponent of nuclear weapons.

When he was still young, his beloved wife was killed during the Nazi invasion of his homeland. In August 1939, Dr Rotblat tried to bring his wife from Poland back to the research institute in the United Kingdom where he was employed, but she fell suddenly ill, and he was forced to return to the United Kingdom alone. Hitler's armies invaded Poland soon after.

In our dialogue,[7] Dr Rotblat related the sorrow he felt at being unable to save his wife. Humanity must remember the huge numbers of lives lost in these brutal atrocities in order to make sure that such a thing never occurs again.

The Polish educator Janusz Korczak (pen name of Henryk Goldszmit) encouraged and cared for children during the turbulence of the Holocaust. When discussing the origins of the Convention on the Rights of the Child, his role must be considered.

Chowdhury: Yes, Korczak loved children and articulated child rights as an area of significance that requires the special attention of all. I loved it when he said: '[Children] are entitled to be taken seriously. They have a right to be treated by adults with tenderness and respect, as equals.'[8]

Ikeda: He was a physician, a noted writer and an educator. The orphanage he founded employed an education system emphasizing the independence of the child. When the orphans for whom he was caring were sent to live in the Warsaw Ghetto, created by the Nazis following their invasion of Poland, Korczak went with them, protecting them in their harsh new circumstances. The Nazis repeatedly offered to free Korczak, who was Jewish, but he refused to leave the orphans and, remaining true to his convictions to the end, ultimately died with the children in the Treblinka extermination camp.

As a matter of fact, just before Korczak and the orphans in his care were sent to the extermination camp (5 August 1942), they performed Tagore's play *The Post Office* (written in 1914). Tagore's works were banned by the Nazis, but Korczak ignored this in what can perhaps be seen as his declaration of the freedom of the human spirit in the face of the harshest oppression.

He loved children sincerely, and his noble ideas, expressed in lofty sentiments – 'Love the child, not just your own'[9] and 'Children are not people of tomorrow; they are people today'[10] – are the spiritual forerunner of the Convention on the Rights of the Child.

Chowdhury: Having the benefit of such a legacy, another Pole, Adam Lopatka, a diplomat, chaired the drafting committee that prepared the Convention, which took nearly ten years to complete. A wonderfully compassionate gentleman and an astute diplomat, Adam and I collaborated often to secure wide-ranging understanding and support for the evolving Convention.

Incidentally, the stained glass mural outside the UN Security Council room at the UN Headquarters in New York, a gift from Poland, is the only national gift to the United Nations to feature a child. My special thanks to Poland, as a nation, for this unique present and, of course, for taking the initiative in drawing up the remarkable Convention. In presenting the proposal, Poland showed very appropriately great concern for children and their rights.

Humanity owes a debt of gratitude to Adam Lopatka for his leadership and guidance in this regard.

Ikeda: For his invaluable contribution to children's rights, Adam Lopatka received the Tolstoy International Gold Medal from the Moscow-based International Association of Children's Funds. Albert A. Likhanov, president of that association, and I have spoken together many times and have in fact published a dialogue titled *The Path to the Land of Children.* On a visit to our Soka schools, Mr Likhanov told our students that, when everything is going well for them, they should remember that there are others who are suffering and be especially eager to help the very small and the old.

In offering this message of reaching out to the suffering and the weak, Mr Likhanov presented our students with a precious gift. Adults need to be models, teaching courageous, caring attitudes through their actions in everyday life. To succeed, they need to make a conscious effort for their own growth. Children reflect adult society.

Back to the Convention on the Rights of the Child, I suspect that many problems arose during the course of its preparation.

Chowdhury: In 1984, I went to Warsaw for some intense and engaging discussions on children's rights. I was the Deputy Permanent Representative of Bangladesh to the United Nations at that time. The issues relating to parental authority, comprehensive reflection of all human rights pertaining to children, and articulation of the best interests of the child in the Convention, attracted a lot of attention from varied perspectives.

Though not in the context of an intergovernmental negotiating forum, my efforts in Warsaw, both personal and as a member of the UNICEF Executive Board, were to identify areas of commonality whereby the proposed text of the Convention could generate wider and quicker convergence of hardline national positions. Back in New York, I could share those with some key delegations to facilitate the drafting exercise that was going on in Geneva at that time.

The Convention, as you know, was available for signatures on 26 January 1990, after the UN General Assembly adopted it on 20 November 1989, and came into force after having been ratified by 20 countries, as envisaged in the treaty itself. Because of my country's strong support of the Convention early on and my own commitment to it, I wanted Bangladesh to sign and ratify it ahead of all other countries. I was in the Bangladesh Foreign Ministry at that time as director-general for multilateral affairs. But things did not work out as I hoped because of the regrettable position taken by one powerful element in the government's decision-taking structure, though I made all relevant plenipotentiary documents available to Bangladesh's UN Mission in New York on time before the Convention was open for signature to enable the country to secure the unique distinction of being the first in the world to sign and ratify the long-awaited Convention.

Eventually, Ghana became the first country to ratify, on 5 February 1990. Finally, only after 19 countries had already ratified did the Bangladesh ambassador in New York become concerned that our country would not even be among the first 20 ratifying nations. With Bangladesh, two other countries, Benin and the Sudan, ratified on the same day, 3 August 1990, bringing the total to 22 and making the Convention operational 30 days later, on 2 September 1990. This is how Bangladesh missed its rightful opportunity to become the first ratifying nation, thereby securing a place of honour in the history of children's rights. What a senseless action by a clueless diplomat! I am immensely agonized over that loss even now.

Ikeda: I can share your painful disappointment. But it is an indication of your greatness that thereafter you worked in Bangladesh and all over the world to spread the spirit of the Convention on the Rights of the Child and help it gain acceptance. I have the highest praise of all for your passionate, consistent work to rigorously protect children's rights and do all you can for children's happiness.

To Protect Human Dignity

Chowdhury: As a foreign ministry senior official, I had the opportunity to encourage UN entities and civil society organizations in Bangladesh to organize broad-based discussions on the implications of the Convention in a Bangladesh context and on how best its implementation could be gradually advanced. On many occasions, I participated personally in those interactions. I also had the Convention translated into Bangla, published in booklet form, and made widely available to those interested.

Being one of the Least Developed Countries of the world, Bangladesh faces perhaps more multifaceted challenges than other developing countries for the survival, development and protection of its children. The most serious is, of course, that of child survival, particularly beyond their fifth birthday. Working with our development partners, particularly UNICEF, Bangladesh has been successful in providing wide coverage under universal child immunization campaigns against six major childhood diseases.

Ensuring proper nutrition is vital to child survival beyond five years of age. Malnutrition is a primary concern and defeating it has remained an uphill task in our development efforts. To prevent stunting of both physical and mental growth, early childhood development has continued to be a key strategy.

Ikeda: All these factors are essential to children's sound growth. Satisfying these basic needs is extremely important to the protection of human rights and human security. It is even more vital for children than adults.

Chowdhury: In spite of its socioeconomic constraints and magnitude of poverty, Bangladesh has taken fairly good care of its children, particularly in the context of survival. Infant and child mortality rates have both gone down. We have adopted measures to protect children from common diseases. Diarrhoea resulting from the scarcity of safe drinking water, aggravated during recurring floods, remains a major killer in Bangladesh. Along with immunization campaigns, a home-grown treatment known as oral rehydration therapy has significantly contributed to child survival in the country. Girls' education, too, has emerged as an essential component in Bangladesh's development efforts. International organizations, particularly UNICEF, and their civil society partners are closely involved in the process.

Women's Education

Ikeda: Educating women is an issue of the greatest importance. President Makiguchi wrote, 'Mothers are the original educators and the ones who will build the ideal future society'.[11] Shedding the light of education on the mothers of the future has a direct bearing on the education of children. The education of one woman represents a boundless expanse of hope.

Chowdhury: You have always emphasized the importance of educating girls along with boys as equals. That is absolutely pertinent, and its positive impact on society is substantive .

In Bangladesh, education for girls is free up to the tenth grade. An informal system provides the much-needed opportunity for girls' education by organizing schools in the remotest parts of the country. Thousands of Bangladeshi villages benefit tremendously from this opportunity for girls' education. The strategy is that if the girls cannot go to schools, the schools would come to the girls.

It has changed the rural scene in Bangladesh in a big way. It has not only generated literacy and self-confidence among girls but also produced enormous social benefits by preventing early marriages, lowering childbirths, providing financial security, and enhancing women's status and rights in the family as well as in the community. It has been proven that investing in girls' education provides the best return of any investment.

Ikeda: I agree completely. In 2006, your compatriot the economist and social activist Muhammad Yunus won the Nobel Peace Prize for his revolutionary concept of microcredit and his Grameen Bank, which makes small loans to help generate income among the poorest of the poor. The majority of the beneficiaries of this kind of financing have been rural women. In his acceptance speech in Oslo, he said, 'I believe terrorism cannot be won over by military action. . . . Putting resources into improving the lives of the poor people is a better strategy than spending it on guns.'[12]

The success of this microcredit initiative, it seems to me, demonstrated to the whole world once again women's latent power to stimulate social development. Tapping the power of women invigorates all nations and societies, and leads to increased growth. The key is to find ways to empower women.

Chowdhury: Along with poverty reduction, the very essence of microcredit has indeed been the empowerment of the poorest women. Among other factors, this is one reason Bangladesh has managed pretty well in reducing poverty for large segments of its 150 million people.

The hard demands of life in Bangladesh for the poorest make it impossible for the children to experience the kind of parental love and care they deserve. In this regard, I would assert with pride that from the dawn of Bangladesh's independence, a proactive and enthusiastic civil society has been at the forefront of the people's struggle for survival and has ensured their wellbeing, especially for those in most need. That being said, I do believe that the family does play a major role in the development of children.

Struggle for Ratification

Ikeda: It is essential for international society to pool its wisdom and work to improve children's environments. Otherwise, we will never break the chains of poverty. In particular, we should reduce our huge military expenditures, including the funds spent on nuclear weapons, and direct these resources toward suffering children in the most critically impoverished countries. This is an issue that leaders of the industrialized nations need to address seriously.

Japan ratified the Convention on the Rights of the Child in 1994. I had long called on the government to do so. As the representative of UNICEF in Japan, you were instrumental in bringing about this result.

Chowdhury: History or destiny brought me back to UNICEF – this time working for the organization. After I had worked a few years as director-general in the Bangladesh foreign ministry, UNICEF head James Grant asked me to take charge of its area office in Tokyo, which I did in July 1990. His objective was to direct the Japanese government's attention and, concomitantly, its contribution level to the UNICEF agenda. In addition to Japan, two other donor countries in the region – Australia and New Zealand – were also my responsibility.

Though my primary focus was on the government, I also decided to expand the support base for children's causes in these three countries among civil society groups, the media, relevant professional organizations and policymakers, particularly mayors and parliamentarians. In retrospect, I feel very encouraged that I persisted in that course and made substantial progress in setting up a broad-based network of support in these countries during my three years' stay in Tokyo.

Australia, Japan and New Zealand signed the Convention in August, September and October 1990 respectively.

Ikeda: The document was signed immediately upon your becoming UNICEF director in Japan. In this capacity, you worked very hard to obtain these three ratifications.[13]

Chowdhury: Of course, New Zealand had its own national commissioner for children, ensuring their close attention from an earlier time. Nonetheless, ratification by these countries needed great effort and wide mobilization of support from diverse quarters. There were serious problems in the cases of Japan and Australia. Finally, Australia ratified in December 1990, and New Zealand in April 1993. Japan came close to ratifying then but did not do so until April 1994, after I had already ended my tenure in Tokyo.

There are three other areas where Japan responded actively to our advocacy efforts. First, the Japanese government was the first industrialized country to prepare a report as was requested of all nations by the 1990 World Summit for Children. Second, the first baby-friendly hospital – specifically, one that promotes breast-feeding – in the industrialized world was certified in the Japanese city of Okayama.[14] Third, the mayors-for-children initiative received wide-ranging support from mayors of big as well as not-so-big cities all over Japan. For this last one, I am especially thankful for the support that local SGI entities throughout Japan provided to me with proactive support by its Women's Peace Committee.

Ikeda: We were most honoured to work with you to increase public awareness of the need to protect children's rights.

What was the biggest obstacle you faced in promoting ratification of the Convention on the Rights of the Child?

Chowdhury: In Australia and Japan, problems resulted from opposition by some groups that feared it might weaken parental control and teachers' authority over children. This common criticism collapses when the Convention is read as a whole. Article 5 states that governments shall respect the responsibilities, rights and duties of parents, the members of the extended family and legal guardians to provide appropriate direction and guidance for the child of rights protected by the Convention. Article 14, which establishes the child's right to freedom of thought, conscience and religion, again stresses the importance of parental guidance. In addition, all these are qualified in a manner consistent with the evolving capacities of the child. I had to expend considerable effort to convince the opposition in these countries that we were not proposing a laissez-faire arrangement for children. Instead, we were asking society to recognize and respect the rights of children.

Ikeda: We owe you a profound debt for the ratification of the Convention. You are a great benefactor to Japan. All thoughtful people are grateful to you for the contributions you have made.

I believe that after this stage you returned to work at UNICEF in New York.

Chowdhury: Yes, from Japan, I was transferred to UNICEF headquarters in New York late in April 1993, as secretary of its Executive Board with the responsibility of facilitating the major structural and organizational reform the Board was about to undergo to harmonize the working of the Boards of various funds and programmes of the United Nations.

In addition, I was part of a small team entrusted with the task of preparing countries to ratify the Convention on the Rights of the Child. As a matter of fact, we challenged ourselves to make the Convention the most universally ratified human rights treaty. We operated in a focused, well-planned manner, country by country, initially opening doors by drawing attention to documents of major international summits and other conferences expressing at the highest level an in-principle commitment to support the Convention. The small team attended these international conferences to lobby delegations urging early ratification by all. This enabled us thereafter to approach countries individually asking them to fulfil commitments already made by their leaders at those global gatherings.

I feel pride when I realize that all the countries of the world – except the United States and Somalia[15] – ratified this landmark, multidimensional international treaty at that time. I believe the Convention provides an effective roadmap for real and sustainable global development that puts children first.

Ikeda: I believe so, too. Your perseverance and continuous efforts led a large number of nations to ratify the Convention. Persevering dialogue and sincere action can move the times. Though apparently circuitous, gradualism is actually the shortest, most correct path to follow.

Tagore wrote, 'To seek new paths in a constant renewal of strength – that has always been the secret of progress'.[16] He also observed that the cultivated person grows by accumulating the wisdom of the masses. The only way to succeed is by patiently lending an ear to others' opinions and reaching mutual agreement bit by bit. Attaining harmony with people of different values and cultural backgrounds requires persistent patience. I am convinced that the persevering efforts expended by you and your colleagues on the team will shine with even greater radiance in the years to come.

Chowdhury: Thank you for saying so. Articulation of the Convention, which was initially proposed in 1979, on the occasion of the International Year of the Child, included many noble ideas and high principles. Later, however, we had to abandon hope of agreement on some points and had to devise compromises.

The final session of the drafting committee was marked by angry exchanges between delegates pressing their respective national points of view. The issues of inter-country adoption and the age at which children might serve in military forces provoked fiery debate. Stronger language on the issue of child soldiers and on sexual abuse could not be retained in the final text. To address these major concerns, we subsequently had to work out two optional protocols to be added to the Convention.

Some countries have entered reservations while ratifying because their governments do not agree with one or more formulations in the Convention. However, I feel that some of their reservations are groundless and inconsistent with the purpose of the Convention.

Moving Steadily Forward

Ikeda: You refer to the Optional Protocol to the Convention on the Sale of Children, Child Prostitution and Child Pornography and the Optional Protocol to the Convention on the Involvement of Children in Armed Conflicts, both dating from 2000. I have called for the ratification of these two in my 2002 peace proposal and on other occasions. Now the big challenge is having the Convention and its two protocols effectively implemented both nationally and globally.[17]

Chowdhury: Your exhortation is much appreciated. The two protocols were negotiated to make up for the Convention's unclear compromise language and have now been ratified by many countries. The compromise was a smart move – it enabled us to reach agreement on the Convention and get it adopted. It took ten years to finalize the Convention. Most of us who wanted it to be agreed upon without further loss of time remained quite flexible. We stood between the so-called purists, who wanted to include each and every right in strong language, and the minimalists, who wanted restrictive language throughout the text. We pragmatists insisted that what is good today can be made better tomorrow. The important thing was to not let the opportunity of adopting the Convention pass us by.

Ikeda: It was a wise approach. As Mahatma Gandhi famously said, 'Good travels at a snail's pace'. Reforms made too fast are fragile. When something untoward arises, they can crumble away to nothing. The way to effect lasting reform is to keep our eyes on distant ideals while moving steadily forward, step by step.

The futurist Hazel Henderson, with whom I have conducted a dialogue,[18] began tackling environmental problems when she noticed soot from polluted air on her child's skin. She told me:

Since we knew what a big task bringing children up is, we were anxious for our children to have the best future possible.

Thinking back, I realize that's what gave us the strength to endure all kinds of persecution and keep pushing ahead.[19]

Starting from her concern with children's environmental issues, today she advises many governments on the environment, welfare, economics and nuclear disarmament.

Whether they are environmental or child-rights issues, trying to resolve problems that arise from doubts and questions about things close at hand often leads to solutions for these issues on a global scale. This is why world leaders must heed the people's voices and tap their wisdom. In this context, the mission and responsibility of the United Nations grow increasingly important.

Chowdhury: The Convention on the Rights of the Child is the culmination of more than half a century of international efforts to set universal standards for these rights. The earlier child rights documents had a welfare focus. The Convention thus represents a major shift toward children having autonomous rights.

To me, two elements in the Convention highlight its unique outlook. The first is the recognition of the principle that the 'best interests of the child' are of 'primary consideration in all actions concerning children'. The other is Article 12, the Convention's most innovative provision, which says,

States parties shall assure to the child who is capable of forming his or her own views the right to express those views freely in all matters affecting the child, the views of the child being given due weight in accordance with age and maturity of the child.[20]

Ikeda: Children have the right to pursue their own happiness and to be respected as individuals. The Lotus Sutra, the quintessence of Mahayana Buddhism, relates how the eight-year-old daughter of a dragon king attains Buddhahood, symbolizing the supreme worth of children's lives, and that they deserve equal respect with adults.

The dragon king's daughter vows to her teacher, Shakyamuni, to do all she can to save suffering people. Even a child can be the protagonist in the bodhisattva practice of helping those who are suffering. This view offers a fresh lesson on the need for adults to regard children as full-fledged individuals. We must seriously consider and speedily implement ways of reflecting in society the all-too-often unheard voices of children.

Chowdhury: As we conclude this part of our dialogue devoted to children, let me recall the profound obligation enshrined in the preamble of the 1959 United Nations Declaration of the Rights of the Child, asserting that 'Mankind owes the child the best it has to give'.[21]

SEVEN

An Effective United Nations

Ikeda: The thirteenth-century Buddhist leader Nichiren wrote, 'If you want to understand what results will be manifested in the future, look at the causes in the present'.[1] Securing a victorious future requires nations, societies and individuals to courageously rise to the challenges of the present and to move steadily forward.

With an annual GDP (Gross Domestic Product) growth rate of more than 5 per cent, Bangladesh now numbers among the 11 most promising developing countries, after Brazil, Russia, India, China and South Africa (the so-called BRICS[2]). Japanese television reported in a programme on Dhaka that considerable increases in income among the poor there have raised the level of the country's economy as a whole.

The spread of microcredit of the kind represented by Grameen Bank has played a major role in the improved economic stability of the lowest earners in Bangladesh, hasn't it?

Chowdhury: Yes, microcredit plays a big part in promoting the empowerment of the poor. As I mentioned earlier (see Conversation Six), Bangladesh is devoting great energy to the education and empowerment of women and girls. Nonetheless, still one of the Least Developed Countries[3] in the world, Bangladesh must consider fundamental issues like meaningful poverty reduction and protecting socially vulnerable segments, while steadily pursuing economic development.

The GDP growth rate should not be the sole objective or criterion of development. To make development sustainable, the most important focus should be the people. We have seen time and again that quality of life can never be improved by just material growth. In my role as representative of my own country and also representing the United Nations, I consistently underscored the importance of people-centred and rights-based development for all countries and all peoples.

Ikeda: As I have also consistently insisted, we must make the people's welfare our focus in all things. This is the way to create a better society brimming with vitality.

There are many young people in Bangladesh. A country where young people and women can grow with hope and courage is certain to flourish.

To return to the topic of microcredit, when you visited Tokyo in 2006, you gave me a beautiful piece of fabric woven by women empowered by that initiative.

Chowdhury: The fabric was done in a traditional Bangladesh design with typical rural motif. At the same time, that beautiful work of art represents the determined struggle of poor women of the present time.

Ikeda: As my wife and I examined the beautifully embroidered fabric with the deepest appreciation, we envisaged the noble image of the Bangladeshi women who created it with pride and skill. Often too much attention is paid to statistics like the GDP, but it is surely a sign of social progress when self-confidence, smiling faces and pride in earning a living return to women who have long suffered in poverty.

In the peace proposal I issued in January 2008, I stressed that the effort to attain the United Nations' Millennium Development Goals must be focused not only on meeting statistical targets but also on restoring suffering individuals' wellbeing.

Chowdhury: The most important mission of the United Nations is to improve comprehensively the living conditions of the peoples of the world. A vital aspect of this undertaking is true commitment and practical action in favour of the weakest and most vulnerable nations and their peoples, who are compelled to face the most daunting challenges in today's world both domestically and externally.

Your repeated statements to this effect in your speeches and peace proposals delight and encourage me immensely. You always speak out for the weakest people and express the urgent need for international support for them, particularly for their social development. In one of your peace proposals, you urged us to remember that our goals must reflect the face of each individual and must be directed toward bringing qualitative change into their daily lives and restoring the happiness that results from human solidarity and feelings of fellowship.[4]

Inner Reform and Peace

Ikeda: The United Nations' role in protecting the weak is increasingly important. This is why, in this conversation, I want to discuss that role in the twenty-first-century world. History demonstrates the undeniable truth that disputes based on conflicting self-interest are destined to arise regularly among nations. The multilateral UN system was devised to regulate such disputes. Such a system is crucial and indispensable for the survival of the Earth's peoples. Our failure to take the United Nations seriously now will bring regrets in the future. Josei Toda always said that it represents the epitome of twentieth-century human wisdom, and that we must protect it as a fortress of world hope and foster it for coming centuries.

Chowdhury: Mr Toda gave wonderful expression to the basic rationale for the creation of the United Nations. Leaders of the world today should lend an attentive ear to what he and, subsequently, you have had to say. During his lifetime, he stood up for universal values and resisted militarism, which seeks to suppress fundamental human rights. I am also impressed by his approach to the abolition of nuclear weapons as an integral part of the process of inner transformation that would eliminate global misery.

Ikeda: The philosophy of human revolution that Mr Toda developed during his two years' imprisonment for struggling against Japanese militarism – the idea that we can transform society and build the foundation for world peace through our inner transformation as individuals – is the principle upon which our movement for peace is based. Supporting the United Nations, the human race must move forward together with the attainment of peace and harmonious co-existence as its guiding principle.

In this effort, as the old saying goes, slow and steady win the race. Though strengthening the various organs of the United Nations might seem circuitous, in fact it is the most direct way to achieve global security for humankind. Exclusive focus on national self-interest is ultimately self-destructive. No nation can enjoy peace and prosperity unless the enduring security of the whole world is ensured. In 'On Establishing the Correct Teaching for the Peace of the Land', Nichiren, whose teachings we in the SGI follow, asked, 'If you care anything about your personal security, you should first of all pray for order and tranquillity throughout the four quarters of the land, should you not?'[5]

The United Nations is an organization embodying the Earth as a whole. This is why we of the SGI continue to believe firmly in making the United Nations a central force and expanding support for it.

The Buddhist ideals of the dignity of life, equality and compassion transcend national and ethnic differences, and articulate a way of life founded on our common humanity. These Buddhist ideas resonate deeply with the principle of peace that is the foundation of the United Nations. This is why we consider support of the United Nations a foregone conclusion and a way of carrying out our mission as Buddhists. On the basis of this Buddhist humanist philosophy, we of the SGI have pursued a course of consistent support for the United Nations.

Case for the United Nations

Chowdhury: I am an ardent and, at the same time, a rational believer in the United Nations, a universal world body that strives to promote peace, development and human rights in a mutually supportive and collaborative world within a multilateral framework.

As you think of the United Nations as the embodiment of a global society, I might compare the organization to the air that we breathe all the time without being aware of its existence. The moment it is taken away, we realize how vital it is to our life. The same is true about the United Nations. Surely the UN has many deficiencies, but it is the only available universal body that is striving to make this world a better place.

Without it, the world would be chaotic, and then we would appreciate how crucial its role has been. That is why it is also critical that the reform of the United Nations addresses these deficiencies to better serve the peoples of the world. In some of my own speeches, I have borrowed your term for the United Nations as the 'Parliament of Humanity'. The organization can be proud to have committed and reliable supporters like you.

Ikeda: In an interview with the Inter Press Service, on 28 March 2008, I talked about my confidence in the United Nations.

Chowdhury: I read the article and was most deeply moved by your explanation of why the United Nations has not brought about lasting world peace even now, decades after the end of the Second World War. You said:

> In other words, the UN is not by nature a powerless institution. Rather, what is weak is the will of the international community to work through the UN to resolve problems. And this lack of will impacts the ability of the UN to function. For my part, I have tried to contribute to creating a better, more stable environment for the UN by urging the various world leaders with whom I have met to offer the UN greater support.[6]

In addition, you said in the interview:

> The members of the Soka Gakkai International (SGI) have been cooperating with UN agencies and other NGOs to raise awareness on issues relating to disarmament and the environment and to promote an ethic of global citizenship. Our stance is not that of bystanders, watching to see whether the UN will succeed or fail. Rather, we want to focus on developing a deeper sense of responsibility – what we can and should do to enable it to function effectively.[7]

It has been encouraging to find that the members of the SGI are far from passive bystanders or irresponsible critics. Time and time again, I have personally witnessed them trying to find out what they can and should do to promote the goals and objectives of the United Nations.

In your peace proposal for 2006, you took as your theme 'A New Era of the People: Forging a Global Network of Robust Individuals'. The idea expressed in this theme should characterize the United Nations' strategy for the twenty-first century. I would say with particular emphasis that we must not leave things up to the politicians, diplomats or to international civil servants alone. The most effective way to begin reform and to create a better world is for the common people to rise up – for civil society to come forward to ask for change for the better.

Ikeda: The ordinary people must play the leading role. The United Nations can manifest its true strengths only when its goal is the welfare of the people.

I think young people at the stage when they are choosing their careers would be interested to hear about your early days as a UN staffer, including how you came to work there. Would you mind telling me a little bit about that period?

Breath of Fresh Air

Chowdhury: Well, I had a diplomatic career spanning four decades. I joined the Pakistan Foreign Service in 1967 and completed my final tenure with the United Nations in 2007. Thirty-five of those 40 years were devoted to multilateral diplomacy, particularly at the United Nations. I represented Bangladesh at the United Nations and in other international forums in various capacities. I also worked for the United Nations. And I also had the honour of being elected to lead a number of intergovernmental bodies, including the two main organs of the United Nations – the Security Council and the Economic and Social Council.

Actually my initial association with the organization was in the context of academic study for a master's degree in contemporary history from the University of Dhaka. My second association with it occurred in 1971, during the Bangladesh Liberation War. At that time, I arranged, on behalf of the government in exile, to dispatch a team of eminent persons to New York to bring to the United Nations' attention the ongoing war of independence. But both of these associations were without my own physical presence at the United Nations.

It was in 1972, soon after the liberation of Bangladesh, that I was sent by my government to the UN Headquarters in New York to work for the admission of the newly independent nation as a member. This was a turning point in both my career and my life.

Ikeda: It was a time when the independence of a growing number of Asian and African nations was bringing a breath of fresh air to the United Nations. On the occasion of my first visit to the UN Headquarters in October 1960, I already sensed the high hopes the peoples of the developing world had for the organization. During that year – known as the Year of Africa – 17 new African nations came into being. The sight of the representatives of these new member nations taking part in the General Assembly and various committees left a deep impression on me.

I have, again, always insisted that the twenty-first will be the Century of Africa. The representatives of those newly independent African nations conveyed an eagerness to work with the United Nations as a way to create a better world. Since then, whenever I have thought about the great mission of the United Nations, I have recalled the sight of those committed representatives.

Chowdhury: That is exactly how we felt. It was only in 1972 that I physically saw the United Nations for the first time. My wife and I were staying in a penthouse very close to the United Nations on 46th Street between First and Second Avenues. The morning after our arrival, I opened a window in our bedroom and saw the row of national flags fluttering in front of the UN Building. I was absolutely thrilled. It was like a dream come true. I called my wife in excitement to come and see that awesome view of the UN Building.

Later, when I started working in the building itself, I used to get goose bumps from feeling that I was actually carrying out my responsibility inside the building we had read about, seen photographs of, and fantasized about. It gave me not only pleasure and a sense of pride but also a kind of confidence knowing that I could work there to pursue a crucial objective for my homeland, for whose independence I had struggled tirelessly with deep conviction. That confidence gradually grew to give me the ability and capacity to be articulate, effective, persuasive and convincing as I interacted with delegates from various countries of the world.

Ikeda: You were an eager youth, filled with an impassioned hope and sense of mission. In May of 1972, the year you first saw the UN Building, I visited Washington, DC. I was on my way home by way of Paris after having initiated my dialogue with Arnold J. Toynbee, who had invited me to his London residence.

Chowdhury: An interesting coincidence – you and Dr Toynbee had a great deal to say about the United Nations.

Ikeda: He was concerned that, though all member nations have a single vote, the pronouncements of different countries carried very different weight. Small and medium countries would probably join together in the future, he thought, noting that African and Arab groups had already formed. Dr Toynbee expressed his expectation that those groups would assist and complement one another in creating unique positions in international society.

He also said that the important thing for resolving global problems, such as pollution, would be for all countries, regardless of size, to come together to form a true world government. While this was a perceptive observation, sadly, his concern has still found no resolution.

I believe that it is absolutely essential to create a system in which all nations, regardless of size, have an equal voice and a shared sense of responsibility in solving global problems in a United Nations that is in name and deed a congress of humanity and a stage for humanity's common struggle.

Chowdhury: It is my strong conviction that it is essential for all world leaders to work together in a cooperative, constructive spirit to, as you emphasize, empower and strengthen our beloved, unduly maligned world forum. As one who has worked with the organization for many years in many capacities, I am fully aware of the extent to which the United Nations is in your debt for your consistent support and efforts in its name. Your annual peace proposals articulate the importance of strengthening the United Nations and the need for constructing a multilateral framework. You have been presenting those valuable proposals for decades, and each year I read them with great interest encouraged by your worthy ideas and life-enriching philosophy.

No Nation Isolated

Ikeda: What was the most daunting challenge for you in carrying out your first assignment at the United Nations?

Chowdhury: The most difficult thing was setting up communications with members of the Security Council, in particular the permanent ones, in the hope of gaining their approval for Bangladesh's admission. As the UN Charter envisaged, a negative vote by any permanent member would frustrate that objective.

In this context, it was crucially important to win the understanding of China, which had objected to our admission in 1972 basically in view of its geo-politically significant relations with Pakistan. China had, of course, said that it was not fundamentally opposed to Bangladesh's admission to the United Nations but wanted to defer the matter to allow reconciliation among the parties concerned.

I was heartbroken when, sitting with my wife in the visitors' gallery of the Security Council chamber on 25 August 1972, I observed the Chinese permanent representative, Ambassador Huang Hua, raise his pencil to signify his country's veto of Bangladesh's bid for membership. As you know, in 1976, he became the foreign minister of China, in which capacity he facilitated friendly relations with Bangladesh.

Ikeda: Unfortunately, Bangladesh membership was not recognized in 1972. How did you react?

Chowdhury: It presented a complex challenge to the Bangladesh team in New York. Right away, we started working with the Chinese delegation on overcoming their objection. I was the main conduit from Bangladesh at the working level in the ensuing discussions. It became apparent that China would be willing to withdraw its objection once Pakistan's concurrence was available. It was said that they wanted to prove that China was loyal to her friends in good times and bad. We understood that. I am confident that China had agonized over the position it had taken because it was only in 1971, after 22 years of fighting for it, that China herself secured her legitimate, rightful place at the United Nations – and because their first veto would be against the membership of another developing country, more so a newly independent, impoverished nation like Bangladesh.

Ikeda: So you proceeded with negotiations fully aware of the Chinese position. At the time, I believed cementing China's position in the United Nations was indispensable to making the organization an effective congress of humanity.

In September 1968, I proposed the normalization of Sino–Japanese relations to an audience of more than 10,000 students. China's Cultural Revolution was still raging, and Japan and the West regarded China with animosity. Still China was Japan's neighbour with a population of 700 million. Persisting with the status quo, in which Japan and China had no formal diplomatic relations, was not conducive to Asian stability or world peace.

On this basis, I resolutely called for recognition of the Chinese government, promotion of economic and cultural exchanges, and the establishment of China's place in the United Nations. I advocated its admission to the United Nations because under no circumstances should a nation – any nation at all – be isolated from the rest of the world. I was criticized for my stance, but I am convinced that history has justified my belief.

Chowdhury: I deeply feel the same way as you do – no nation should be isolated and denied membership of the world body. That is why we continued with renewed efforts to overcome all obstacles to the admission of Bangladesh to the United Nations. We set up a group of friends of Bangladesh composed of five senior and influential ambassadors to the United Nations. This group started working on Pakistan and China to pinpoint the difficulties, figure out the best way to overcome them, and determine how long it would take to clear the way.

On a bilateral level, my focus was to maintain regular contact with China, which was through Zhou Nan, who was then Counsellor of the People's Republic of China's Mission to the United Nations. He was a sharp diplomat who later became the leader of China's negotiation team responsible for the reversion of Hong Kong to Chinese rule. We developed a frank, cooperative and mutually helpful working relation.

It took two years before we were admitted, in 1974. Bangladesh functioned as an observer nation at the United Nations for these two years. On 17 September 1974, finally the flag of Bangladesh was hoisted in the row of UN flags in front of the headquarters building, signifying its full acceptance into the world body and the international community.

Ikeda: I can well imagine the joy you must have felt on the grand occasion when your homeland became the 125th member nation, and I cannot fail to appreciate how hard you strove to achieve this result.

As Dr Toynbee stressed, the effectiveness of the United Nations in the years to come will depend upon whether it succeeds in rallying the strengths of as many nations as possible and promoting cooperation among them to overcome the numerous problems the world faces. We have a Japanese expression, 'Allowing a precious treasure to rust'. We must not allow this to happen to the United Nations. We should employ it effectively, so that it can shine its brightest for us.

Property of Humanity

Chowdhury: The United Nations will never be effective in the true sense unless and until its membership collaborates, inspired by its enormous potential for the good of humanity. For me, the day-to-day involvement in Bangladesh's admission was a wonderful opportunity to get to know the organization, to internalize its concepts, to be familiar with its working culture, to enter its operational labyrinth, and even to find out personally all the nooks and crannies of the sprawling headquarters building. When I came back as the Bangladesh ambassador in 1996, I used to tell my younger colleagues that to be functionally effective in the UN Building, they must also know the physical dimensions of every part of it – which stairs lead to which place, which corner is the best place for quiet diplomacy, and where to get a cup of coffee during late-night negotiations. Continuing to be a truly effective UN diplomat is a lifelong engagement – all the more as the working culture of the world body keeps evolving.

Ikeda: This is important advice for success in diplomacy and negotiation. On a different level, whenever I visit Soka Gakkai community centres in Japan or SGI facilities in any part of the world, I encourage supervisors and staff members who work behind the scenes to inspect places like storerooms that are usually not visited. I have always taken great pains to ensure that our centres and facilities are places where our members feel safe and to do my utmost to prevent serious accidents or fire. I consider this my responsibility as a leader.

Chowdhury: Now you give me new insight into the depth of your caring and humane concern for SGI members.

Talking about physical facilities, the delegates lounge at the United Nations was active in the early 1970s but not as crowded as it is now. The media area and the delegates lounge were the two places I used to go a lot in order to meet people, for gathering information and finding out what was going on.

For me, such close and all-embracing involvement with the United Nations first turned into an infatuation, then into an attraction, and then into an enduring love for the world's most universal entity that continues to mature even now.

Ikeda: Many NGO leaders supporting the organization in New York and Geneva praise the love and passion you have for the United Nations. You deserve to be called Mr United Nations.

Having experienced two world conflicts and numerous other armed clashes, humanity should never again repeat the tragedy of war. The creation of the United Nations was the outcome of a vow to create a peaceful world, in which humankind can live happily and in ways true to our best capabilities. This is why it is so important to work to protect the United Nations and help it keep up with the times, as you have done.

Although the United Nations faces many problems and challenges, we cannot ensure that humanity has a future unless the United Nations is strengthened, and the nations of the world work together in harmony. In this sense, to protect the United Nations is to protect our nations, ourselves, our children, and our future. We SGI members hold this as an immutable conviction.

In particular, we believe that a network of awakened people has the power to move and change the times. The United Nations is the property of humanity. I hope that we can further discuss and study ways to pool the might of the masses for the sake of strengthening this property.

EIGHT
The Congress of Humanity

Ikeda: The struggle for peace advances one step at a time. On 19 July 2008, the Toda International Advisory Council of the Toda Institute for Global Peace and Policy Research, a Soka Gakkai-affiliated peace organization, convened a conference at the Catholic University of Louvain, Belgium. Thirty scholars from 16 nations participated, and a variety of peace issues, including UN reform, were discussed. Former International Peace Research Association Secretary-General Luc Reychler delivered a congratulatory address, and Secretary-General Kevin Clements sent a message.

The elimination of nuclear weapons and strengthening of the United Nations are two issues the Toda Institute has focused on from its inception. You kindly attended the international conference hosted by the Toda Institute in Los Angeles in February 2006, which addressed the theme 'Transforming the United Nations: Human Development, Regional Conflicts and Global Governance'. As founder of the Institute, I thank you again for your contributions during conference deliberations.

Chowdhury: I thank you for inviting me. Focusing on the reform of the United Nations, Director Majid Tehranian and his team skilfully organized the brainstorming. Several representatives of the

United Nations, including myself, welcomed this opportunity. Also I personally benefited from the richness and diversity of perspectives introduced by other participants, who included academics and civil society representatives. The Toda Institute should be commended for bringing together such a brilliant group of scholars to talk about the future of the United Nations.

The complete freedom with which participants at the Los Angeles conference expressed their opinions was impressive. Their openness, the respect they showed for one another's views, their thoroughness and the sincere interest they demonstrated in the effectiveness of the United Nations impressed me deeply.

You founded the Toda Institute for Global Peace and Policy Research and the Ikeda Center for Peace, Learning, and Dialogue, both of which do wonderful work in stimulating serious and purposeful exchanges of views on issues that are of concern to humanity. To that end, the pursuits of these organizations are truly worthwhile.

Ikeda: Thank you for your warm words of understanding. Dr Tehranian served as institute director from its founding in February 1996. He was succeeded in his post in 2008 by Olivier Urbain. I hope you will continue supporting the organization as you have.

Chowdhury: In my exchanges with Majid Tehranian and his successor, Olivier Urbain, as well as with Masao Yokota, representative (now advisor) of the Ikeda Center, I had the pleasure of sharing my thoughts about bringing some of the burning issues of our times into the mainstream activities of these two forward-looking organizations. I believe both of them are well positioned to undertake activities including research on the culture of peace that, to our great encouragement, you have been championing so enthusiastically. I look forward to supporting both these organizations, which are hallmarks of your intellectual inspiration, in any way I can, as they chart their courses for the future.

Ikeda: University of Denver Vice Provost Ved Nanda highly praised the 2006 conference because people speaking from different vantage points frankly expressed their ideas on the United Nations' future outlook. I was pleased to see that the conference covered how to reform and strengthen the United Nations from a variety of viewpoints.

The Toda Institute for Global Peace and Policy Research is dedicated to promoting open dialogue on the welfare and needs of the people, transcending ethnicity, religion and cultural differences, to find solutions to the problems confronting the world. Supporting the institute's ideals and efforts, approximately 600 representatives from more than 65 countries and regions participate in the Toda International Advisory Council. Through the cooperation of researchers from many fields around the world, we have built this institution for tackling the issue of peace. Former director Tehranian referred to this worldwide network as a family-like circle of cooperative research. Cool-headed, objective discussion based on reality is important. I hope this warm, familial atmosphere will be preserved.

Chowdhury: Speaking of a good family-like atmosphere reminds me of the Los Angeles conference. After each day's meeting was over, we participants had dinner together. It so happened that the first day of the meeting coincided with one participant's birthday. At dinner, we all joined in singing 'Happy Birthday'. The following day – 5 February – was my birthday; that evening I was the focus of the participants' singing.

But the bouquet of flowers and the warm wishes you sent on that occasion made me happier than anything else. They were special. I shall always remember that evening for the heart-touching gesture of your deep sincerity and warm friendship, and the cordiality that I received from everyone at the conference.

First-hand Experience

Ikeda: What I did was very small, but I am delighted that it pleased you. The Toda Institute was founded in 1996, the Ikeda Center for Peace, Learning, and Dialogue in 1993. The Ikeda Center's mottoes are: 'Be the heart of a network of global citizens. Be a bridge for dialogue between civilizations. Be a beacon lighting the way to a century of life.' Through lively seminars, lectures and publishing, it brings together thinkers from around the world and communicates its message. The Center's publications are highly regarded and used as textbooks in more than 500 courses at 220 universities.[1] I have contributed prefaces and commentaries to a number of those publications, including *Subverting Hatred, Subverting Greed, Educating Citizens for Global Awareness,* and *Ethical Visions of Education.*

As a person active not only in the United Nations and UNICEF but on a broader international stage, how do you think we can make the work of these two peace-related organizations even more significant?

Chowdhury: Before answering your question, I should like to mention an experience that might be a useful reference. In November 2001, I was invited by the Woodrow Wilson School of Public and International Affairs at Princeton University to speak on the 'third world' perspectives of the work of the UN Security Council. At the time, Bangladesh was still a member of the Council. The lecture-room gallery was filled with students and faculty members, and most of the students were pursuing master's degrees in international affairs. During the question-and-answer period following my talk, I was disappointed by the direction and substance of their questions, as they had no connection with the reality of how the United Nations, more so the Security Council, works after more than half a century of existence. The students had read textbooks, they had studied thoroughly, and their teachers had presented in-depth academic lectures. But they had had no opportunity to hear from practitioners who knew first-hand how the current Security Council works – how it had evolved in every way since it was set up.

The way the Council works and its members operate has evolved greatly over the decades. It is absolutely essential that a student specializing in international affairs should have a real understanding of the current situation and, if possible, be exposed to how the organization actually works and does not work. Often so-called UN experts are deficient in this area, and there exists a huge gap between textbook knowledge and on-the-ground reality.

Ikeda: Yes, it is important to understand how the United Nations actually functions. Closing this gap between knowledge and reality is always an important point on which institutions of higher learning need to focus in every area.

For ten years, I received private instruction on a wide range of subjects from my mentor. Highly skilled in mathematics, he had in the pre-war period published a book titled *Suirishiki shido sanjutsu* (A Deductive Guide to Arithmetic), which became a bestseller with more than one million copies. His teaching was rooted in applying the knowledge acquired through study to actual life and society, and to the creation of value. In instructing youth, he never clung to textbook knowledge but discussed every subject in light of social issues. His lectures concentrated on finding ways to transform knowledge into wisdom, always centred on the welfare of human beings. The living learning I acquired from him is an integral part of my whole being to this day.

Chowdhury: Yes, I can understand how it would remain with you. Learning must stay in contact with actuality to avoid lapsing into armchair theorizing. Unfortunately, at the Princeton meeting, the students' questions had no real connection with reality on the ground. I suggested to the concerned teacher that to be meaningful and worthwhile, their curriculum on the United Nations needed restructuring because students could have the mistaken impression that getting a master's degree in the international system and mouthing the textbook-ish knowledge they got in school would give them credibility. He, too, must have sensed the need because he asked me to craft a course on the United Nations from practical, realistic perspectives. Knowing theory, history, philosophy, conceptual underpinnings and so on is necessary, but, to be what it really should be, that knowledge must be combined with an understanding of how an organization has evolved and currently functions within the contexts of its objectives, mandates and working methods.

Ikeda: Though a scholarly foundation is important, without access to the real-life experiences and opinions of people who have actually sweated and struggled on the job, it is impossible to grasp how things really are. Herein lies the importance of connecting the scholarly with the practical.

Concrete Proposals

Chowdhury: That is why I would like to see the Toda Institute and the Ikeda Center serve the function of a bridge. Although it has its inherent value, the scholarly approach alone is not enough. We must include the practical application of peace research if we are to make it relevant and valuable.

As far as advice goes, I recommend that the Toda Institute preserve the format it adopted for the 2006 Los Angeles conference and, in addition to scholars, include people of practical experience within the framework of its debates. In terms of structuring the agenda on the United Nations, preliminary informal consultation with people who are involved and know the concerns of the United Nations and areas where scholarly support is needed could help determine topics of discussion and make the deliberations more fruitful, more meaningful.

Ikeda: Again, it is impossible to take effective action without paying attention to what is happening on the ground. Practical steps based on concrete reality are the key to building a better future.

Cooperation between both the scholarly and practical aspects is essential to UN reform.

Chowdhury: Looking ahead into the future with the active engagement of scholars and people with practical experience is relevant to the future of the United Nations itself. Unfortunately, the United Nations lacks a mechanism to do that. There are offices to deal with daily business and management functions but none that I might call a 'futures unit' that can look well ahead and identify the coming concerns of humanity.

Of course, we benefit from outside research and studies, but the UN Secretariat, too, must look into the future; not the immediate future, but say ten years ahead. I always underline this point when people ask me about reforming the United Nations. Preparing well ahead of time to address the concerns of the future would help the United Nations better serve the needs of our world.

I appreciate the wonderful work the Toda Institute and the Ikeda Center do and should like them to take up a UN-related agenda through increasingly practical approaches. It would also be worthwhile to organize panel discussions or symposia or roundtables to introduce the work of your two organizations on global issues at the United Nations itself.

Ikeda: Thank you for your valuable advice. What kind of reforms and reinforcement does the United Nations need to function as a congress of humanity and to meet the expectations of the world's people? This is a question to which I, too, as a global citizen, have given deep thought. I have exchanged ideas with secretaries-general and numerous other UN-related individuals, and I have offered concrete suggestions in my annual peace proposals.

This comes from the teaching of my mentor, who insisted on concrete proposals and actions for the peace and progress of humanity. He frequently told us that such concrete ideas and actions, though they might not be realized immediately, will act as the sparks that eventually ignite and spread the flame of peace. While empty theorizing never gets you anywhere, he said, concrete proposals can become pillars supporting real change, holding up a roof that protects humanity. I hope to make whatever small contribution I can to this kind of peace-building.

Chowdhury: You are the one person in the whole world who has been speaking in a substantive way for more than 25 years about the United Nations, its effectiveness, and the need for its improvement. Some UN functionaries and scholars have addressed similar issues but none for as long and as consistently as you have done. Your annual peace proposals always bring up issues that relate to the work of the United Nations and, on quite a few occasions, were largely devoted to the subject.

Your concrete approach is truly wonderful and embraces both current and future issues. You keep abreast of what is happening at the United Nations and incorporate your wisdom and perspective in your peace proposals in ways that benefit not only SGI members worldwide but also humanity as a whole, promoting understanding of the relevance of the United Nations in a big way.

Ikeda: You are most generous to say so.

Chowdhury: I am only highlighting what is reflected in your proposals. I would like to express my heartfelt gratitude to you for the consistent support and encouragement you have given the United Nations.

You last visited the Headquarters in 1996. In the time that has elapsed since then, the world has altered in significant ways, its context has changed, it has become more complex, while you have evolved a consistent philosophy of support and encouragement for multilateralism with the UN system at its core. The United Nations needs to know about this support.[2] For all your commitment and

Mr Ikeda's first visit to the UN headquarters (October 1960)
© Seikyo Shimbun

UN Secretary-General Kofi Annan welcoming Ambassador Chowdhury in his office at
UN Headquarters on the latter's first day at work as Under-Secretary-General and
High Representative of the UN, New York (March 2002)
©UN Photo/Evan Schneider

Ambassador Chowdhury with Bangabandhu Sheikh Mujibur Rahman,
Father of the Nation of Bangladesh and Prime Minister of India Mrs Indira Gandhi
during the former's first foreign visit as Bangladesh Prime Minister to Kolkata,
India (February 1972)

Ambassador Chowdhury chairing a UN Security Council meeting as its President
(March 2000) at UN Headquarters
©UN Photo/Eskinder Debebe

UN Secretary-General Javier Perez de Cuéllar (left), Prime Minister of India and
winner of the first UN Population Award Mrs Indira Gandhi (centre) and
the Award Committee Chairman Ambassador Chowdhury at
UN Headquarters, New York (30 September 1983)
©UN Photo/Yutaka Nagata

Mr Ikeda with Dr J. Forbes Munro at the honorary doctorate conferral ceremony at the
University of Glasgow, UK (June 1994)
© Seikyo Shimbun

Mr Ikeda with Dr Bishambhar Nath Pande, former vice chairperson of the
Gandhi Memorial Hall (February 1992)
© Seikyo Shimbun

Mr Ikeda visiting the SGI-USA Boston centre
(September 1991)
© Seikyo Shimbun

1976 Nobel Peace Prize laureate Dr Betty Williams, UN High Representative
for Alliance of Civilizations Ambassador Nassir Al-Nasser and Chair of the event
Ambassador Chowdhury at the book launch of *A Forum for Peace* by
Dr Daisaku Ikeda at UN Headquarters (20 February 2014)
© Seikyo Shimbun

Ambassador Chowdhury with 2011 Nobel Peace Prize laureate Leymah Gbowee at the
launch of Global Campaign on Women, Peace and Security during the Global Summit
to End Sexual Violence in Conflict in London (12 June 2014)

Mr Ikeda talks with Dr Joseph Rotblat
(October 1989)
© Seikyo Shimbun

Mr Ikeda talks with Dr Arnold J. Toynbee
(May 1975)
© Seikyo Shimbun

Mr Ikeda talks with Dr M. S. Swaminathan
(April 2004)
© Seikyo Shimbun

Ambassador Chowdhury with President Mikhail Gorbachev at the Assembly of the World Political Forum after the former's keynote speech on poverty at Stresa, Italy (22 October 2004)

Ambassador Chowdhury with Jigme Singye Wangchuck, the King of Bhutan and the global proponent of the concept of Gross National Happiness (GNH) at King's Royal Office in Thimphu, Bhutan (March 2006)

Mr Ikeda talks with Dr John Kenneth Galbraith
(September 1993)
© Seikyo Shimbun

Mr Ikeda meeting Ms Wangari Maathai
(February 2005)
© Seikyo Shimbun

Mr Ikeda talks with Dr Hazel Henderson
(January 2001)
© Seikyo Shimbun

UNICEF Executive Board Chairman Ambassador Chowdhury launching the
nationwide mass child immunization campaign with President Corazon Aquino
of the Philippines at Malacanang Palace in Manila (April 1986)

Ambassador Chowdhury with 1984 Nobel Peace Prize laureate Bishop Desmond Tutu
at the Church of the Epiphany at Gramercy Park in New York City (1985)

Ambassador Chowdhury (front row centre) at the inauguration of the first-ever
exhibition on *Building a Culture of Peace for the Children of the World* at
UN Headquarters in New York (February 2004)
© Seikyo Shimbun

Mr and Mrs Ikeda attending the World Peace Youth Culture Festival at Carnegie Hall
(June 1996)
© Seikyo Shimbun

Mr Ikeda with Mr Nelson Mandela (October 1990)
© Seikyo Shimbun

Mr Ikeda, the founder of the Soka University, attending a class (January 2004)
© Seikyo Shimbun

Ambassador Chowdhury (back row left) in his youth with his parents and his younger
sister Anarkali in Dhaka, erstwhile East Pakistan, now Bangladesh (1967)

Ambassador Chowdhury with his mother at the residence of
Bangladesh Ambassador to the UN in New York (1998)

Ambassador Chowdhury with his wife, Mariam, in Tokyo soon after presenting his
commencement speech at Soka University in Japan (18 March 2016)
© Sakura Goto

Ambassador Chowdhury and Mr Ikeda at Soka University in Japan (30 August 2006)
© Seikyo Shimbun

After receiving the Honorary Doctorate presented by Soka University in Japan
Ambassador and Mrs Chowdhury join Mr and Mrs Ikeda for the official photograph
at the University campus (19 March 2003)
© Seikyo Shimbun

Ambassador Chowdhury and Mr Ikeda commence their dialogue at Hachioji in Japan
(19 March 2003)
© Seikyo Shimbun

contribution to the world body, you deserve special recognition from the United Nations.

Connecting Youth

Ikeda: I will do my best to live up to your generous estimation of my contributions.

Many students at Soka University of America, which has as one of its goals training leaders for a pacifist world, are deeply interested in the United Nations' activities. The UN Study Tour Project, which started a few years ago and which you have generously supported, provides our students with a precious opportunity to learn about the United Nations.

The first tour, in 2006 entailed 50 hours of discussion and interaction with more than 30 people, including yourself, when you were among the United Nations' senior management; Nobuaki Tanaka, Under-Secretary-General for Disarmament Affairs; Carolyn McAskie, Assistant Secretary-General for Peacebuilding Support; Pera Wells, Secretary-General of the World Federation of the United Nations Associations; and Aye Aye Thant, President of the U Thant Institute.

A visit to the UN Headquarters and the opportunity to meet and learn from many officials and staff members strengthened the students' conviction that the United Nations ought to serve, not as an arena for conflicting national interests, but as a forum for dialogue promoting the prosperity of all humankind. I am convinced that such educational programmes, though they may seem modest, help to forge a connection between the United Nations, the congress of humanity, and young people, who bear responsibility for the future.

Chowdhury: The Soka University of America UN Study Tour is a highly significant undertaking. Connection with students and, for that matter, with all young people, should be an essential theme for the United Nations in the twenty-first century.

In my vision statement presented to the 2006 Los Angeles conference of the Toda Institute, I expressed my firm belief that the world of the future will have abundant positive-minded, global citizens if the young people of today better understand and appreciate the values of the United Nations and of multilateralism. I stated, 'In the future, the United Nations should be an organization that interacts more closely and substantially with young people to benefit from their ideas and enthusiasm in shaping the future of the world'.[3]

My specific enthusiasm and belief in the involvement of young people emerged in a concrete and transparent way as I was developing the UN General Assembly's Programme of Action on a Culture of Peace. I felt that, if we really want to create a peaceful, non-violent and secure planet, we must engage the people who will be in charge of the world for at least the next 30 or 40 years. Since they are now entering the prime of life, we must assist young people in developing a global outlook and in familiarizing themselves with the work of the United Nations, so that a lifelong engagement of mutual support, benefit and solidarity is developed.

Ikeda: Young people are the protagonists who will create the future. I have devoted my full energies to the cultivation and education of young people, on whom the future depends. I have made education the crowning focus of my life.

In August 2006, I submitted a proposal for a United Nations focused on youth.[4] I did so based on my conviction that to solve global problems, we must abandon narrow national interests and expand our horizon to embrace a shared responsibility. This must be based on the interests of our planet and the human race as a whole, and young people must play the leading role in this new endeavour. I firmly believe that vigorous participation by young people in the United Nations' work can be the Archimedes' fulcrum from which the groundswell toward a peaceful world can gain new impetus.

Chowdhury: Many of the decisions that the United Nations makes in the areas of peace, development, human rights, the environment, climate change and so on have a strong impact on all people, of course, but mostly on the young, who will be on this Earth long after we will and with whom we must engage, not ignore. Unfortunately, however, the United Nations lacks an effective mechanism for communicating with them. Exchanges between them need to be substantive and attentive to the issues that are important to young people.

Programmes like the World Programme of Action for Youth to the Year 2000 and Beyond are only token expressions of the United Nations' involvement. Youth issues should be given higher priority and youth a greater opportunity to participate in the activities of the United Nations system than now.

You touch on a very sensitive point when, in your UN proposal, you call for deliberation on the establishment of a global entity to deal specifically with action of and for the young people of the world and suggest the creation of a department of youth within the UN structure. I agree with you wholeheartedly.

Ikeda: Our times are calling for vibrant youth in all countries who desire peace to join forces and become the impetus for the United Nations' activities. New UN reforms need to be promoted through their youthful ideas and passion.

There is also a rising demand in civil society for the establishment of a special organization to advance coherent, coordinated policies in the interests of women – who, after all, make up half the population of the world. The United Nations needs to advance the empowerment of women, who are facing harsh situations in many parts of the globe. With the establishment of ways enabling greater participation in the United Nations by young people and women, a greater diversity of ideas will be vibrantly reflected in all its policies. This is the key to building a bright new future for the organization.

Chowdhury: Coming as I do from one of the most vulnerable countries of the world with a large, young population, I am painfully aware of the need for the United Nations to embrace the youth agenda and enter the twenty-first century in the real sense. It is high time that Member States include young people in their delegations and facilitate their contribution in the decision-making process. The UN Secretariat has to work out effective ways to reach out to and engage young people. Otherwise, we will have a sceptical generation that is not in a position to appreciate the value of the United Nations in addressing the complex challenges that we all face. That is why I believe that, in the future, the United Nations must interact more closely and substantively with young people. The youth agenda needs to be creatively placed in the mainstream. My efforts and experience in promoting the culture of peace have made me fully aware of the critical need to engage youth in a meaningful manner in the global agenda.

Ikeda: Solving problems of poverty and the environment, as well as creating the culture of peace, will demand strong, persistent efforts over several generations. In his later years, Joseph Rotblat worked hard to develop the International Student/Young Pugwash, a group of younger-generation scientists. In our dialogue, he said:

> The passion, energy, and enthusiasm of youth sometimes become excessive and too extreme. Yet, even so, they are important. I always make an effort to be gentle and avoid crushing or discouraging a young person's enthusiasm. I also try to cheer them on so that their passion can continue burning brightly.[5]

Dr Rotblat's words are the powerful expression of the profound insight of a great world leader who, though in his nineties, remained an impassioned, dedicated activist for peace. If we wish to continuously create greater, deeper value, making the present better than the past and the future better than the present, then we must treasure our young people.

Chowdhury: You devote your head and heart, your entire soul, to Soka University of Japan and Soka University of America. The students of those two remarkable institutions are immensely fortunate. I have frequent opportunities to interact with students from both universities through programmes like the UN Study Tours and my own visits. I had the pleasure of meeting the students from the United Nations Club of Soka University and receive regular communications from its members, updating me on their activities toward building the culture of peace.

Ikeda: I am grateful to you. The students are all delighted by your support of their activities.

Chowdhury: In all my exchanges with these students, I am struck by their openness, eagerness to reach out to the peoples of the world, ability to appreciate the diversity of peoples, and yearning to be a part of the global community. Their remarkable life force encourages me and convinces me that the United Nations needs to work with young people who are open-minded and free-thinking.

Besides the students at SUA, there must be quite a lot of young people in the world who hope to work for the United Nations and for world peace. However, the dilemma is that their perspectives tend to become narrowly focused, and they lose the enthusiasm to become global citizens as they enter their respective professional lives. How do you think we can resolve this predicament?

Education Builds Peace

Ikeda: This is a major challenge, but I am not pessimistic. As you point out, the problem requires a paradigm shift by adults. We need to make it possible for young people not only to participate but to play a major role in the organization's activities. For example, as you mentioned earlier, positive outreach efforts, such as creating a youth department within the Secretariat, must be made.

In addition, reforms to reflect the wishes of grassroots movements in the United Nations are essential. Efforts to forge a closer relationship between the world citizenry and the United Nations are important, too. As I once told Secretary-General Boutros Boutros-Ghali, a United Nations lacking the support of the ordinary people has no future. The United Nations Charter begins with the words 'We the peoples . . .'. The organization can manifest its true strengths only when it is firmly rooted in the solid earth of the world's people.

Most necessary of all is education that cultivates world citizens capable of contributing to the peace and happiness of all humanity. Instead of concentrating on knowledge acquisition, education needs to ignite in young people's hearts a lifelong flame of dedication to others' welfare.

In speaking of non-violence (*ahimsa*), Mahatma Gandhi said it is not something we can put on and take off at will, like our clothes, but must become an inseparable part of our existence.[6] Likewise, we need to offer our young people an education that engraves deeply a sense of responsibility and awareness of being a citizen of the world. The passion of youth will determine the future of the Earth. This is why we need to devote all our strength to education that evokes the limitless possibilities of youth and an environment in which such education can thrive.

Chowdhury: Like you, I strongly believe that a key ingredient in building the culture of peace and global understanding is education. Never has it been more important for the next generation to learn about the world and understand its diversity. Education for peace, sustainable development and human rights needs to be accepted in all parts of the world, in all societies and countries, as an essential element of learning and knowledge.

To meet effectively the challenges posed by the complexities of our time, the young of today deserve a radically different education – one that does not glorify war but educates for peace, non-violence and global cooperation. The task of educating children and young people to find non-aggressive means to relate with one another is of primary importance. They need the skills and knowledge to create and nurture peace for their individual selves, as well as for the world to which they belong. Learning about the culture of peace that has the potential of individual transformation of youth should be incorporated in all educational institutions as part of their curricula and become as essential a part of our educational process as reading and writing.

NINE
To Protect the Vulnerable

Ikeda: Because of the financial crisis that erupted throughout the world in autumn 2008 – with a severity that is said to occur once a century – international society faced an unprecedented challenge. When such crises occur, and the situation degenerates, it is always the poorest nations and their peoples who are most adversely affected. As UN Secretary-General Ban Ki-moon warned:

> Many developing nations lack the resources to rescue financial institutions in emergencies, as wealthier nations have done. . . . Today's crisis will affect all countries. But those who will experience the greatest hardships are likely to be those least responsible – the poor in developing countries.[1]

The United Nations has a responsibility to lead world public opinion and encourage prompt action in each nation to protect the most vulnerable, who will be hardest hit. This is why in this chapter, I want to discuss the United Nations' mission and responsibility as an ally of the vulnerable.

Chowdhury: Virulent unfolding of the current financial crisis on top of food and fuel crises poses a serious challenge to millions in the most vulnerable nations of the world. As you say, in this context, the mission and responsibility of the United Nations to these countries in special need and their impoverished peoples are highly relevant and potentially meaningful. You have quoted the UN Secretary-General, who I believe should take a proactive role in ensuring specific measures so that the poorest in these countries do not suffer any more. Ban Ki-moon has an opportunity to take the lead and prove his credibility.

Ikeda: In such a serious crisis, it is particularly urgent to promptly adopt appropriate measures, limiting the damage to a minimum.

Coincidentally, the global financial crisis of 2008 occurred just when the United Nations Millennium Development Goals reached a crucial turning point – a reduction in the number of people enduring extreme suffering around the world (from the baseline of 2000, when the MDGs were established).[2] But without more intense efforts, achieving the goals will prove difficult in sub-Saharan Africa and some countries of the Commonwealth of Independent States, which was set up after the collapse of the Soviet Union. The United Nations Millennium Campaign's Stand Up and Take Action programme[3] is an attempt to promote such intense efforts.

In 2007, 43 million people in 127 countries took part in this programme, and in 2008, the numbers increased to 117 million in 131 nations. Now in the face of the global financial crisis, it is even more important for people around the world to unite and insist that the current situation must be addressed.

Chowdhury: It is important for the international community to realize that the situation remains grave, particularly for the world's most vulnerable countries. These countries – identified as the Least Developed Countries[4] – continue to be the voiceless, marginalized and poorest countries of the world since the category was established more than four decades ago. These countries do not attract the world's attention unless they are engulfed in conflict or devastated by natural disasters.

The global crises of recent years have shown that all the programmes and commitments meant for LDCs did not provide any respite to the common people of these impoverished countries. They suffered beyond comprehension and are still doing so. A global safety net for LDCs is needed to reduce the suffering of the millions of vulnerable people in the weakest segment of humanity. Such a safety net needs to be structured in a way that would automatically trigger measures to protect the vulnerable in LDCs in times of crisis.

To show leadership, to regain some credibility, and to live up to their responsibilities, the United Nations and its Secretary-General and Member States need to be at the helm, steering the international community's efforts to get these countries out of the morass made worse by the global development crisis.

LDCs and their development partners are responsible for organizing bilateral assistance programmes. It is increasingly apparent that these assistance programmes are based not on the objectives of the programme of action adopted by the United Nations for LDCs but rather on the agendas of those LDCs motivated by domestic political aspirations of their leadership as well as constrained in many cases by the conditionalities of their development partners. This mutuality of national interests of the LDCs and those of their development partners is now increasingly visible. In the past, this self-serving dimension has been kept out of the multilateral process – using the excuse of the bilateral nature of these discussions. However, whatever is decided on a national level should be under the umbrella of the broader multilateral policy decisions agreed upon by all.

A major contributing factor to LDCs' misery continues to be the rate of their population growth, which must get special attention both at the national and global levels. By 2015, the LDCs' population of 880 million will increase by another 200 million people. Even with the present size of their population, achieving the MDGs of halving poverty, enhancing school enrolment, and lowering infant, child and maternal mortality is an uphill task. An additional 200 million persons by the target year for the MDGs would make the goals absolutely impossible to reach in LDCs.

The silver lining is that some LDCs, such as Bangladesh, Mozambique, Senegal and Uganda, may be able to reach these goals, at least to a large extent. But such an achievement will be beyond the capacity of most LDCs by 2015.[5]

Century of Africa

Ikeda: Global society must find a way to respond to the harsh reality of nations suffering from poverty. With the recognition that they are our dear friends who share the planet with us, we need to reach out and do our best to offer assistance in the way most suited to each country's particular situation and needs.

As I said earlier, for the last 50 years I have declared that the twenty-first century will be the Century of Africa (see Conversation Seven). In December 2007, I held a meeting with nine African ambassadors to Japan – from Senegal, Gabon, Republic of Congo, Zambia, Zimbabwe, Eritrea, Kenya, Rwanda and Egypt. I said to them, 'It is impossible to overestimate the profound significance of friendly relations with Africa to the future of Japan and to the peace and prosperity of the world'. In my peace proposal for 2008, too, I made several suggestions concerning Africa.[6]

Chowdhury: I read your annual peace proposals with keen interest. In one, you set forth your African youth partnership programme, which stresses empowering youth and training people to address the challenge of overcoming Africa's problems. Your proposal must have greatly encouraged not only the nine ambassadors you mentioned but also, I am sure, all Africans.

Ikeda: Actually my proposal for youth empowerment was inspired by the message you have been stressing for many years: Young people possess the energy for innovation and new solutions, and their empowerment is the key to breaking the vicious cycle of poverty. I proposed starting by changing the circumstances of the youth population, knowing this would result in improvement for all age groups, liberating society as a whole from the grip of poverty and reorienting it in a positive direction. Many thinking people have expressed their agreement and sympathy with this approach.

In the same proposal, as a means of accelerating the achievement of the United Nations' Millennium Developmental Goals, I called for the establishment of a world fund to ensure the water supplies that are indispensable to life. Improving people's living conditions by focusing on measures for ensuring safe water and good sanitation is an urgent necessity.

Voiceless People

Chowdhury: The United Nations emphasizes the importance of addressing the human dimension in overcoming development challenges related to water and sanitation. I am deeply impressed by the way you take the viewpoints of developing nations fully into account in connection with these issues. It is important for the UN system to accord priority to the poorest countries, helping them reach their development goals.

Otherwise, the United Nations will lose credibility as the organization that stands by the weakest and the most vulnerable. If you cannot take care of your own poorest nations, how can the UN speak about achieving the Millennium Development Goals? The focus should be on these neediest countries.

Along with the least developed nations, we need to remember that the landlocked and small island states are also among the most vulnerable countries and therefore need the attention of the United Nations and the international community. Helping them get that attention was what I did as part of my responsibility as the UN High Representative for five and a half years. With all humility I recall that these three groups of countries in special need – least developed, landlocked, and small island – were targeted by the United Nations for the achievement of the MDGs at my behest less than a month after I accepted this responsibility in March 2002.

Ikeda: That is just the kind of prescient action I would expect from you, Mr Chowdhury.

My mentor's cherished wish was misery's elimination from the world. Having adopted this mission, which he entrusted to me, I have expanded the movement for human revolution that aims, based on Buddhism, to enable all people to lead fully human and happy lives. The individual's dignity and worth are human society's foundation.

In order to relieve the misery of poverty and hunger that threaten this dignity, I have placed great emphasis on offering proposals that emphasize, along with human rights and human security, human development. In the dialogue we shared, the world-renowned agricultural expert M. S. Swaminathan argued, 'If you want to help a society, begin with the poorest, most neglected person and work upwards'.[7] Lacking this perspective, no society can enjoy peace and prosperity.

In an interview you gave to the *Seikyo Shimbun* newspaper,[8] you said you considered making improvements, however small, for the world's people to be the United Nations' most important mission. You also emphasized the importance of taking action for the weakest nations and those condemned to live in the harshest circumstances. I agree completely. Your words perfectly sum up the United Nations' role in the twenty-first century. Most important, however, is that you have personally taken the initiative to carry out this mission and set an example within the United Nations. Your achievements there are immortal.

Chowdhury: I thank you for your warm understanding. As the first High Representative for the Least Developed Countries, Landlocked Developing Countries and Small Island Developing States, a position that was established by the UN General Assembly in January 2002, I felt an immense sense of pride to have the opportunity to be the advocate, champion and spokesperson for the 'voiceless' nations in the world. I realized that one of the greatest constraints of such nations is the absence of opportunity to make their voices heard.

In addition to resource constraints and limited staffing, these countries are constantly engaged in an uphill task with their very small missions to the United Nations, having to compete for the world's attention to their concerns. Supporting them in this endeavour was the role of my office. I think that my five and a half years as the High Representative helped raise their profile significantly and put their issues high on the global agenda.

Ikeda: Your efforts were important and resulted in drawing greater attention to the least developed, landlocked, and small island states in the United Nations. On an earlier occasion, you described your thoughts at the time, which impressed me deeply: you were haunted by the feeling that you would not be able to complete everything you wished, but the difficulty and challenge of the work also made it rewarding, and the issues themselves were a form of encouragement. You added that you felt blessed to have a job of such weighty responsibility and importance. I can't help but feel that your willingness to work for others' happiness without concern for your own pains must correspond to what Buddhism teaches as the bodhisattva way.

Chowdhury: Your appreciation for my work is far too generous. I was only doing what a responsible global citizen should do. Even after leaving the United Nations formally in July 2007, I continue to advocate for these most vulnerable countries in my public speaking commitments at various forums in different parts of the world.

Earlier in this dialogue, I mentioned the UN Conference on the Least Developed Countries, which is convened outside of the UN Headquarters approximately every ten years. I am one of the very few to have attended all three previous meetings, in 1981, 1990, and then in 2001. At the third, held in Brussels, I represented the LDCs and negotiated their Programme of Action, speaking on behalf of the developing countries caucus, the Group of 77.

Despite the United Nations having organized three global conferences with lots of commitments, the number of LDCs increased from 25 in 1971, when the group was created, to 50 in 2001. This necessitated the creation of an effective, efficient and high-profile entity to monitor the UN Programme's implementation nationally, regionally and globally. Recognizing this need, the Brussels conference asked Secretary-General Kofi Annan to present his recommendations regarding the role and structure of such a mechanism to the General Assembly.

Spirit of Empathy

Ikeda: I believe that the Secretary-General's advice resulted in the decision of the General Assembly to establish the UN Office of the High Representative for the Least Developed Countries, Landlocked Developing Countries and Small Island Developing States (UN-OHRLLS).

Chowdhury: Yes, that is correct. Kofi Annan's report laid down two guidelines: first, he believed the Office should be located in the UN Headquarters in New York. He also believed it should have a broad political profile and report directly to the Secretary-General.

Second, he decided that it should be headed by someone at the under-secretary-general level who could deal with high-placed partners on an equal footing. Having made these determinations, he started looking for somebody to be the first occupant of the office to set up the entity as envisaged and also to articulate its operational direction. He consulted the Member States fairly extensively about the role he had in mind. I had just finished my term as Bangladesh Ambassador to the United Nations and was preparing to return home when Secretary-General Kofi Annan asked me to join his senior management team and set up this new office, articulate its direction and give it the profile it needed.

Ikeda: His selecting you only goes to show how greatly you had won the trust of the Member States in general, as well as the Secretary-General.

Chowdhury: Of course, I was not the only person who was considered, but the Secretary-General honoured me by saying, 'You are the best person that I can think of – can you join us?' I officially became the first High Representative on 18 March 2002.

Kofi Annan later told me that he wanted somebody knowledgeable about the United Nations, familiar with LDC issues, committed to the cause and available full-time. He also felt that the first head of the new office should be from an LDC.

I continued in this position until 30 June 2007. For me, this was the opportunity of a lifetime, because as a representative of a least developed country and leader of the Group of LDCs for ten years during Bangladesh's chairmanship, I felt very close to the cause. A rather unique feature of my appointment was that the Secretary-General felt that his selection of me met all the requirements of the post so comprehensively that it was not necessary for him to consult my government, which is normally done for such senior-level posts.

Ikeda: You have striven tirelessly to alleviate the plight of people suffering from poverty. It seems to me that your post as High Representative was much more than a mere job to you; it was a noble mission that can rightly be described as your natural vocation.

Buddhism identifies the spirit of empathy that feels the pains and sufferings of others as one's own as the source of compassionate, courageous deeds to realize a better society. The essence of the bodhisattva way is, first, a vow or pledge to which one devotes one's entire being and a life dedicated to overcoming numerous challenges to fulfill this vow.

A second aspect of the bodhisattva way is described in the Lotus Sutra by the metaphor of the lotus blossom blooming from muddy water. The bodhisattva does not seek to flee the 'muddy water' of the real world, but lives to make a pure, noble flower bloom from its depths. To save those suffering, the bodhisattva plunges into the raging breakers and helps them safely board the great ship of peace and happiness, dedicating him- or herself to others' welfare.

Chowdhury: Setting my own life aside, it is you and the members of the SGI who have unflaggingly striven to practise the way of life of the bodhisattva in our world of deepening confusion. I am very grateful to you, nonetheless, for generously describing my work as a UN High Representative in such glorifying words.

When the Secretary-General asked me to join, two other vulnerable groups – Landlocked Developed Countries (LLDCs) and Small Island Developing States (SIDS) – were added to the original mandate of the new office. Thus I became the advocate for as many as 90 countries out of the United Nations' total membership of 192. I was truly encouraged by this enhanced opportunity.

I knew of the staffing and budgetary constraints of our small office but felt that enthusiasm, determination and commitment would enable us to accomplish much more than spacious office and a big budget could. In fact, we proved that more can be done even with less.

Ikeda: The important thing is not an organization's scale or budget. Even a small group of people can stir waves of reform when its members strive with all their might to overcome the challenges they are facing. I am sure that the great achievements of you and your staff members shine like a beacon of hope for many other UN entities compelled to work within greater restrictions.

The Soka Gakkai, too, started out as a small organization. But Tsunesaburo Makiguchi and Josei Toda utterly devoted themselves to thoroughly cultivating even a single person of genuine character and ability, building the foundation for the growth we have attained today.

Mr Toda used to urge we of the youth division to train a single individual of true character, because *kosen-rufu* – a Buddhist term for the realization of peace and happiness for the human race – would advance if we were able to train even one individual willing to continue the struggle undaunted, regardless of being imprisoned or exiled. I have always based my actions on this lesson from my mentor.

Chowdhury: Your words make me even more deeply aware of the way a vow to uphold what you learned from your mentor has provided the driving force for your dedicated work for world peace. I deeply value the idea that a single person can be of key importance.

Triumph of the Insulted Man

Ikeda: New movements always face uncomprehending criticism. In our early period, the Soka Gakkai was ridiculed as a collection of the sick and destitute. President Toda taught us to respond to such criticism by asking our critics how many sick and destitute people they had helped. His unshakable conviction and passion ignited the hearts of us youth.

As his disciple, I regarded the slanders levelled at us as a source of the greatest pride. The Lotus Sutra teaches that 'there will be many ignorant people / who will curse and speak ill of us'.[9] When asked what made him happy, President Toda often said that hearing reports of Soka Gakkai members becoming happy and gaining good health made him happier than anything else. I feel exactly the same way.

Chowdhury: I have the profoundest respect for the Soka Gakkai members, who work day and night to alleviate the sufferings of society's weakest members. Your deeds have much in common with my own work at the United Nations. In my work with the most vulnerable nations, what brought me the greatest happiness was learning of significant improvements in their conditions.

Serving as advocate for these nations with special needs and championing their cause brought great satisfaction to me personally. As the first head of the UN-OHRLLS, I am proud to have been able to lay the groundwork, set up the operational framework, and elevate and expand the presence of our office in various multilateral forums, so that we could bring the concerns of the neediest countries to the centre of the global development deliberations.

As a result, for the first time a number of LDCs were in a few years in the channel for graduation off the LDCs list. Still a major and deliberate effort and support on the part of the United Nations in favour of these countries needs to be undertaken.

Ikeda: I can only speculate about the large number of smiles you and your staff have brought to people's faces. Economic growth alone cannot bring smiles of genuine happiness.

I am reminded of a story about Sir Isaac Newton related by the American philosopher Ralph Waldo Emerson. Someone asked Newton what had enabled him to make his great scientific discoveries, and he replied, 'By always intending my mind'.[10]

Unfailing concentration of head and heart on the issue at hand accounts for your great achievements as High Representative. For example, I understand that you contributed greatly to the creation of a system for monitoring the extent and nature of support provided by the international community to vulnerable countries.

Chowdhury: The achievements were made possible by the support I had from staff members in my office. While monitoring the implementation of the LDCs programme, we also undertook advocacy for them. Thus we spent half our time advocating and half monitoring.

I termed my office's advocacy role as 'substantive advocacy', because alongside advocacy in the traditional sense, we also provided empowering knowledge and information, as well as negotiating support for the delegations. That also complemented our monitoring efforts; the two were mutually reinforcing. In addition, we set up an interagency consultative group consisting of 20 agencies of the UN system to discuss, monitor and coordinate support and assistance in favour of the Least Developed Countries.

Ikeda: The matter of creating interagency consultative groups has been an issue at the United Nations for some time. A report issued by the Commission on Human Security in 2003 states, 'With a focus on protecting people rather than adhering to institutional mandates, the current compartmentalization among the numerous uncoordinated actors should be overcome'.[11] In 2004, with the same thing in mind, I proposed a peace rehabilitation council to bridge the aid gap in strife-torn regions and to promote and regulate activities ranging from humanitarian aid to peacebuilding. I have high hopes for the work of the Peacebuilding Commission, established by the United Nations in 2006 to concentrate mainly on rebuilding the lives of and restoring happiness to people suffering in the aftermath of conflict.

Chowdhury: The creation of the Peacebuilding Commission, along with its support office, has become a pillar of UN reform. Its operations are proceeding smoothly. I feel that any UN entity embracing both civil society and Member States works well.

The first two countries chosen by the Commission for its post-conflict peacebuilding support were Sierra Leone and Burundi, both on the list of Least Developed Countries. That put my office and the Commission and the support office headed by Carolyn McAskie in close contact and collaboration.

You emphasized rebuilding the lives of and restoring happiness to people suffering in the aftermath of conflict. This is surely the best way to make peacebuilding more meaningful and worthwhile and to prevent conflict from recurring. I believe that in view of its mandate, creating the culture of peace should be a central aspect of the work of the Peacebuilding Commission and the support office. That is why I hope the new Commission will make creating the culture of peace one of its major undertakings.

As you know, Japan played the important role of chairing the Commission in 2007 and partly in 2008. I hope that in the future, too, Japan will take the initiative to make the work of the Commission more productive.

Ikeda: To build a peaceful, humane, global society, Japan must work in tandem with international society, exhibit greater leadership, and contribute more. In the words of Rabindranath Tagore, 'Man's history is waiting in patience for the triumph of the insulted man'.[12] Now is the time for us to summon all our wisdom to the fullest, work together, and respond to this heartfelt cry.

TEN
Redefining Development

Ikeda: Protecting the environment is undeniably one of the biggest issues confronting humanity in the twenty-first century. Climate change in particular is deeply interconnected with a wide range of problems, including poverty, regional conflicts, accessibility of energy and resources, the food crises and our troubled economic systems. Climate change is believed to be one of the causes of the meteorological disasters that have been occurring with great frequency around the world in recent years.

Chowdhury: Global warming is indeed a major cause of increased occurrences of natural disasters in all parts of the world. In recent years, such disasters have been occurring in greater frequency and intensity in many places, one after another.

Ikeda: Hurricanes Gustav and Ike ravaged Cuba and the United States in September 2008. Floods victimized three million people in eastern India. These kinds of disaster are increasing each year. Between 2000 and 2004, a yearly average of 326 such disasters afflicted about 262 million people, doubling the figures for the early 1980s.

Especially severe damage has been done to developing nations, where one in 19 people has been adversely affected and where the risk of being stricken by natural disasters is 80 times higher than in developed nations.[1]

Chowdhury: As your remarks indicate, weather damage causes extensive suffering and drainage of resources in developing nations. The ones to suffer most are the LDCs, which are structurally too weak to cope with such calamities. The majority of the 150 million-plus people of Bangladesh frequently encounter floods, cyclones and abnormally high tides, called tidal bores.

In the summer of 2007, we had the worst flooding in a decade. It inundated about 40 per cent of the country's territory, displacing 10 million people in search of shelter and safety. In November 2007, cyclone Sidr hit the country, affecting thousands. Environmental damage was enormous. For example, half of our tropical forests were damaged. A deltaic, riverine lowland crisscrossed with hundreds of rivers, tributaries and waterways equal to a length of 15,000 miles, Bangladesh is subject to water-caused destruction every year.

Ikeda: Once again, my heartfelt sympathy for your people's suffering.

Major natural disasters, taking the lives of beloved family members in an instant and destroying the foundations of people's lives, leave horrible psychological scars. With its profound understanding of life, Buddhism teaches that they have an enormous influence on humanity and alter the destiny of society. Nichiren wrote, 'It is perfectly clear that if heaven itself crumbles, then the body of the individual likewise will crumble; if the earth breaks asunder, the body of the individual too will break asunder'.[2]

A report by the United Nations Development Programme records the experiences of the people of Bangladesh and other parts of South Asia suffering from severe flooding in the summer of 2007: 'There are more floods now and the river banks are being washed away faster. There's nowhere to go. My land is in the river, I have nothing now' (Northwest Bangladesh).[3]

'We had never seen such floods before. Lots of houses were destroyed, lots of people died, our agricultural land was submerged, crops stored in houses were lost. Many livestock were lost too' (West Bengal, India).[4]

The Japanese people, who have suffered from seasonal typhoons from time immemorial, understand your people's plight all too well.

Chowdhury: As one who was closely involved in the United Nations as Bangladesh representative as well as the United Nations' senior official to secure greater international support for the world's most vulnerable countries, I do always identify with their outcries, anguish and distress. Most of the people of countries hit hardest by natural disasters are seriously poverty-stricken as well. They are, therefore, vulnerable to even slight sea-level rise and climate change.

As Kofi Annan has rightly asserted:

The countries most vulnerable are least able to protect themselves. They also contribute least to the global emissions of greenhouse gases. Without action, they would pay a high price for the actions of others.[5]

On top of recurring natural disasters, they are now facing additional vulnerability due to the risk posed by climate change.

Geographical features – in the case of Bangladesh, being flat and only a few feet above sea level – make a number of countries susceptible to the worst consequences of climate change. Even a three-foot rise in sea level as a result of global warming threatens small island nations such as the Maldives, Vanuatu, Tuvalu and Kiribati as well as many coastal countries.

Many opportunities that I had at the United Nations as the advocate for these countries to visit them and interact regularly with their representatives made me deeply aware of their concerns and the need for increasing global support of their own national and regional development efforts. A key aspect of the climate change catastrophe is that it will not happen as one huge global disaster at a given point in time. As has been rightly described, what the world's poor are facing is a relentless increase in the risks and vulnerabilities associated with climate. The source of these incremental risks can be traced in a big way to multifarious human activity, notably in the unsustainable lifestyle of overconsumption in the industrialized world.

Ikeda: The lifestyle of excessive consumption was a major topic of discussion at an international conference held in Hawaii in November 2008, sponsored by the Toda Institute for Global Peace and Policy Research. More than 25 scholars from all over the world took part in the conference, the theme of which was 'Facing Climate Change with a Renewed Environmental Ethic'. As might be expected, discussion focused on the current conditions of developing nations suffering major damage as a result of climate change.

When I met with Tommy E. Remengesau, Jr., former president of the Republic of Palau, an island nation, in June 2002, he told me:

> Global warming is an extremely serious issue for the people of Palau. Ocean levels have risen and salt water is invading the aquifers. . . . The destruction of our coral reefs is progressing. Greatly increased water temperature has caused the coral to turn white and die.[6]

As you have said, we need to share the threat felt by people vulnerable to climate change and must work together with them. As part of such efforts, it is vital that we emphasize support in terms of human development, encompassing such things as health and longevity, education and culture, and freedom from violence.

I have always urged, in looking to the United Nations' future activities, the necessity of making three themes, capped by the word *human* – human development, human security and human rights – our pillars. The reason is that I believe the primary mission of the United Nations, symbolized by the reference to 'We the peoples' in its charter, is to work for the welfare of all peoples and to eliminate the very word *misery* from the globe.

Gross National Happiness

Chowdhury: Your emphasis on the importance of human development, human security and human rights is truly profound. The three areas are indivisible and deserve top priority in the activities of the United Nations. The key focus of my work with the United Nations for nearly four decades had been on its role in improving the quality of life of the needy millions throughout the world. I consider human development especially important, because it directly affects people's lives and can prove extremely effective in ensuring human security and human rights in developing nations.

In addition, it is the area in which the United Nations has impacted positively on the lives of millions of people in those nations. There is close interaction between climate-related vulnerability, poverty and human development. I have long insisted that, unless the United Nations deals squarely and seriously with human development challenges in the most vulnerable countries, its credibility will come into question.

Ikeda: I am well aware of your praiseworthy efforts in this area. Pakistani economist Mahbub ul Haq established the Human Development Index as a gauge of a nation's degree of development. From the time the Toda Institute for Global Peace and Policy Research was founded, he was one of the people who placed great hope in its work.

He is famous for pioneering the concept of human security, which he connected with human dignity, insisting that it should be reflected in people's lives in concrete forms, such as 'a child who did not die, a disease that did not spread'.[7] In a keynote address delivered at an international conference sponsored by the Toda Institute in June 1997, he said, 'It is easier, more humane, and less costly to deal with the new issues of human security upstream rather than down-stream'.[8] Though he passed away more than a decade ago, Dr Haq's achievements are immortal.

Chowdhury: I am very happy that you refer to his outstanding achievements. I knew him personally, had the opportunity to interact with him on many occasions, and have deep appreciation for his work. When he proposed the Human Development Index, many people did not accept it. For superficial reasons, some UN members raised their voices in opposition. Today, it is widely accepted, used and quoted by researchers, policymakers, educational organizations, the media and civil society in elaborating global, regional and national development scenarios.

The multidimensional concept of poverty and development has been further elaborated by the United Nations' *Human Development Report* (HDRs),[9] which go beyond the definition of poverty as mere income deficiency and shows that poverty is also vulnerability and lack of voice, power and representation. This immensely significant conceptual redefining and refining has been made possible through HDRs.

We have even moved one step forward and are already discussing Gross National Happiness (GNH), coined by His Majesty the Fourth Druk Gyalpo Jigme Singye Wangchuck of Bhutan. My meeting with him in 2006 in Thimphu was one of my most delightful experiences as the High Representative of the United Nations. Though he was still king at the time, he was most informal and engaged in substantive discussion about the development prospects of his least developed and landlocked but forward-looking nation. I was extremely impressed by his willingness to lend an ear to what others have to say and to do everything in the best interest of his people.

He shared with me the basic philosophy and rationale behind the GNH. After subsequent study of the subject, I have come to believe that with some required national adjustments to reflect the current Human Development Index, his GNH has considerable relevance for all countries of the world, particularly those that are deeply engaged in sheer materialistic pursuits.

The ultimate goal of all development is the happiness of the people. The most spectacular economic growth is not always conducive to this end. We should never make the mistake of thinking it is.

Fulfilling the Mission

Ikeda: Development must always be in the pursuit of human happiness and a means for the realization of global peace and cooperation. Overlooking this ultimate purpose and concentrating solely on economic and income growth rates only broadens the gap between rich and poor, and misses the real mark – human happiness. We should not mistake the means for the end.

The late economist John Kenneth Galbraith, with whom I met, said that we should convert from economic power built on the victimization of others through war and structures of economic oppression to an economics of compassion, enabling all the peoples of the Earth to live in happiness. He strongly urged all of us, especially young people, to understand the reality of our world today – that most of the tragic deaths occur in the poor countries. Death is a daily routine in some countries, he emphasized, and the young people in wealthy countries must awaken to their responsibility to change this.

Chowdhury: A truly worthy sentiment. Having visited many of the most vulnerable countries in connection with my UN work, I understand the enormity of their development challenges. Of course, these countries need to put in their own efforts, but I believe that the developed nations need to assume increasing responsibility for the attainment of the UN Millennium Development Goals, about which we spoke in the preceding conversation.

We must also engage the entire UN system including the World Bank group to give special attention to the development of these 90 most distressed nations. If we succeed in doing that, we can proudly say that the United Nations has lived up to its purpose. At any rate, striving to this end must be the core responsibility of the United Nations and the focus of its leadership for the coming years. I am convinced that this will increase both the United Nations' effectiveness and credibility, and show the world that the United Nations can actually deliver and contribute to global human development.

Ikeda: In August 2006, when I met you in Tokyo, I handed you a proposal to the United Nations titled 'Fulfilling the Mission: Empowering the UN to Live Up to the World's Expectations'.[10] I want to thank you for delivering it to Secretary-General Kofi Annan and other leaders in the organization. The proposal title represents my hope that the United Nations will fully recognize the urgent popular longing for peace and perform the role of an international organization protecting humanity. I included the following quotation from Dag Hammarskjöld, the second UN Secretary-General, as symbolic of the United Nations' mission:

> 'The Uncarved Block' – remain[s] at the Center, which is yours and that of all humanity. For those goals which it gives to your life, do the utmost which, at each moment, is possible for you. Also, act without thinking of the consequences, or seeking anything for yourself.[11]

Chowdhury: Many people at the United Nations have great respect for Dag Hammarskjöld and his achievements. His noble aspirations ring forth in the words you just quoted. I revere him as the philosopher Secretary-General.

As part of my work as the United Nations' champion of its 90 most vulnerable members, I have travelled extensively from Benin and Burkina Faso to Uganda and Paraguay, from Sudan and Senegal to Mali and Mauritius, from Bhutan and Kazakhstan to Laos and Mongolia, and from Samoa and Fiji to the Bahamas and Grenada. I have acquainted myself with their development efforts and, at the same time, advocated for the international community's support to them. I have witnessed first-hand their determined efforts for development, as well as the multifaceted support that the United Nations is providing in improving the common people's lives.

At the same time, I have also felt it my duty to urge these countries to do their best to take special care of the neediest among their own citizens. These include, of course, women and children plus the disabled, the elderly, migrants, indigenous people, and people affected by conflict and post-conflict conditions. While these poorest and weakest countries themselves require international support, they themselves must lend a helping hand to their own vulnerable population as part of their efforts for human development and human security.

Ikeda: Providing aid to developing countries is indeed not enough. As you say, we must also encourage the governments of developing nations to implement policies protecting their weakest members. Aid and development assistance must always be based on the perspective of helping individuals. Their happiness and sense of satisfaction in life are the essential criteria. This is why it is important to heed the voices of people whose human dignity is threatened, who are suffering.

The World Bank spent seven years surveying 60,000 people in 60 nations for an analytical report titled *Voices of the Poor*, which was published between 1999 and 2002, and which recommended three points for consideration in promoting aid policies:

(1) Promoting economic opportunities for escape from poverty.
(2) Facilitating empowerment enabling people to choose their own employment.
(3) Enhancing security for daily living plus security for emergencies.[12]

These recommendations are still valid.

Chowdhury: Yes, they are, though globalization and the vulnerability of the world economy have made things more complex. The third recommendation that you mentioned from the report has been reflected in my suggestions for a global safety net for the Least Developed Countries in the context of relevant United Nations gatherings. Incidentally, as Bangladesh's UN ambassador, I served as a panellist at the forum organized for the launch of this landmark World Bank study in Geneva in July 2000.

To generalize a little bit without citing specific incidents, I consider two things very important. First, most people of developing countries are hardworking and willing to do whatever they can to improve their conditions. They have simple objectives in life. All they ask for is a regular income to feed themselves and their children, a shelter, education and health care, and human security. They are not asking for the moon. They require only what is within their reach. They are resilient, industrious and sincere. We must remember that sometimes lack of opportunity is a greater blow than a lack of income. For the people in LDCs, poverty of opportunity is a much more serious threat than poverty of earnings.

Ikeda: On my many trips to developing countries, I, too, have been greatly impressed by the hardworking people I encounter. The eyes of the young men shine, and the women's smiles sparkle. The same qualities were characteristic of the Japanese before our period of rapid economic growth. In the period immediately after World War II, we were compelled to start life afresh amid burned-out ruins. It is no exaggeration to say that industriousness was our only asset.

Chowdhury: Their poverty does not mean that developing countries lack hope. Many people in those countries are, as you agree, industrious and hardworking.

My second point: Gradually more and more women are entering the area of development, contributing to each society's objectives and goals of improving their lives. In many countries, the microcredit system, which we discussed earlier (see Conversation Six), is empowering women, who, in turn, are making a difference in their communities, in their societies with the result that even in rural areas, they are breaking out of poverty and gradually becoming capable of fulfilling their basic needs. Because of developments like these, I am always encouraged by the people's enthusiasm and hard work.

Ikeda: This enthusiasm and hard work must be remembered in connection with the promotion of human development. Amartya Sen made a noteworthy point about promoting human development:

> The people have to be seen, in this perspective, as being actively involved – given the opportunity – in shaping their own destiny, and not just as passive recipients of the fruits of cunning development programs.[13]

People must be regarded not as the recipients of assistance and development aid but as the proactive protagonists of change. The role of international society should be to support from the sidelines the people's efforts to pull themselves up by their own bootstraps.

Global Marshall Plan

Chowdhury: In this connection, I recall that Professor Sen characterizes human development from the standpoint of expanding human abilities and possibilities, and greatly emphasizes the importance of individual freedom and human rights. He sees 'development as freedom'.[14] Poverty and hunger rob people of their dignity and self-respect, thus making a hopeful, valued way of life impossible. Citizens of the poorest, weakest countries are vulnerable in all kinds of ways. They are too vulnerable to perform or behave in ways expected in an organized Western society. Still we must not underestimate or ignore them.

During my work at UN advocating for these poorest nations, I used to say that I had the best post in the United Nations for several reasons. It offered a wonderful opportunity to work for the poorest and the weakest. I always told my staff to cultivate that spirit in their heads and hearts. Many of the tasks they would be required to perform would not appear in their job descriptions but had to originate in the heart and the head of a committed individual. I advised them to consider their work as a mission.

I also told my colleagues that timely and quality performance are very important. I said that if we are talking about the LDCs shaping up, we in the UN system also need to shape up. We must respond more efficiently, effectively and sensitively to the needs of the most vulnerable.

Ikeda: What a wonderful philosophy of public service in the noble bodhisattva spirit! Each of your precious words should be engraved in our hearts. Your achievements are sure to grow more lustrous with the passing years.

A society with a weak foundation has a hard time developing under its own power. Japan's outstanding recovery after World War II was due, in addition to the industriousness of the Japanese, to outside aid in the form of two American funds – the Economic Rehabilitation in Occupied Areas fund and the Government Appropriations for Relief in Occupied Areas fund – plus financing from the World Bank. Thanks to international assistance, Japan laid the foundation for growth and development.

In Europe, as is well known, aid in the form of the Marshall Plan facilitated recovery from the devastation of World War II. In 2002, I proposed the implementation of a global Marshall Plan drawing on these past experiences and centred on the United Nations to vanquish the poverty that afflicts so many nations. International aid has taken many forms, but we now need to build a structure for more inclusive, consolidated financial cooperation not only to address the problem of poverty but also to assist in achieving the UN Millennium Development Goals.

Chowdhury: I am delighted that, at such an early time, you made a constructive proposal for solving the poverty problems plaguing some nations. A global Marshall Plan is a wonderful idea. The words 'Marshall Plan' might seem to suggest that such a plan can be implemented only after great destruction like that of World War II. But in the context of the Millennium Development Goals, the idea of the plan could infuse special energy into this global development initiative in achieving quick and sustainable economic and social progress in developing countries.

Ikeda: In the world today, a small group of nations are consuming most of our natural resources and maintaining a luxurious lifestyle, while the citizens of the majority of countries live in abject poverty under conditions that constantly violate their human dignity. The global financial crises we are currently experiencing increase in the perils faced by these societies and further undercut their already weak positions. Rectifying such social injustice is an urgent issue and duty for humanity.

Following the G8 summit held in Germany in 1999, funds have been made available for aid to heavily indebted, poor nations, earmarked for social improvement in areas such as poverty relief, education, health and medicine. To intensify the international drive for a solution to poverty and to further strengthen the flow of international aid, we urgently need bold, purposeful ideas and actions.

Chowdhury: I attended that summit as Bangladesh was the chairman of the Non-Aligned Movement (NAM) at that time.[15] As an outcome of the G8 summit in Germany, the multilateral debts of 19 countries were cancelled. I am happy to say that 13 of those 19 were LDCs. Nine more LDCs were then in the pipeline to have their multilateral debts to the World Bank and IMF cancelled. Unfortunately, since then practically no further development has taken place in relation to exemptions of the bilateral and commercial debts of the LDCs.

It is important to ensure a system whereby the money received from debt relief or debt cancellation is utilized for particular social and economic programmes, particularly – as you say – for dealing with poverty, education, and health care. Such a system will encourage further debt relief because of the pledge by debtor nations beforehand to use their resources to promote human development and human security.

Our Own Power

Ikeda: Crises resulting from uncontrolled capitalism make people everywhere acutely aware of the dangers of runaway globalization. At the same time, such crises stimulate international society to seek ways to order and regulate world capital while simultaneously solving problems of poverty and the environment.

One measure under consideration, which I discussed in my 2009 peace proposal, is the introduction of a form of international taxation called 'solidarity levies'. France has already introduced a tax on international air travel, and other financial steps such as taxes on international currency transactions have been debated.

In September 2008, with the formation of a nonpartisan parliamentary federation, the Japanese government officially announced its intention to participate in the Leading Group on Solidarity Levies to Fund Development. As you have noted, exemption and cancellation of liabilities, though significant, are only temporary measures. It is critical for international society to work together to establish a new system that can provide developing countries with steady support. Perhaps international solidarity levies can play an effective role in building a global governance of peace and harmonious coexistence.

Some time ago, at a meeting with then UN Secretary-General Boutros Boutros-Ghali,[16] I proposed the creation of a world people's fund to support the United Nations, because I believe that each individual ought to feel responsible for global society as a whole. It is no longer possible for anyone to be indifferent.

Chowdhury: We need an innovative, sustainable mechanism to provide financial support to impoverished, vulnerable nations. International solidarity levies are one approach. A global safety net to protect these nations from being affected during global economic instability is absolutely essential.

Ikeda: Rabindranath Tagore thought highly of judo, which he called a source of spiritual inspiration. He included it in his school's curriculum and even wrote the following poem on the spirit of judo. Let me quote it as indicative of a good mental attitude to have when crises arise:

> *Be not embarrassed by ignorance*
> *Be not afraid of danger.*
> *Do away with your fear.*
> *To overcome all obstacles,*
> *Call forth your power.*
>
> *Aid the weak and outdo the strong.*
> *Do not despise yourself as weak and pitiable.*
> *Do away with fear and have faith in your own power.*[17]

ELEVEN
No Peace Without Women

Ikeda: Rabindranath Tagore wrote, 'Women have the vital power more strongly in them than men have'.[1] I agree, and I believe that the power of women is a key to a new stage of history.

In 2008, the Tokyo Fuji Art Museum, which I founded, held an exhibition titled *Happy Mothers, Happy Children*, in which about 140 domestic and overseas artworks in various genres – oil painting, traditional Japanese painting, sculpture, prints and photographs – were organized around the mother–child motif. They included the famous *Happy Mother* by Ernest Barthélemy Michel, an artist in the French Academisme tradition. Presenting an image of a warm, loving realm of children's innocent smiles and mothers' gentle gazes, the exhibition was well received.

Everywhere around the world, nothing is stronger or more beautiful than the bond between mother and child. We must strive to make the twenty-first century one in which the smiles of children and mothers shine more radiantly than ever before.

Chowdhury: An exhibition on the theme of mothers and children of the world was a wonderful idea. My long involvement with the United Nations convinced me that, as you say, women are more caring, more mindful of what is in the best interests of society for present and future generations than men are. In that sense, they are the main anchor of any society. They keep a society together.

Their spirit of sacrifice, mission of service, empathy and compassion make them ideally equipped to work for social good, for the greater good of everybody. Just think of the enormous burden that women in many parts of the world undertake on a daily basis. At the same time, for generations, women have also been contributing significantly, albeit on most occasions from behind the scenes, to resolving conflict, strife, and tension in their families, in their communities, in their societies.

Ikeda: More attention should be paid to this reality. The Buddhist scriptures expound: 'Just as a mother would protect her only child at the risk of her own life, even so, let him cultivate a boundless heart towards all beings. Let his thoughts of boundless love pervade the whole world.'[2] Buddhism encourages us to be compassionate and do all we can for others, just as a mother nobly devotes herself entirely to protecting her children.

Without this beautiful, compassionate maternal spirit, we cannot build a peaceful, humane world. As I have said repeatedly, we must listen attentively to women and mothers, and make full use of their abundant wisdom, keen sensitivities and great vitality in the creation of a better society. I am convinced that if we do so, the world will be a more humane, peaceful and liveable place.

Chowdhury: Care and compassion come naturally to women. I believe that women are by their very nature much more stable and balanced as human beings. Hardship does not deter them from doing things that are good for their children, for their family, for their society in general.

Human society has survived and been sustained mainly because of women's nurturing qualities. But this is not recognized, respected and reflected in the way women are treated in all parts of the world. Discrimination against women continues to manifest in many different ways everywhere. Concerted efforts by all – individually and collectively – are needed to rectify this totally unacceptable situation.

Courageous Examples

Ikeda: No politicians, scientists or educators can compare in greatness to mothers. We all owe these glorious women our deepest respect and gratitude.

The futurist Hazel Henderson, as I mentioned before (see Conversation Six), stood up as a wife and mother to initiate social reforms to ensure a healthy environment for children. The citizens movement that began in New York in the 1960s to curb air pollution was driven by the joint efforts of mothers, including Dr Henderson, concerned for their children's future. She was branded the most dangerous woman in America, and some even sent letters denouncing her to her husband's company.

But she never gave in. Burning with a determination that was more than a match for her opponents, she continued to rouse people and institutions to take action until she won the environmental improvements she sought.

Another courageous woman is Wangari Maathai, who for more than 30 years waged a relentless struggle against tyrannical authorities and ultimately triumphed with her Greenbelt Movement, which sponsored the planting of 40 million trees in Africa. The way she smilingly related her story to me when we met in Tokyo made a profound impression.

A driving will to leave future generations a beautiful planet and protect children's environments inspired both Dr Henderson and Dr Maathai to take action. It was not calculation or considerations of profit and loss that drove them on; it was deep, maternal love and a sense of responsibility.

Chowdhury: I have met both of them and have found them to be possessed of deep convictions and unwavering determination. Their spirit-uplifting leadership qualities were key to achieving their objectives.

Women are more self-composed than naturally volatile, irascible men. They have a better, more rational understanding of life's difficulties. They can face such situations with composure, which many men cannot do. Men are challenged too easily. Women look for non-violent, harmonious ways of facing challenges, whereas men are confrontational more often than not.

Ikeda: Yes, they are. Hazel Henderson also says that she inherited her constructive, pacifist attitude toward life from her mother, to whom she has dedicated the following poem:

> *Dear Dorothy — mediating conflicts, instilling ethics*
> *By her actions more than her words.*
> *What fortunate people*
> *We who grew up under her wing.*
> *This is true courage:*
> *To toil each day for others.*
> *This is true valor:*
> *To keep faith with the future,*
> *Without compensation or recognition.*[3]

If we ask who are the people who want to give children the best possible future and support the humane bonds of society in the truest sense, we surely will answer that they are the countless women and mothers who are the real sages of peace.

Women Enjoying Happiness

Chowdhury: Reflecting on my work at the United Nations and what I have seen in Bangladesh, I can say emphatically that the most impressive of all are the poor, landless, uneducated women in rural areas in the developing world. Given the odds they face, the challenges they encounter, the obstacles they have to overcome, it is obvious that they are the real leaders. They are the vanguard of women's struggle to emerge from poverty and make a better life for their children, risking even their own safety and security. In the undertakings of the United Nations and other organizations working for women's development, we must give special attention to uneducated, poor rural women because, as I found in my own country, they bring about real, remarkable change.

Let me add here one important dimension to advancing the full and effective enjoyment of women's rights: the role of men in that process. It is necessary that men be involved fully in ensuring that women's rights are internalized, truly recognized and substantively implemented by all of us, along with other human rights.

Ikeda: My dialogue with M. S. Swaminathan emphasized precisely this point. He said: 'If you do something for a woman in a family, everybody benefits. The reverse may not happen.'[4] In other words, doing something for a male family member does not necessarily benefit all other members — an observation that contains a sharp truth.

The SGI emphasizes the cherishing of women in order to create a society in which they enjoy the fullest degree of happiness. This is also the spirit of Buddhism. And in fact, women and mothers play a major part in the humanistic movement for peace, culture and education carried out by the SGI in 192 countries and territories.

The traditional spirit of the Soka Gakkai and the SGI alike is to cherish all women and fight for their happiness. I recall how Josei Toda once said with great emotion, as he watched women arriving for a Soka Gakkai meeting, perspiring in the summer heat, 'Without these people, we could never advance our peace movement based on Buddhist principles'. He turned to me and said, 'I want you to protect these precious children of the Buddha throughout your life'.

Chowdhury: I feel very proud of the contribution that the Soka Gakkai women's division and young women's division make in promoting the culture of peace, the rights of women and children, the status of women in society and the overall objectives of humanity. In my interactions with them over so many years, I have found that they are among the most energetic, enthusiastic and empathetic members of the SGI. I hope they will keep up their spirit, creativity and good work, even more so now, as we face increasing challenges to peace, women's participation and human rights.

Ikeda: The Soka Gakkai women's and young women's divisions are expanding a grassroots movement for human happiness and world peace, based on their firm conviction that women's voices and actions can change the world. Many central leadership positions in SGI organizations all over the world are held by women. Having overcome various hardships, they have become shining suns of hope causing the flowers of happiness and friendship to bloom in their regions and communities.

The peace scholar Elise Boulding had the following words of praise for them:

> Women have a tremendous role to play in the local community. But, for long ages, in many countries, not just in Japan, they remained shut up at home with no place in society. That is why the appearance of women stubbornly persisting in peace work in their communities, like those in SGI organizations, is so important.[5]

Chowdhury: Women of the SGI should be proud of their work on behalf of a wonderful organization that recognizes, respects and advances the role, rights and equality of women.

Ikeda: A Buddhist scripture tells the story of Queen Shrimala, who made the following vow to Shakyamuni:

> If I see lonely people, people who have been jailed unjustly

and have lost their freedom, people who are suffering from illness, disaster, or poverty, I will not abandon them. I will bring them spiritual and material comfort.[6]

True to her promise, Queen Shrimala thereafter devoted herself to the wellbeing of people weighed down by life's sufferings. I believe that what we need today, as rapidly advancing globalization spawns division and conflict, and widens the gap between the rich and poor, is the power of women who possess the dedication to others embodied by Queen Shrimala.

Mahatma Gandhi said that it is women who must teach pacifism to a world where people thirst for the 'nectar' of peace even while engaged in hostilities.[7] The reason that, in addition to Gandhi, so many other world leaders in the cause of peace place their hopes in women is the resourceful, determined nature of women, embodied in their gift for healing desolate hearts and their practical, deeply grounded commitment to preventing violence, nurturing life and promoting peace. Tapping these qualities and building a grassroots network based on them are the key to success or failure in creating the culture of peace.

What role do you expect women to play in creating the culture of peace?

Chowdhury: Instead of comparing themselves to men, instead of trying to emulate them, women should be women. They do not have to change simply because the world still remains a man's place. Women must bring out what they are. I believe they are not the weaker but the stronger sex, stronger than men in many positive ways. It is unfortunate that, though they have so much power, authority and control over almost everything, men remain selfish and egocentric by denying women equal rights and equal opportunities to contribute their share to global progress.

In spite of this reality, women in many societies no longer wait for men to grant rights or create opportunities. They create them on their own through determination and perseverance. I believe this is a welcome development of which we are going to see more and more, especially the more that men try to put obstacles in their path to equality and empowerment.

Ikeda: It is the inevitable current of the times. Any nation or organization that ignores it forfeits its continued development and viability.

In September 2008, the United Nations Development Fund for Women issued a report titled *Progress of the World's Women 2008/2009: Who Accounts to Women?* According to this report, women at present hold only a fourth of the seats in the world's national legislatures, and on average, working women's wages are 17 per cent lower than those of men. About a third of the women of the world are victims of gender-based violence. The report goes on to say that just as nations have the responsibility to articulate and fulfil their promises in women's rights, women's participation, given this present situation, is essential to maintain good governance.

At the United Nations, you worked hard to expand women's role in peace work, thus inspiring the UN Security Council to make its first proclamation on the issue in 2000. Your pioneering statement for the UN Security Council's recognition of women's peace roles was reported in Japan, too.

Breakthrough of UNSCR 1325

Chowdhury: The International Women's Day in 2000 – 8 March – was an extraordinary day for me and will be so for the rest of my life. It was a landmark day for humanity as well. That day, after intense stonewalling by fellow UN Security Council permanent members, it was possible for me, as the President of the 15-member Council – during the first of my two terms – to issue a statement that formally brought to global attention the contributions women have been making to preventing war, to building peace and to engaging individuals and societies to live in harmony. It recognized peace is inextricably linked with equality between women and men. Till that time – 55 years since the Council was established – such substantive contributions were unrecognized, underutilized and undervalued.

The Council determined that equal access and full participation of women in power structures and their full involvement in all efforts for the prevention and resolution of conflicts are indispensable to the maintenance and promotion of peace and security. The statement underscored the 'importance of promoting an active and visible policy of mainstreaming a gender perspective into all policies and programmes'[8] relating to peace and security.

It is unfortunate that the intrinsic role of women in peace and security remained unrecognized since the creation of the United Nations Security Council. For a long time, there has been an impression of women as helpless victims of wars and conflicts. That inexplicable omission was reversed on 8 March 2000 by this conceptual and political breakthrough, thereby sowing the seeds for Security Council Resolution 1325, which was adopted in October of that year by consensus after eight months of negotiation. The need to involve women at all decision-making levels, including in the peace process, is now globally recognized by the international community.

Ikeda: Such involvement is absolutely necessary. Consisting of 18 articles, the resolution is epoch-making in urging 'Member States to ensure increased representation of women at all decision-making levels in national, regional, and international institutions and mechanisms for the prevention, management, and resolution of conflict' and encouraging the Secretary-General to 'implement his strategic plan of action (A/49/587) calling for an increase in the participation of women at decision-making levels in conflict resolution and peace processes'.[9]

Noeleen Heyzer, then executive director of the United Nations Development Fund for Women (UNIFEM), highly praised the resolution:

Today, members of the Security Council established a new precedent for the 21st century. Without international action, women caught in conflicts have no security of any kind. And without women's full participation, the peace process itself suffers.[10]

Chowdhury: I recall with great appreciation the energetic role Noeleen herself played in raising the profile of the issue as head of UNIFEM. I would also pay tribute to the energizing role of civil society organizations. Resolution 1325 carried women's voices to the Security Council. It is amazing that in the ten years since its adoption, just four numerals – 1-3-2-5 – have generated a global enthusiasm that is unprecedented in many ways. Adoption of Resolution 1325 in 2000 by the Council opened a much-awaited door of opportunity for women who have shown time and again that they bring a qualitative improvement in structuring peace and in post-conflict architecture. Women and many men all over the world have been energized by this resolution.

Even the UN Security Council, which is known for being a closed club, showed a forward-looking approach by adopting four follow-up resolutions related to women and peace and security. One of the best-known Security Council resolutions, 1325 conveys a strong political message to the international community that there can be no lasting peace without the active and equal participation of women.

Ikeda: I can imagine the untold efforts that must have gone into making this a reality; it is a great achievement. Radhika Coomaraswamy, UN Under-Secretary-General and Special Representative for Children and Armed Conflict, also praised it highly in a special report to the UN Human Rights Council on the causes and results of violence against women:

The adoption by the Security Council of Resolution 1325 (2000) has been very important in recognizing the vital role of women in promoting peace and calling for an increased use of women's expertise in conflict resolution and at all stages of peacemaking and peace-building.[11]

Chowdhury: I am glad that I could sow the seeds for Resolution 1325 during my presidency of the Security Council. Since then, reports on its implementation show the comprehensive nature of the resolution in clearly setting forth national responsibilities, regional cooperation and international engagement.

Again, the main focus of the resolution is the participation and involvement of women in all aspects and levels of peace processes. For this reason, it urges Member States to take specific actions to ensure women's equal and full participation as active agents in peace and security. The resolution is historic not only because the Council for the first time systematically addressed the manner in which conflict affects women and girls differently from men and boys but also because it acknowledges the crucial link connecting peace, women's participation in decision-making and the recognition of women's life experiences in conflict situations.

Because it was adopted by the Security Council, according to Article 25 of the UN Charter, the resolution is binding on the international community as a whole and all Member States and entities of the United Nations in particular. It has created a tremendous opportunity for NGOs, particularly women's NGOs, to organize them in their work for equality, rights and empowerment of women and girls.

True Parity

Ikeda: On the several occasions thereafter when women, peace and security were topics in the Security Council, you often insisted on the absolute necessity of women's participation in the peace processes. Every October, the anniversary of Resolution 1325's adoption, substantive discussions have been held in the Security Council on its implementation.

Chowdhury: Let me acknowledge here that there are growing complaints that the political thrust of the historic resolution remains unimplemented. Gender perspectives are not yet fully integrated into the terms of reference in peace operations. We continue to receive reports that women are still often ignored or excluded from formal processes of peace negotiations and elections and in the drafting of new constitutions or legislature frameworks. The historic and operational value of the resolution has been undercut by the disappointing record of its implementation. The complicity of the Security Council in international practices that make women insecure, basically as a result of its support of the existing militarized interstate security arrangements, is truly frustrating.

Ten years of expectation and exasperation have to end. The time to act was yesterday. Anniversaries are good to lift the spirit and energize us, but our work and advocacy should be every day – never to give up. Now we need to look ahead, bearing in mind that progress has been minimal.

The United Nations has to take the lead in implementation. The Secretary-General has to lead the United Nations in taking that lead. It is obvious that governments of developing countries, particularly of the poorest and most vulnerable, would not move for implementation unless there is international support and encouragement. That should come from the United Nations – with UN Resident Coordinators who represent the United Nations and the Secretary-General taking the initiative to encourage national-level leadership for the implementation at country level.

I consider 1325 one of my two humble contributions to the UN system and – I say in all humility – to the rest of the international community (the other being the UN Declaration and Programme of Action on a Culture of Peace). As you point out, the role of women is absolutely essential to the culture of peace. Their involvement strengthens its roots. Promoting anything that will be good for the future of society advances the culture of peace. That is what Resolution 1325, in the broader interpretation of its focus, would ensure.

Ikeda: Women's empowerment and their role in the peace process are major themes of the peace proposals I issue annually to commemorate the establishment of the SGI. All the world thinkers with whom I have held discussions join me in agreeing that women's viewpoints must be reflected in all attempts to cope with our global problems.

When I met (in 1996) President José María Figueres Olsen of the Republic of Costa Rica and his mother, Karen Olsen de Figueres of the Figueres Foundation, Mrs Olsen's words to me were unforgettable:

> I believe in the future. To believe in the future means to have a dream and advance and develop toward it. By 'develop' I don't just mean technological and economic development; I mean the development of human happiness. It is a 'struggle without end' for a better society, based on the sanctity and value of human life.[12]

What must we do to ensure that these views are reflected in all the United Nations' actions?

Chowdhury: In spite of all our efforts, we are still far from establishing 50/50 parity between women and men working throughout the UN system. This parity is particularly important at the senior levels. Equality must be not merely statistical but also substantive. Some organizations like the United Nations Children's Fund and the United Nations Population Fund have done well in moving toward achieving that target. Others have not.

Ikeda: Ann M. Veneman, UNICEF executive director, and Thoraya Ahmed Obaid, UNFPA executive director, are both women.[13] More than a decade ago, Nafis Sadik, who was UNFPA head at the time, discussed this same topic at the book presentation ceremony at the United Nations for *A People's Response to Our Global Neighborhood*, hosted by the Ikeda Center for Peace, Learning, and Dialogue.

Speaking of the importance of UN and other international conferences in encouraging the participation of civil society in world governance, she expressed the regret that many such conferences ignore the voices of women, who constitute half of any society, and exclude them from decision-making.

She added that she was not simply referring to ensuring women's participation in such areas as health, education and rights but everything that influences daily life and children's future: war, military expenditures and economics. We need to pay attention to the voices of women – voices from the future – in dealing with all issues of importance to humanity.

Chowdhury: Unfortunately, in the area of peace and security, the United Nations is still predominantly a man's organization. For the first time, Resolution 1325 opened the door to changing that perception and the unacceptable reality behind it. We must make sure that this potential is effectively realized rather than lost.

Ikeda: The question is how to implement the article of Resolution 1325 that 'urges the Secretary-General to appoint more women as special representatives and envoys to pursue good offices on his behalf.' This is the crucial point.

Chowdhury: Participating at the international Wilton Park Conference 816[14] in Britain in 2006, along with Liberian president Ellen Johnson-Sirleaf, whose contribution to 1325 is well known, I declared, 'It would be purposeful for the United Nations to have a fulltime advocate and monitor for 1325 – a kind of Special Representative of the Secretary-General for 1325'.[15] This single step would go a long way toward advancing the 1325 objectives. Since then, the appointment of a special representative on sexual violence against women and the setting up of UN Women[16] with a broader mandate to pursue all women's issues, including 1325, have changed the dynamics and given us expectation for forward movement.

We also need a set of tracking indicators to determine what countries lack and what deficiencies can be made up with regard to the implementation of 1325. It will also be important for senior women secretariat officials to speak up more strongly in favour of appropriate reflection of women's role and issues in the work of the United Nations.

But the same is true of men. Male and female members of the senior management group must advocate and support the real involvement of women and true recognition of their role.

Women and Men Working Together

Ikeda: All the points you make are important. To build real gender partnerships, active steps to open the way for female involvement alone are insufficient. Men must change their way of thinking and overcome their prejudices.

In an essay, I once set forth the following qualities that men need to cultivate for the future:

1. The generosity of spirit to accept women's abilities without feeling threatened.
2. The honesty to welcome women's integrity and candour.
3. The self-reliance to refrain from making unfair demands on women's patience.
4. The sensitivity to consider women's feelings and point of view.

If men can improve themselves by developing these traits, it will be a great advance toward a society in which all human beings – men and women alike – can manifest their strengths equally. I believe that the current of the times is moving in this direction.

Chowdhury: The genuine gender partnership that you mention is extremely important. In many countries, the cabinet portfolio of women's affairs goes to a woman. In my opinion, however, either a man or a woman should be feeling empowered to do the job. It is important for the women's movement to reject the idea that leadership positions in women's ministries must be allocated only to women.

By the same token, cabinet posts, traditionally given to men, should be open to women. The same guideline should apply to intergovernmental organizations as well.

Ikeda: The point you make tends to often be ignored. It is essential to avoid being distracted by superficial issues and to take practical, effective steps to enable men and women to together build a better society. I agree with Hazel Henderson when she says, 'I think we can restore balance to human society, including the economy, if men and women work together as equal partners'.[17] Equal partnership is the important thing.

Chowdhury: She makes a vital point. In recent years, general portfolios traditionally allocated only to men have in a number of cases been given to women: ministries of foreign affairs, finance, justice, the interior, trade, and so on. In the developing world, this kind of wonderful development is occurring in a number of African countries. In Bangladesh, in addition to having a dynamic Prime Minister, women have filled top cabinet posts as ministers of foreign affairs, agriculture and the interior. This indicates that the basic objectives of Resolution 1325 can be achieved through conscious, determined and structured implementation.[18]

The potential of the resolution is limitless. I believe strongly that 1325 belongs to humanity – it is the common heritage of humankind – it is owned by us all, it is for the benefit of all.[19]

TWELVE
The Road to Hope

Ikeda: I reiterated the importance of the culture of peace in my peace proposal for SGI Day in 2009, designated by the United Nations as the International Year of Reconciliation. The UN General Assembly then proclaimed 2010 the International Year for the Rapprochement of Cultures. It is urgent, as you always say, to establish the culture of peace around the world. We of the SGI are resolved to intensify our efforts in this direction.

I want to focus our discussion now on the role of the family, the smallest, most basic social unit for spreading the culture of peace at the grassroots level, because I think this is perhaps the most effective way to demonstrate the relevance and meaning of the culture of peace to the majority of people. Regarding this, in your congratulatory address at Soka University graduation ceremonies in Tokyo in March 2003, you said:

> As the oldest institution in human history, the family is absolutely at the core of the promotion of the culture of peace. Younger members of society, growing up in a family that teaches them the virtues of tolerance, harmony, and understanding, will grow up with the right values that inculcate the culture of peace. We should remember that the work for

peace is a continuous process. Each of us can make a difference in that process.[1]

I frequently hear students comment on how memorable your commencement address was.

Chowdhury: I, too, have the fondest memories of that graduation event. The desire to have a family is a basic human instinct. In different cultural contexts, the constituent members of the family change considerably. Nonetheless, we must ensure that this basic instinct will always remain to perpetuate the values of love and happiness, of caring and sharing. Naturally children form an important part of the institution. At the same time, they grow up with the family influencing the shaping of their mindsets.

I believe that we must encourage the family in our individual contexts. That is why I keep on emphasizing the role of family in building the culture of peace. Couples must be fully aware of the importance of the involvement of the family in any big endeavour. Indeed no initiatives either of the government or of society will succeed unless the family gets involved in the real sense.

Ikeda: Elise Boulding once told me: 'Peace is not only about acting in times of danger, it is also about assisting one another in daily life. The family and local community are key starting points.'[2] Peace is indeed founded on the family.

The Great Earth

Chowdhury: The continuing experience of mutual support and assistance in daily life is the soil in which the culture of peace grows. The indispensable role of the family is the mutual cultivation in parents and children of a caring spirit and shared love, understanding and solidarity.

When I was growing up, my supreme good fortune was to learn

from my parents to love people, to care about the underprivileged, to take a total, compassionate view of things and to extend a helping hand to everyone. Seeing my mother and father put these values into practice in daily life inspired me to emulate them. They created a congenial home atmosphere, where I could sense, absorb and internalize these attitudes. From this experience, I came to understand that, in dealing with children, parents must maintain a good balance between instructing and stimulating personality formation on the one hand and providing opportunities to develop individuality, originality, and creativity on the other.

Ikeda: President Toda considered it one of the Soka Gakkai's social missions to become the 'great earth' stimulating the growth of magnificent human beings. In keeping with his wish, the SGI has developed into a network of men and women of all ages connected by humanistic ideals and active in 192 countries and territories.

Many of the industrialized nations of the world are experiencing an attenuation of human relations in various respects. As you suggest, these nations face the major challenge of not only strengthening family connections but also expanding open-minded interactions in the community and throughout society.

Chowdhury: Striking differences in family conditions in both developed and developing countries are found in various parts of the world. Traditionally all Bangladeshis have big extended families. In my youth, cousins who lived close by were part of the immediate family. I grew up surrounded by my father's and mother's siblings, cousins, and distant relatives, in frequent contacts with extended family in many different places.

Older people treated all younger ones like their own children, whether they were or not. In fact, in Bangladesh, we called cousins 'brother' and 'sister' and treated them as our own siblings. Next-door neighbours who were our parents' friends were called 'aunt' and 'uncle' and respected accordingly. And they looked on us as nieces and nephews.

Someone was always on hand to help us if we found ourselves in trouble. For instance, there was always somebody available to help out if one was sick or otherwise preoccupied. On religious or festive occasions like weddings or birthdays, relatives, friends and neighbours all gathered. Though today this is changing in urban areas because of modern social pressures, big families in Bangladesh still get together in times of happiness or during difficult times to share the experience and to benefit from such sharing.

Succeeding as a Family

Ikeda: In the past, the warm, supportive family environment you describe was commonly seen throughout Japan. Now, however, like other industrialized nations, things have changed dramatically, and with urbanization and the increasing prevalence of the nuclear family, a growing number of young people have relocated from their hometowns, where their extended families are centred, to the cities, establishing their families there.

Against the background of this social shift, the Soka Gakkai members have reached out in friendship to the families in their communities, creating activities to which parents can bring their children – from elementary through high school. We have a tradition of promoting this familial atmosphere in our communities, with young adults acting as brothers and sisters to their juniors, listening to their problems and encouraging them.

In addition, at the monthly Soka Gakkai discussion meetings held at the neighbourhood level, members of different generations and fields of endeavour get together like a big family to discuss matters of faith, share joys and sorrows, and encourage and support one another. At the same time, since the time of second president Toda, the creation of harmonious families through faith has been a top priority in the SGI.

You have built a model family, and I want to ask you about achieving this goal. What points do you consider important?

Chowdhury: First, the value of the family should be seen not only in the context of hardship but also in the context of happiness. We should avoid monopolizing the good times by ourselves and turning to the family only in bad times.

Second, there should be ground rules for behaviour and interaction between husband and wife and between parents and children. But those rules should be flexible enough to provide children with opportunities for creativity, originality, independence and confidence-building.

Third, harmony and sharing require a kind of forum – perhaps family meals – providing opportunities for the family to sit together and talk. Gathered around a table for meals, people can share joys and difficulties, problems and pleasures. In addition, the dining-table forum provides a wonderful chance to express dreams, goals and hopes. Parents can describe the things they are currently doing or their plans and hopes.

After thinking things over in their own way, children might then express the wish to participate in their father's and mother's wonderful activities. I think it is important to talk about and share dreams together as a family through exchanges of this kind.

Ikeda: Thank you for your concrete, precious suggestions. It also reflects the warm, open approach to children you and your wife have, treating them as individuals and equals. It is certainly true that children dislike being constantly ordered about, even if it is in their best interests. And assuming that they will understand your true intent just because you're their parent can lead to serious misunderstandings. It is precisely in the family setting that openhearted dialogue and voicing one's thoughts are most important.

The foundation of the family, of course, is the relationship between husband and wife. I understand that your wife, Mariam, whom I had the pleasure of meeting when she visited Soka University of Japan with you, took great interest in volunteer work from the time she was a young girl, offering nursing care at home and in the neighbourhood, and that she continues to contribute to society since your marriage. Such wonderful compassion in itself embodies the culture of peace.

What does she mean to you? As a married couple, what do you emphasize in your domestic daily life?

Chowdhury: I always say that husband and wife are an inseparable pair whose harmonious teamwork is reflected in the activities of both. In my work, I get tremendous encouragement, support, and intellectual and moral backup from my wife. In a similar way, I offer my assistance in her work, which sometimes goes beyond the home, since she is involved in initiatives contributing to social and human development.

At the same time, I contribute to the fulfilment of her responsibilities as a homemaker. Mutuality is important. That is why I call husband and wife a team. Mutuality develops respect and recognition but avoids undue expectations.

Ikeda: A commitment to inspiring and encouraging one another is important. I, too, am deeply grateful to my wife.

About 40 years ago (in 1969), while travelling around Japan, I came down with a high fever, caused by acute pneumonia. I was relieved when my wife rushed to my side from Tokyo to care for me. Since then, at my doctor's suggestion, she goes with me everywhere, in Japan and overseas.

During one of our meetings on my first visit to China in 1974, Liao Chengzhi, chairman of the China–Japan Friendship Association, asked my wife to express her thoughts. At first, she demurred, but then, since she had been asked, said: 'In Japan, I had always been told that Communism is something to be feared. For that reason, I had come to perceive China as a scary country.' At first I was anxious, having no idea what she might say next. She added with a smile, 'After talking with all of you, however, I have come to see clearly that China is a warm country overflowing with love and humanity.'[3] Delighted by this, Mr Liao applauded her warmly and said: 'You have spoken truthfully and honestly. That's the way to make friends!'[4]

When meeting with important world figures, my wife's presence has often contributed to creating a warm, congenial atmosphere. Women have a remarkable ability to create the culture of peace wherever they are.

Chowdhury: My wife and I have fond memories of Mrs Ikeda. Both of you attended the SGI fifteenth World Peace Youth Culture Festival held at New York's Carnegie Hall, 18 June 1996, to celebrate the fiftieth anniversary of UNICEF. When speaking at Carnegie Hall representing UNICEF, I glimpsed you and your wife from a distance. When we met again in 2003, your wife reported to mine how you had predicted that I would go far in life. Until then, we had never heard such flattering comments. I was touched that Kaneko did remember it and pass it on to my wife. Her gesture revealed her perceptiveness and inner qualities in a wonderful way.

Ikeda: It is kind of you to say so. Nichiren writes about how important it is for husband and wife to proceed through life in harmony and unity: 'Explain all this to your wife too, and work together like the sun and moon, a pair of eyes, or the two wings of a bird.'[5] My wife and I have always held this spirit in our hearts and joined in striving to realize the vision of President Toda, who stood up valiantly for the peace and happiness of all humanity.

In appreciation to her, I wrote the following verse:

Opening the path
As I walk with you,
My irreplaceable support.[6]

Chowdhury: Wonderful words. As the poem says, I am sure that your wife is your irreplaceable mainstay. The strength I sense in her characteristically calm gentleness emerges from her profound compassion and determination to work for the good of society. I also find that you deeply respect and adore the role she plays. This appears in the mutual support and respect you demonstrate whenever you talk or undertake something together.

Ikeda: Thank you again. To return to your wife, I'm sure it must be challenging for her to both fulfil her domestic roles and participate in activities for the social good. It is indeed a wonderful life, and I'm sure her example must have made a great impression on your children.

Chowdhury: Our children have been very supportive and aware of what we do. It is important for children to grow up knowing that life is not always a bed of roses and to be aware of the hardships their parents encounter for their sakes. This knowledge enables them to be good parents themselves in later life.

I am pleased that our three children – Shantonu, Sudeshna and Anando – have turned out to be wonderful individuals, confident, happy, full of compassion, and willing to do something for humanity. My wife and I are proud of them and now of our four grandchildren.[7] Two grandchildren are still very young, but the other two – both granddaughters – are actively involved with people and enthusiastic about global human issues as well as about other countries, cultures, and societies. It is wonderful to watch them grow up. My wife and I learn also from their ideas and their creativity.

Adversity as Education

Ikeda: It is important to stay in touch with the young people who embody the future and keep moving forward inspired by the growth and dynamism of the young. My mentor always insisted that only the young can be trusted, and he trained us young people with both great strictness and love. Looking back, it's hard to believe that a half-century has passed since his death (on 2 April 1958). I have kept his legacy alive by striving tirelessly for world peace and stirring a groundswell of dialogue.

During this time, I have been frequently misunderstood and criticized, but I was prepared for that. For instance, as I mentioned earlier, I visited China in 1974 and then, in the same year, the Soviet Union. For days on end, people condemned me, as a man of religion, for travelling to a socialist country. But I was confident that if I took the first step, many young people would follow.

In fact, Soka University was the first Japanese university to admit state-financed Chinese students after World War II. I personally stood as the students' guarantor. Today, a total of 900,000 Chinese students have come to Japan to study.

Chowdhury: Your contributions not only to Sino–Japanese amity but also to global peace and support for the United Nations have been truly remarkable in so many ways.

In my long years at the United Nations, my family and I have confronted various tribulations. Most of our challenges have been generated less by physical challenges than by human smallness of mind, jealousy, meanness, discontent with our achievements, and disregard for the values we adhered to, genuineness of our hearts and far-sightedness of our initiatives. On many occasions, our openness and desire to be inclusive have been frustrated because of narrow-mindedness.

As you and I discovered in 2003, we share similar experiences. We are both victims of our own good intentions and openness and willingness to work for the benefit of people. Human unkindness and narrowness have hurt us more than external physical hardships. But these experiences enabled us to grow even stronger. Without them, we might have become complacent and lax. Challenges renewed our energy and determination.

I always try to derive energy from challenge, failure and mistakes that should be regarded as opportunities to learn. My failures have taught me many things. I believe firmly that failure opens up a new door for success by telling us what went wrong the first time. One should not be afraid of failure. I now talk about this point to a wider group of young people in universities and colleges. Challenges are worthwhile. True they can be sometimes devastating, but as long as you are really determined, you can overcome any physical, intellectual or moral or even institutional challenge. It is important to bear this in mind.

Ikeda: One of my favourite sayings goes, 'There is no greater education than adversity'.

THIRTEEN
The School of Life

Ikeda: Summits held in London in April 2009 between the leaders of Russia and the United States signalled a new dawn for the reduction of nuclear armaments following the Strategic Arms Reduction Treaty (signed 1991). Against this background, US President Barack Obama announced a new, comprehensive vision of a nuclear-free world in Prague, Czech Republic. We must vigorously pursue all such opportunities for nuclear-arms reduction and make them the incontrovertible tide of the times.

We of the SGI, taking as our fundamental starting point the Declaration for the Abolition of Nuclear Weapons issued in September 1957 by President Toda, have created a movement demanding the total elimination of such weapons. Working in cooperation with UN bodies and NGOs, we have continuously engaged in activities like delivering to the secretary-general a petition bearing the signatures of ten million people and holding exhibitions in many countries around the world demonstrating the threat of nuclear weapons. In 2007, on the fiftieth anniversary of President Toda's declaration, we made a fresh start by declaring the People's Decade of Action for Nuclear Abolition.[1]

The time has come not only for government action but also for bringing together a broad spectrum of voices within civil society to galvanize international public opinion on this issue.

Chowdhury: Yours is a much-needed, meaningful, and forward-looking undertaking. For a world free of nuclear weapons, we must ask not only for non-proliferation but also for destruction of all existing weapons. It is therefore necessary to get more support for a nuclear-weapons-free world and genuine assurance through real action by the existing nuclear-weapon states to fulfil their obligations under the Treaty on the Non-Proliferation of Nuclear Weapons (NPT).

Fear and the desire for power and respect motivate nations to develop nuclear weapons. This can be reduced significantly if nuclear-armed nations fully comply with their NPT obligations. I believe strongly that global as well as national public opinion would support positive action in this direction. Today's young people in particular play a crucial role in such an opinion-building process.

Ikeda: It's an important point. Both US President Obama and Russian President Dmitry A. Medvedev are currently in their forties, and many around the world have high hopes for these two youthful leaders. Today's severe global economic crisis offers an excellent opportunity for the United States, Russia and other countries to change their way of thinking and make dramatic arms reductions. Though the task is long and hard, we must, for the sake of humanity's future, halt the proliferation of nuclear arms and press steadfastly onward to their total elimination.

I put special hope in the vitality and fresh ideas of young people, on whom the coming age depends. Youth have the power to stir waves of change to make the world a better place. Working in solidarity, young people cannot fail to open the doors to a new epoch.

You have continued to express your firm faith in young people, affirming to them that they have the power to make the world a better place and that, given concerted cooperation and will, we can eradicate famine and disease, eliminate malnutrition and poverty, and create a future in which everyone can lead a fulfilling life.

President Toda, again, also treasured young people and had high expectations for them. Having been trained by such a great teacher,

I also place my faith in youth, work in their midst, and share their joys and sorrows as we work together to pioneer a better future. My determination to do so remains unchanged today. Their strength is of the greatest importance to the creation of a better future and to making the culture of peace the foundation of a new global society.

Chowdhury: As a matter of fact, I not only agree with you that the future belongs to the youth, but I go even further, to say that the present also belongs to them. The youthful, vibrant, and open mind of the new generation has the potential to bring a sea change that will enable the world to look at itself in a much more understanding way.

You have asserted very rightly that young people will create a better future and build the culture of peace as the foundation of a new global society. The culture of peace by itself has the potential to develop a world of understanding, cooperation and solidarity. I am deeply inspired by the high expectations that your mentor, Josei Toda, had for young people. I believe the strength of the SGI comes from that focus of its past and present leadership.

Ikeda: We have always advanced in the spirit of the 'youthful SGI'. As those responsible for creating the new age, our youth have been vibrantly active. I am happy that in all of the 192 countries and territories where the SGI is active, young people take the lead and, burning with ideals and a great sense of mission, continue to expand our network of peace and friendship.

Chowdhury: I have personally seen how sincerely the young members of the SGI have taken up the initiative to promote the culture of peace and thereby take a leading part in the global movement for the culture of peace. The sooner we recognize the value of the contribution that the youth can make to move away from prejudice and hatred toward tolerance and non-violence, the better it is for our present and future generations.

Cherishing the Young

Ikeda: Unfortunately, however, today many young people lack hope and ideals. We of the older generations are responsible for this. In all too many cases up to now, those in power have exploited and sacrificed youth for their own ends.

A real leader loves young people and wants to cultivate their abilities. Society's leaders have the mission and responsibility to make it possible for young people to make the most of their abilities and take active roles in society. Though still modest, we are seeing steady growth in a wide spectrum of youth volunteer activities around the world. We must all prize, encourage and foster these emerging efforts. In your encounters with youth around the world, have you noticed any particularly noteworthy developments?

Chowdhury: I have the opportunity to interact with young people in a number of ways but mostly through two approaches. One is to stimulate them to learn more about the culture of peace, tolerance, understanding, and respect for diversity and pluralism, as well as to encourage them to practise those values in their own lives. The other is to make them aware and concerned about the plight of the poorest, most vulnerable countries and realize that nearly 90 out of 192 UN Member States – nearly 45 per cent of the membership – fall into this category.

As young people grow up and begin their working lives and professional careers, they should comprehend fully the needs of and be compassionately supportive of these nations. It is absolutely unconscionable that in this age of human progress, we allow such a vast segment of humanity to continue to be impoverished.

Ikeda: This is indeed the essential factor in uniting humanity and achieving world peace. We must give young people the widest field of vision possible. If we can lift and expand their focus from the narrow realm of their immediate personal circumstances and inculcate in them a sensibility that regards occurrences in the far corners of the world as relevant and meaningful to their own lives, their existence will be greatly enriched and deepened.

I hope that young people will become global citizens with a sense of justice, who empathize and feel solidarity with the distressed everywhere. As long as they feel responsible for both the future and the whole world, they will be capable of manifesting immeasurable strength.

Another way of expressing this idea of responsibility is mission. Elevating young people's awareness of this mission is the key to transforming the world. You proposed the following measure in this connection:

A very important way of promoting the culture of peace is through the spreading of peace education. . . . Peace studies in all educational institutions should be incorporated as part of their curricula.[2]

I agree entirely. How do you envision the content and curriculum of the peace studies and peace education that you think should be conducted in educational institutions?

Peace Education

Chowdhury: Efforts to cultivate understanding and internalization of the culture of peace must start at an early stage of education. Simple things about what peace means, how one benefits from knowledge about other peoples, how one should behave with others, and similar topics need to be made a part of the daily interaction among teachers and students at all levels. As the family is the first place where such interaction commences, parents have an important role to play.

Like all kinds of education, peace education should be an integral part of life; it should be people-oriented and commonly understood instead of theoretical or academic. We must learn how to be naturally non-violent and peaceful. It should be our serious and sincere effort to encourage others to build the culture of peace in their interaction with others. This process, I believe, is easy and simple when well-intentioned and done with determination.

Ikeda: I completely agree that peace education should be an integral part of life, and that it should be people-oriented. This is the heart of the Soka Gakkai regional peace-culture forums, in which women play the principal part, and our efforts to foster peace awareness in young people. It is a form of consciousness raising conducted by the people themselves.[3]

Chowdhury: People's involvement in generating popular awareness about peace and its value in our lives is absolutely necessary. Unfortunately, human history has glorified war and war heroes. Peace and people's efforts for peace in our society and in our world have not found the place and prominence that they deserve. The time has come to change that convoluted recording of history.

At the same time, at higher levels of education, it is important to create a curriculum that educates and empowers individuals in the culture of peace. I am not an expert on curriculum development, but I believe that the culture of peace – peace studies or peace education – must be seen in the context of self-transformation as well as in interaction with others. It is self-empowerment in both these contexts that I am emphasizing.

To make the culture of peace a global movement, the nations of the world should make a genuine effort to introduce peace education in all their institutions at every level. Learning about the culture of peace can be more effective when the teaching method is suitable to the level of the students. Civil society has a major role to play in this regard, by asking for the introduction of peace education and by providing non-formal education to develop the culture of peace for all from their very childhood, particularly for those who do not have the opportunity to benefit from the formal system of education.

In addition, it should be compulsory to include materials on the United Nations in peace education, as was done in the case of human rights education during the UN-declared decade between 1995 and 2004. A similar decade devoted to education for the culture of peace would be a meaningful step forward.

Ikeda: Adults need to take the initiative in promoting peace education. As a follow-up to the Decade for Human Rights Education to which you just referred, the United Nations began its World Programme for Human Rights Education in 2005. The SGI cooperated with other NGOs in promoting this programme, too. Our steady efforts with many countries and other NGOs bore fruit when the General Assembly in December 2004 unanimously agreed to establish the programme. In addition to continuing to promote the World Programme for Human Rights Education, the SGI is taking further steps to work together with various NGOs in order to reflect as many voices from global civil society as possible – another example being the UN Declaration on Human Rights Education and Training, drafted by the UN Commission on Human Rights.

The SGI has been engaged in grassroots-level activities, including human rights and peace education, since the Cold War days; above all, continuity and accumulation are essential for these activities. We are determined, while expanding the friendship and solidarity of global citizens, to persevere in our support for UN activities from the perspective of peace, culture and education.

Chowdhury: The value-creation aspect at the core of the Soka schools is truly remarkable. I am privileged to have witnessed this first-hand during my teaching of the culture of peace course at Soka University of America since 2009.[4]

As I no longer formally work for the United Nations, I now spend more time speaking to young people. I have accepted many invitations to address students at colleges, universities, high schools and even elementary schools. I believe that speaking to students at all levels helps build the culture of peace in the most deep-rooted manner. Though there are pressures on my schedule, I always accept invitations from educational institutions because those are excellent opportunities to interact with and empower young people.

I have found the youth in the United States and many other countries to be very open in their outlook and eager to reach out to and learn about other societies and cultures. I am struck on many occasions by their fairly good understanding of situations and conditions in other parts of the globe. Generally they are quite supportive of and friendly toward other countries, especially those in difficulty. As I have said, their open-mindedness is very impressive.

Openness of Youth

Ikeda: You and I are both, again, extremely fond of Rabindranath Tagore. In one of his poems, he wrote, 'Youth alone knows how to surmount barriers / Infinite is his hope, unlimited his powers!'[5]

Youth has boundless potential. And as you point out, young people are first and foremost open-minded. This outstanding characteristic distinguishes them from their seniors, who are more likely to cling to preconceived notions. We must therefore strive to build a society that encourages and makes best use of the purity, flexibility and openness of youth.

Chowdhury: Whenever I talk with young people, I inquire about their future ambitions. While they are studying and completing their education, they keep open minds about everything. But when they enter professional life, many of them tend to change and seem to lose their openness and empathy for the world's impoverished. What triggers this change, and why does it happen? Although this still puzzles me, I continue to expect a great deal from young people.

Now is the time to direct their attention to peace, education and building the culture of peace. I believe strongly that in this way it is possible to make their open, positive and youthful mindset last permanently. This is the responsibility of the adults — us — who unfortunately have not been able to make our world less violent and more peaceful. We need to take every step so that our future generations at least have the opportunity to internalize the culture of peace in their lives.

Ikeda: Providing peace education to youth is going to be a major issue for the future of society and the world. In a sense, social systems possess a structural power to control human thought and action. People's values and viewpoints change according to their situations or positions. Reality is harsh. Even people who had a keen sense of justice and burned with great ideals in their youth find it hard to make it through life unless they have faith as solid as a boulder and the support of a firm philosophy.

Nichiren wrote, 'To accept is easy; to continue is difficult'.[6] In this sense, as you have said, the focus needs to be on implementing lifelong peace education in a way deeply rooted in people's lives as well as on the continuing effort to impart great courage, hope, and inspiration to young people.

Let me ask you several questions in this regard. What points are you especially careful to keep in mind when talking with young people?

Chowdhury: I make no special mental preparations as such. I approach young people always with confidence in their open-mindedness and eagerness to learn. I am always happy to devote part of our time together to questions and answers. I want not only to speak but also to listen to what they have to say. I am always encouraged to find their positive outlook and impartial, independent analyses. My only preparation is to make sure I speak less and listen more. Greater interaction with students is always so refreshing.

Ikeda: Listening is an act of respect, trust and encouragement of young people. This is the kind of philosophy we can expect from a person like you, a master of dialogue dedicated to drawing out the limitless potential of youth. I have heard many young SGI members from all over the world say what a deep impression talking with you has made. In your extensive international experiences with students in such countries as the United States, Japan and Bangladesh, what similarities and dissimilarities have you noticed?

Chowdhury: No matter where I go, I am impressed by young people's openness, which, with a global outlook, constitutes a common thread among them all, both in industrialized and developing countries. They want to know about other countries and other cultures and believe that globalism is very much part of their education and knowledge-base. This is as it must be. They cannot afford to remain focused only on themselves.

We need to ratchet up this eagerness among them to know more about the rest of the world and develop a global solidarity. It should be a conscious effort of all education systems to help their students become truly global citizens. As the world has become a 'global village', it is absolutely essential that our youth make the much-needed connection with the rest of the world.

Ikeda: Students' desire to learn is itself the hope of the future. And joining young people in the learning process is rejuvenating. It's an important lesson for adults.

What books would you especially like young people today to read? What movies and music would you introduce to them?

Chowdhury: All such things are important, but I would put slightly greater stress on visual content, which is retained longer and engages the intellectual faculty in a much more effective way. The reader's mind can waver, whereas actually seeing something holds the attention and makes a stronger impact. Visual experiences are especially important to today's children, accustomed as they are to working on computers, playing video games and watching television. Even reading skills, which are vital, can benefit from inspiring visual content.

Ikeda: The skilful use of visual content considerably improves educational effectiveness. A single photograph or a film can communicate a powerful message. For this reason, the SGI has employed visual content in exhibitions and other media in conducting its movement for peace.

At the same time, as many express their concern for the decline of the culture of the printed word in modern society, it is impossible to stress enough the importance of reading. Visual images tend to be fleeting and don't always leave a deep impression on the mind. This is because they encourage the passive absorption of information, which weakens the ability to think on one's own, to imagine and come up with new ideas.

It's important to employ both the printed word and visual media as effectively as possible, exploiting their synergy. We need to enrich young minds by making effective use of both the printed word and the best of visual media.

Encounters with the Great

Chowdhury: To the various means of communications we have already mentioned, I want to add one more: contacts with knowledgeable human beings who have experienced life and who have the credibility and the ability to communicate. Such people physically personify the struggles they have experienced as part of humanity.

For instance, Nelson Mandela requires no introduction. Everyone knows that he is a personification of the struggle for freedom and against oppression and apartheid. So when he speaks, people listen and get inspired. Of course, he is unique.

Nonetheless, every human being has something from which others can learn; we all can serve as an example to others. For me and millions of others, you are such a personality. Your philosophy of human revolution urges all of us to empower ourselves. You talk extensively about always growing, always moving forward. That encourages us immensely.

Ikeda: You are too generous. Putting myself aside, encounters with outstanding people do as much good as reading countless volumes. My mentor urged us to make the effort to meet and listen to great people, even if it was from the back of a large auditorium. There is no better education, he said, stressing how much we could gain from such experiences.

Based on this, I have met and spoken with outstanding people from all over the world and have taken all possible steps to invite such people to meet directly with the students of the educational institutions I have founded, such as Soka University and the Soka schools.

I receive messages from former students on a daily basis attesting to the huge, enduring impact these encounters have had on them over the years. Encounters with the world's great minds in various fields are rare opportunities and the most precious treasure of the intellect.

Chowdhury: As a practical idea, I believe, educational institutions should consciously budget for introducing people with deep and varied life experiences, who are just as important to the learning process as reading and visual exposure. This is even more vital at earlier learning stages than in higher education. This school of life provides more knowledge than anything else.

Ikeda: I like the phrase *school of life*. What words of advice do you have for young people in the twenty-first century? What can we hope for from them?

Chowdhury: Many of the people whom I encourage to join the global movement for the culture of peace ask me what they as lone individuals can do to promote it. Each person, particularly when they are young, considers himself or herself rather insignificant. But I tell all such people that to contribute to the culture of peace, they must begin with themselves. A person who grasps the essence of the culture of peace and becomes peaceful, non-violent, understanding and respectful of diversity will develop the capacity to be confident, strong and self-empowered, to face the challenges of life.

In this way, he or she can contribute to the building of the culture of peace not only in an individual sense but also in a much broader context. Each individual who transforms in this way can then add two, three or four other people over time, who become committed to the culture of peace: to be personally peaceful and non-violent. This is fascinating and transformational.

Ikeda: One must stand up as an individual. Some words of Mahatma Gandhi have been with me since my youth: 'The greatest men of the world have always stood alone.'[7] 'Strength of numbers is the delight of the timid. The valiant in spirit glory in fighting alone.'[8] All reforms begin with a single courageous individual.

Nichiren teaches, 'A single individual has been used as an example, but the same thing applies equally to all living beings'.[9] The individual is of ultimate importance. This is the core idea of the human revolution that we in the SGI advocate. The revolution of a single individual can change a community, a society, a country, and ultimately the whole world. This is the unchanging formula, now and in the future. In short, the global revolution starts with the individual human revolution.

Chowdhury: In addition, I tell people to discuss the culture of peace with family and close friends. Each individual empowers himself or herself and thereafter is able to motivate a few more people to the cause. Each of these other persons continues to spread the process.

Everybody's empowerment will not be the same, but everyone empowered in this way will be committed to the culture of peace, addressing challenges, resolving problems of life peacefully, and refraining from countering violence with violence, whether it be verbal, physical, cultural, structural or any other kind. To those who doubt their capacity to contribute to the culture of peace, I emphasize that 'This is what you as an individual can do'.

Ikeda: As you have shown by your example, we need to speak in an accessible way that opens people's hearts and minds, and engage in one-on-one dialogue with as many as possible. You have faith in the tremendous potential of each individual. Though it may sound simplistic, I believe that heartfelt encouragement is the key to awakening people so that they can manifest their potential.

Every day, all over the world, SGI members encourage one another in striving for their mutual development and empowerment. They urge one another to never give up, to realize their own immeasurable power, to have self-confidence, and to work together for the sake of peace.

A Buddhist scripture teaches, 'The voice carries out the work of the Buddha'.[10] The human voice has the power to encourage, impart bravery, destroy evil and guide society in the direction of happiness. I am convinced that spreading the powerful voice of encouragement, hope and justice throughout the world is the best way to build the culture of peace.

Chowdhury: As a practice, I tell children and young people to empower themselves first, then address the empowerment of the people around them. I underscore the empowerment of parents, who belong to older generations, often suffering from prejudice and transmitting to their children – sometimes subconsciously – their own negative values. Instead of being changed by them, children should strive to change parents' attitudes by freeing them from ingrained, unnoticed prejudices.

Ikeda: The idea that children can enlighten parents is extremely important. Buddhist scriptures teach the importance of repaying one's debts of gratitude to one's parents but also that children who correct parents' prejudices and mistaken religious views demonstrate true filial piety.

As they grow into mature adults, children should care for their parents and make them feel secure. The insight that children can transform their parents is essential for transforming people's out-looks, building an age of renewed creativity and progress, and bringing innovation and fresh advancement to our world.

FOURTEEN

Opening the Book of the World

Ikeda: Humanistic education is the wellspring of the culture of peace.
You delivered a lecture series on the culture of peace for four weeks
at Soka University of America in early 2009. Following the success
of your 2008 lecture series, you have forged a deeply significant
history with us, and as university founder I am very grateful. The
students found your lectures, which looked at history and current
events with a multifaceted approach for building the culture of
peace, enlightening and stirring. Many of them reported that your
talks taught them the importance of mutual understanding, trust
and cooperation, and inspired their enthusiasm and ardent sense
of mission for peace. I understand that, in addition to delivering
lectures, you and your wife warmly encouraged students by visiting
them in their dormitories and meeting them in the dining hall. For
this, I thank you once again.

Chowdhury: And I should like to say how happy and satisfied I am
each time I visit SUA. My first visit there was in 2005, when I delivered the university's first commencement address as its first class
graduated. Since then, I have visited a number of times. Each of my
visits has been meaningful, providing me an immense opportunity
to interact with bright young people.

Students there are absorbed in their studies and learning because they are keen on becoming better global citizens. They are eager to strive for peace and non-violence, not only in their own lives but also in their interactions with the rest of the world. In this way, they help realize your longstanding support of the United Nations. Their positive attitude impresses me greatly, and my continuing visits to SUA further encourage me to promote the culture of peace together with you and those students who imbibe your ideals.

Ikeda: I am delighted that, at the Soka Universities in Japan and America, students are deepening their understanding of the culture of peace and are strengthening their support for the United Nations.

Chowdhury: During my January 2009 visit, one of the lectures I delivered – organized by UNICEF volunteer leader Ruby Nagashima with the joint support of UNICEF and the SUA United Nations Club – dealt with the topic 'Water for Life'. Students from SUA and neighbouring educational institutions filled the auditorium to listen intently to an exposé on the conditions of the poorest and the most vulnerable peoples on the frontline of the global water crisis now looming large on our planet.

Thereafter, I was encouraged to learn that a number of the young people present later decided to become UNICEF volunteers to raise local contributions to finance projects in the neediest countries. The spirit of today's young people inspires me and makes me hopeful about our world of tomorrow.

Happiness as the Basic Goal

Ikeda: 'Water for Life' is an important theme. Clearly your speech on the supreme importance of human development had a profound impact on the students. It is gratifying that, through occasions of this kind, SUA is serving as a source of information and enlightenment in the community. This is only possible because you and other thinkers of your calibre from around the world have so graciously visited the university to share your wisdom.

I consider education, the key to determine the future of humanity, my crowning task. But education today is in crisis and faces many difficult challenges. In your view, what are some of the major issues confronting education today?

Chowdhury: I believe that in many countries the basic purpose of education has been lost. I get deeply disappointed when I find that most people consider getting a job to be the sole aim of education. Of course, jobs are important to maintain you and your family and have a better quality of life. Parents have an important role in instilling in their children the real value of education, which, in simple terms, is to become a better human being in every sense and a global citizen to serve humanity.

I am pleased that you and I are discussing education, which is the first of the eight specific action areas in the UN Declaration and Programme of Action on a Culture of Peace. I recall that, after those eight key action areas had been identified toward the final stages of negotiations of this document by the General Assembly, UN Member States were nearly deadlocked about their order of priority. Finally, I recall that, as the chairman of the General Assembly's nine-month-long drafting of the document, I managed to convince them all to agree that 'education' stands out as making the most important contribution in building the culture of peace.

In today's increasingly globalized and interdependent world, instead of making the narrow goal of acquiring material possessions the sole objective, our education system should focus mainly on making the younger generations better prepared to become global citizens.

Ikeda: What is the purpose of education? Some say it must be for the good of society; others think its goal is to produce capable individuals to serve national interests. There is something to be said for each of these positions, but I believe that education's primary purpose is the happiness of children and students.

This was the starting point of Tsunesaburo Makiguchi's educational philosophy. Soka education aims for the happiness of the young, for cultivating whole human beings with a proper balance between intellect and character, and is based on the fundamental principle of education to be a world citizen. This is why we have advocated the philosophy that one individual's happiness must not be built on the unhappiness of others. Because Soka education is based on this foundation, I believe it will produce individuals capable of contributing to the community, society, nation and whole world.

Education for Everyone

Chowdhury: Undeniably, knowledge and skills have important roles to play in enabling human beings of all ages to make a living to support themselves and their families. Such education must be suited to the needs of the particular society.

In many rural areas of Bangladesh, for instance, an impressive, non-formal school system mainly intended for girls who are not in the position to receive formal education focuses on basic education and simple knowledge of life skills. For the poorest of the poor in Bangladesh, such education ignites a craving for more knowledge and prepares girls for formal institutions where schooling is free and where practical facilities are somewhat better.

As we know, investment in girls' education has proven to give the best return of any investment whatsoever. Educating girls gives the world the opportunity to benefit from the true contribution of the 50 per cent of its population.

Ikeda: A century ago, realizing the importance of educating women, President Makiguchi initiated correspondence courses for them. Carrying on in the same spirit, Soka education has consistently aimed at developing complete education for women.

Chowdhury: I am very impressed by the importance accorded to girls' education by the Soka system. I would also like to emphasize the need for our education systems to have a real impact on preparing each student to become a total human person, of use not only to the self but also to the family, community, society and whole world.

While studying for academic degrees, young people must also learn to face the challenges of life. How to overcome greed and prejudice? How to get rid of hate? How to grow empathy for all? How to express passion in positive, creative ways? How to avoid violence? How to fight the demons inside us? These are very crucial aspects of becoming a complete human being. Education should focus on making us better human beings and – today more than ever – better global citizens.

Ikeda: Education must provide knowledge and technical skills. At the same time, it must cultivate the needed courage, wisdom and empathy to live out our lives together with others while overcoming hardships and challenges. It must foster a genuine spiritual strength and richness.

Your questioning how we can confront life and our internal issues falls into the category not of knowledge but of wisdom. My mentor often said that mistaking knowledge for wisdom is one cause of the impasse at which modern society finds itself.

Just as knowledge and wisdom differ, so do success and happiness. Education should be a driving force for our victorious, happy lives, teaching us self-control and to improve and strengthen ourselves. Education is the heart of philosophy for us today.

From these perspectives, what is your vision of the ideal university in the twenty-first century?

Chowdhury: Your question brings to mind again the open-system Visva-Bharati University created by Rabindranath Tagore. In that institution, students learned the totality of the meaning and purpose of life, putting themselves in the context of humanity and nature.

On occasions, they even studied outdoors squatting in the shade of the trees.

Classrooms should not be limited to four walls, desks and blackboards. Those are practical tools, but openness of surroundings is extremely important to building character and creating harmony with nature. Any place or opportunity can teach us something relevant to our lives.

Universities should bring young people closer to life itself. Inviting inspiring individuals to share their experiences with students is one way to do this. Revealing the outside world to them is another. Universities should continuously endeavour to make the education they provide as close to life as possible instead of making it too academic and theoretical.

As the world becomes increasingly connected and globalized, universities should upgrade their education systems on a regular basis to make them relevant and purposeful. I believe that a global effort could be made to prepare standard textbooks to be taught universally at all educational institutions to lay the basic intellectual foundation for future citizens of the world. At the same time, students must be encouraged to consciously study diversity in order to learn about and respect our diverse, interconnected, interdependent and heterogeneous planet.

Ikeda: Wisdom resting on keen insight and rich experience is evident in each of the points you make. It is vital for young people to learn through experience in the real world, opening the 'book of the world' and the 'book of human beings'.

President Makiguchi became aware of this early on, while in teachers training in his late teens. This led to his proposed programme whereby half of a student's day would be devoted to classroom work and the other half to labour outside the class. In explaining this system, he wrote, 'Study is not seen as a preparation for living, but rather study takes place while living, and living takes place in the midst of study'.[1] His aim was to break down the barrier between living and study, and provide an education in which the two were intimately linked.

Today the importance of young people's experience – for instance, volunteer activities – is generally recognized. As you say, education open to society is essential to the balanced, sound development of both mind and body.

President Makiguchi's pedagogic ideas embraced lifetime study for working adults, too. Education is not only for the young. Through it, adults can, as community members, parents and global citizens, continue learning and assimilating new things, elevating themselves as human beings.

Reforming education requires improvements in teacher quality. What are your thoughts on this?

Chowdhury: I agree entirely that educational reform should pay greater attention to teacher quality. It is more important, however, to give primary attention to the objectives of education, particularly from the young, foundational years of boys and girls. When we know what students must learn to be prepared to face life's challenges, it is easier to select suitable teachers.

Good teachers are in short supply in all parts of the world – developed or developing. Most societies fail to accord the attention and importance that teachers, among all professional groups, need. In developing countries, of course, budgetary and financial situations are major constraints. But recruitment and training of teachers and, most importantly, the honour and dignity shown to them, are deficient in a big way; even, as I have seen, in some developed countries. In any country, appropriate national policy – reached through national dialogue – as well as close community and parental interest are absolutely essential to making education meaningful and worthwhile at all levels.

Bigger educational budgets do not necessarily result in the quality education we must have. What we need now is overall improvement in the orientation and quality of the education we provide. As I mentioned earlier in our dialogue (see Conversation Thirteen), peace education is an important component of such improvement. Curricula should include peace education as an integral part at all levels. Teachers need to build an understanding of and commitment to the culture of peace and non-violence from an early stage of a student's life.

Here I would like to bring in what my dear and coactivist friend Cora Weiss, president of the Hague Appeal for Peace and herself a globally recognized peace leader, said:

> To raise new generations of people with the skills, values, and knowledge to create and maintain peace, we need peace education. Peace does not come with our DNA. It must be learned. Peace education is not a separate course. It is a holistic participatory process that includes teaching for and about human rights, non-violence, social and economic justice, gender equality, environmental sustainability, international law, disarmament and human security. It prepares us for democratic participation and is based on values of dignity, equality and respect.[2]

Ikeda: Improving educational quality requires support for educators from all angles by the community and society as a whole. But the creation of the culture of peace cannot rely on the classroom alone; it requires a broad-based educational and consciousness-raising effort directed at the general populace. Recognizing this need, the Hague Appeal for Peace in 1999 launched the Global Campaign for Peace Education, to which you devoted great effort.

As you have said, the culture of peace means the empowerment of ordinary citizens. Whether such a culture endures depends on the youth of future generations. The masses, especially young people, play the leading role. The power of youthful passion can reform society.

The SGI employs a grassroots dialogue movement to promote global peace education at the popular level. An example of this kind of activity is the Victory Over Violence movement being steadily carried out mainly by the SGI youth division, with your strong support, in many parts of the United States. Expanding its work to empower youth, the movement restarted from Hawaii in January 2009, at several locations, including President Obama's high school alma mater, with the aim of making definite reductions in local violence.[3]

Chowdhury: I have had occasion to mention the SGI-USA VOV movement in several of my speeches and interactions, particularly with young people. This wonderful undertaking must continue and should be expanded to include all the 192 countries and territories where the SGI is active. It could be a very effective way of promoting the culture of peace.

I would encourage the SGI in all parts of the world to structure its individual programmes to build the culture of peace in close collaboration with local communities. We should work together to include peace and non-violence, as well as study of the United Nations, in schools and institutions of higher learning.

Ikeda: Your remarks should make the young Americans promoting the VOV movement happy.

Another important issue is finding ways for young people to express their energy. It is often said that young people today are reluctant to engage in social activism and reluctant to work together and get involved in social movements. I disagree.

Chowdhury: Today's young people can surely organize and initiate actions that promote understanding and solidarity but in a different way from before. In this day and age of information technology, they have the opportunity to connect instantaneously with any part of the world. IT-empowered young people of today are able to get information about what is happening in the rest of the world and, for that matter, about any subject at any time.

Of course, such information can be used for good or not-so-good purposes. I believe very strongly that interest can be inculcated at schools for things like nature conservation, good health, non-violence, and anti-gun, anti-smoking, anti-drug and anti-alcohol campaigns. Here the young ones need the positive guidance of their parents, family, teachers and mentors.

From the Grassroots

Ikeda: We should create the maximum possible number of venues in schools and communities where young people can be stimulated and encouraged to take interest in social issues, because this can be an excellent opportunity to learn about life. And we need to recognize that young people have their own sensibilities and ways of doing things, and that these change from generation to generation.

As such, it is counterproductive for adults to impose preconceived notions on young people or force them to conform; we need to create an environment in which adults learn along with young people, and young people initiate their own actions. Thus they can fully muster their youthful energies for the sake of peace and a better future.

My mentor used to say that the future belonged to the young. He encouraged us to do things our own way and said he would take full responsibility. He gave us a great deal of autonomy, and he trained us through actual practice.

Given this freedom, young people will sometimes fail. But leaders should continue to support them, allowing them to learn from their mistakes. In every realm, experience is important – a great teacher.

Chowdhury: To inspire young people to undertake social action, adults need to come up with motivation and creativity. When my youngest son was at school in New York in the 1980s, Ed Koch, who was the mayor of the city at the time, came up with a wonderful idea for dealing with a serious water shortage: he appointed all the city's very young students as 'deputy mayors for water conservation'.

They received buttons proclaiming their new responsibilities. Each child monitored and supervised water usage at home to prevent wastage. For example, I was allowed only four minutes to shower. If I took longer, my little son banged on the bathroom door, telling me my time was up and ordering me to turn the water off. The system worked because parents are willing to listen to their children and want to encourage them in their efforts to help the community. The mayor's objective was successful in a big way, as small efforts on the part of children in each household resulted in large overall savings in water volume, thus compensating for that year's scarcity. So that is why I believe that social movements by young people can be very effective, but that motivation should begin early in life.

Ikeda: A splendid idea and an enlightening story. It certainly is important to create opportunities for young people to become independent, responsible, self-aware and enthusiastic. This promotes the full development and exercise of their abilities.

As I have said, in the Soka Gakkai movement, from its earliest stages, young people have taken the lead. I trust them entirely, and I have worked with them to direct and develop our movement. We have always operated in accord with President Makiguchi's admonition that action should be initiated from the membership. Mahatma Gandhi adopted the same approach, stirring the people to action and thus changing the consciousness of society's leaders.

Chowdhury: Absolutely no big social movement has ever succeeded unless it started from the grassroots. This equation is applicable in all cases. Presence of an energizing leader is complementary.

The movement for the culture of peace, too, must start at the ground level and spread forward and all around. Movements against apartheid and racism, for women's suffrage, for non-violence and for human rights have all started this way – slowly and gradually – and have been made possible by the commitment of people, both individually and collectively, who believe in the cause.

Student Exchanges

Ikeda: They are, as I have learned from experience. What curriculum or other approaches do you consider effective in promoting peace education?

Chowdhury: Of course, schooling and curricula are important, but I believe strongly that the most lasting impressions on a child's mind start with the parents – and also, if I may add, the grandparents as an extension. As we have already said, a practical approach rooted in the evolving nature of global society is essential if students are to grow up in a wholesome and worthwhile educational environment.

Peace education will be effective if we create opportunities for students from different cultures, societies and countries to come into contact and interact with one another. Such exchanges can be achieved in many ways and through many means.

One such way is the well-prepared annual 'study abroad' travels that SUA students make to various parts of the world for a semester during their junior year and subsequently report on that experience. I was very impressed, learning first hand from the students how these study travels had widened their perspectives and broadened their understanding of other countries and their peoples. They felt that those 'study abroad' opportunities helped them redouble their efforts to become true global citizens, as SUA's mission statement aspires. At the same time, I would recommend that the programme should include visits also to countries facing real socio-economic challenges to help students develop a balanced understanding of global reality.

Another student initiative that attracted my attention was the annual Soka Education Conference held at SUA.[4] Many educational institutions have community service as part of a compulsory course for each student.

Ikeda: International student exchanges contribute to the creation of a peaceful future. With the advancement of the information age, it has become possible to communicate and exchange ideas without actually meeting face-to-face. We must work to build an unshakable solidarity among global citizens by expanding exchanges among the young and all people.

Chowdhury: The world owes you a lot for promoting international understanding and solidarity. For decades, through your efforts to spread value-creating education and particularly through your annual peace proposals, you have earned the universal gratitude of millions of peace-loving people throughout the world. I believe strongly that, as the most universal global body, the United Nations should have an opportunity to listen to your message of peace. I have been making every effort to bring this about, especially since 2002, when I became the United Nations Under-Secretary-General with the mandate to draw attention of the global community to the poverty and vulnerability of the nations of the world.

Practical education, as you say, is vital not only to students but also to young people in general. One-third of the world's population is considered young. By young, I mean up to the age of 25, or well beyond the age of 18, which is the universal cut-off age for childhood, according to the Convention on the Rights of the Child, the most universally ratified human rights treaty of the world. This third of the population must be prepared, by exposure to peace education, to become global citizens fully empowered for future decision-making roles. Ignoring them now would be giving up our global responsibility as adults, as unfortunately many of today's grownups have done. But we must not fail to give our young the opportunity to prepare themselves for their upcoming challenges.

Ikeda: In my exchanges with many thinkers around the world, I have found agreement on the importance of empowering young people and the danger that the loss of youthful passion poses for the entire world. Devising concrete measures, one by one, for fostering youth is of supreme importance.

Chowdhury: We can no longer afford to ignore the young. Mariam and I feel proud that all our three children now have their own families and are inspired to bring up our four[5] sweet and adorable grandchildren in the same spirit of the culture of peace that they grew up with.

In June 2008, I was invited by UNESCO to moderate a global conference on the topic 'Youth at the Crossroads: A Future without Violent Radicalization' in Bahrain's capital, Manama. It covered an impressive array of innovative ideas on how best to address the problem of violence in schools. During the conference, I was introduced to an imaginative initiative called 'Peaceful Schools International', which supports schools that have declared a commitment to creating and maintaining the culture of peace. PSI was founded in 2001 and is now a respected and innovative source of support for more than 300 schools in 15 countries. It acts as a catalyst and clearing-house for innovative ideas aimed at creating a school-wide culture of peace.

Ikeda: This is an important effort. I am completely in accord with your moving plea against ignoring young people. Youth are the key to the future and the destiny of the human race. Gandhi said, 'If we are to reach real peace in this world and if we are to carry on a real war against war, we shall have to begin with children'.[6] We adults must take action to sow the seeds of peace in the minds of as many young people as we can.

A New Global Society

Chowdhury: Your comments inspire me to emphasize another dimension of not ignoring the role of young people. I am talking about girls and women, who constitute more than 50 per cent of the world's population. Both for demographic and democratic reasons, global society must see to it that they are treated equally, empowered fully, and given all the rights that are due to them.

In my life, I have personally experienced what my dear respected friend Professor Betty Reardon of Columbia University said in an interview in the *SGI Quarterly* in 2008:

> Women have done a great deal that could be a lot more effective if it were done in complementarity with men. I think that what women have done reflects the concerns they embrace as a consequence of their gender socialization. . . . It is the learning acquired through their roles as caregivers and sustainers of life and well-being that influences their cooperative behavior. . . . Women's traditional roles socialize them toward cooperation and inclusion to produce more well-being for more people.[7]

Ikeda: We cannot change the times and build the culture of peace without women's voices and powers. Young people and women are the ones who will take the lead in creating a new global society. There can be no doubt that the surest, most creative path to building the culture of peace is to vigorously promote their empowerment, and I wish to emphatically reiterate the importance of educational efforts on all levels to achieve this.

Chowdhury: No time is more appropriate than now for building the culture of peace. No social responsibility is greater and no task more important than that of securing sustainable peace on our planet. Today's world and its problems are becoming increasingly more interdependent and interconnected. The magnitude, complexity and globalized nature of these problems require all of us to work together in a respectful, collaborative way for the benefit of all. Global efforts toward peace and reconciliation can only succeed with a combined individual and collective approach built on trust, understanding, dialogue, cooperation and global solidarity.

For that, we have to build a grand alliance for the culture of peace among all, particularly with the proactive involvement and participation of young people. Women's proactive engagement will continue to be pivotal to this endeavour. I believe that the global movement for the culture of peace should be the substantive contribution today's society can make confidently to tomorrow's world.

Ikeda: Whether we accomplish this will surely determine the nature of the twenty-first century. I am determined to continue striving with you to create a magnificent network of people connected by the culture of peace. Let us join forces and work all the harder to advance a new global society and attain humanity's victory – together with youth, who are the treasure of humanity, and women, who forever shine with the glory of peace.

You and I both love the great poet Tagore. I will conclude this dialogue between us with his words:

> I have great faith in humanity. Like the sun it can be clouded, but never extinguished. . . . . For men to come near to one another and yet to continue to ignore the claims of humanity is a sure process of suicide. We are waiting for the time when the spirit of the age will be incarnated in a complete human truth and the meeting of men will be translated into the Unity of Man.[8]

Epilogue
by Co-author Ambassador Anwarul K. Chowdhury

The dialogue between Dr Daisaku Ikeda and me upon which this book is based concluded nearly ten years ago, and dramatic shifts in the global scenario have taken place since then – for better and for worse. This epilogue is intended to make the readers aware of what we think are some of the major developments since this dialogue initially occurred. The most disturbing and disappointing thing to note is that the world has become much more violent; the future of our planet has become even more uncertain; and the confidence in the success of collaborative multilateral work on an international level has been shaken. Electoral changes in leadership in some major countries have accentuated those in a stark way.

However, at the same time, there have been many positive and significant developments, which if pursued with sincerity and earnestness, could make our planet a better place to live for all of us.

I have often reflected on how the insights Dr Ikeda and I shared relate to the major and often unexpected developments unfolding on the international landscape. The very unpredictability of emerging challenges will naturally create distance between then and now, but far more meaningful are the timeless principles and essential elements for human civilization that we underscored. Those are more critical than ever.

Highlights of global engagement

In the dialogue between Dr Ikeda and me, we addressed many issues that continue to be of utmost importance in the global arena. This epilogue is intended to provide brief highlights of the areas that I believe continue to be issues central to global engagement. These issues are: the United Nations as the most universal global organization serving the best interests of our planet; the culture of peace as the agenda for a new global civilization; the emergence of global citizenship and the oneness of humanity as basic components of a just and peaceful world; the recognition of the human right to peace as a step in the right direction; accepting multilateralism as the sole modus operandi for international relations; the centrality of the sustainability of our planet and its people in becoming global goals in the 15-year UN agenda leading up to 2030, popularly known as SDGs – Sustainable Development Goals; half of the world's population receiving long-overdue recognition through the women's equality and empowerment agenda; and all these ideas getting a boost from the ever-expanding activism of the people, for the people and by the people in a heightened engagement of civil society.

Convergence of the dialogue issues in UN actions

As I crafted this epilogue, I was struck by how many of the observations presented by Dr Ikeda and me have been borne out, often in encouraging ways.

Our shared emphasis on the primacy of the individual – and the importance of realizing results that make meaningful difference in people's lives – has gained wider ground in many international agreements. My longstanding position that development goals must reflect individuals and bring change to their lives, along with Dr Ikeda's philosophy of individual human progress to achieve change across society, have found reflection in international decisions across all three pillars of the United Nations: peace and security, development and human rights.

Our shared conviction that women must enjoy full equality found expression, during our dialogue, in a joint call for more action within and beyond the United Nations. We discussed the value of an international agency for this purpose, and in 2010, the UN General Assembly created UN Women, a shortened name for the entity to address women's issues on a broader scale.

Dr Ikeda and I also hold a common conviction that investments in youth are critical to the future of humanity. Re-reading our dialogue on this issue through the prism of more recent events, I am struck by the fact that there have been significant international advances in this area. The 2011 Arab Spring certainly raised the profile of youth as well as women in movements for democracy and human rights. The creation of the post of United Nations Youth Envoy could be seen as the realization of the vision we shared. UNSCR 2250 on Youth, Peace and Security was adopted in 2015, recognizing the role that youth play in promoting and maintaining international peace.

My recommendation surfacing in the dialogue that the United Nations establish its own Futures Unit may not have manifested concretely yet, but I am hopeful it is gaining ground as leading thinkers come to appreciate its value. Such a unit would function as a kind of advanced think tank that anticipates global development with an eye towards the future, say beyond 15 years, so the world body can address issues appropriately before they turn into catastrophes. The current preoccupations are so engrossing and overwhelming that no one is anticipating in a forward-looking way what the future may hold.

This dialogue's emphasis on the culture of peace, women's equality, involvement of youth, education, global citizenship, human rights and human dignity and the protection and empowerment of the world's most vulnerable people resonates powerfully today; these issues have only become more pressing since the original edition was published.

Multilateralism

Multilateralism is even more complex today than ever before and is confronting varying challenges. Multilateralism is not restricted to nations but is increasingly involving non-state actors such as non-governmental organizations (NGOs), transnational or multinational corporations, and violence-based entities which include terrorist groups. The SDGs, created through inter-governmental negotiations, were made possible because it is widely accepted that our global problems do need global solutions – that the issues we now face, such as climate change and migration, go beyond isolationist national interests.

UN to take lead

During the decade that passed by, the United Nations has gone through major changes with electing two successive Secretaries-General following the two brilliant five-year terms of Kofi Annan who left us in August 2018: Ban Ki-moon serving two terms totalling ten years and, since 2017, António Guterres in his third year in office. The new head of the UN has earned the enthusiastic appreciation of all in his practical reflection of women's equality in the UN leadership team reaching for the first time in UN history 50-50 parity in the senior management group. With Dr Ikeda's unique record of invariably incorporating support and new initiatives for the United Nations for 37 years in annual Peace Proposals and my own engagement with the world body for 46 years through all three motors which make the UN move – Member States, Secretariat and, of course, civil society – both of us share a deep appreciation of the value of the work of the United Nations and a desire to see its potential fulfilled in the true sense. I have been disappointed to observe successive secretaries-general consumed with day-to-day events and operations at the expense of longer-term and more visionary planning for 'the future we want'.

I often say that there are four main constraints on the Secretary-General being a more effective leader that most people of the world want to see:

• The veto-wielding members of the Security Council, which influences matters in all areas of the UN system. (Yes, believe it or not, it is that pervasive.)

- Promises and commitments made by the Secretary-General as a candidate to secure his or her election.
- The Secretary-General's aspiration from day one of the first term to get re-elected for a second term.
- The labyrinthine UN bureaucracy.

The UN Secretary-General is expected to be a global leader with a global vision that benefits all. The Secretary-General should find ways to rise above those constraints and emerge as a global transformational leader. The Secretary-General, in particular, should focus on the future of humanity, not just the UN's nitty-gritty, protocol profiles, which his or her deputies can handle. If the world needed a manager, we could have chosen a manager. But what we need now – and always – is a true global leader with a true global vision. The world also needs a woman secretary-general as soon as possible, not least to correct the historical injustice of having the post occupied by nine men for its entire existence.

Relevance and Efficacy of The Culture of Peace

The urgent imperative of establishing the culture of peace is among the most encompassing and most relevant of the points we discussed. The United Nations was born in 1945 out of World War II. The UN Declaration and Programme of Action on a Culture of Peace was born in 1999 in the aftermath of the Cold War.

As the chair of the nine-month-long negotiations from December 1998 to September 1999 that produced the 'United Nations Declaration and Programme of Action on a Culture of Peace', I have continued to devote considerable time, energy and effort to realizing its implementation. The Declaration and Programme of Action – a document explaining, outlining and defining everything that the international community has agreed on as the focus of the culture of peace – was adopted unanimously by the General Assembly of the United Nations on 13 September 1999. I was deeply honoured and privileged to introduce at the 53rd Session of UN General Assembly on its concluding day that resolution for adoption without a vote presenting the consensus text reached under my chairmanship.

Ever since the initiative taken by me in July 1997 to formally propose inclusion of a separate agenda item on the culture of peace in the UN General Assembly and its decision to do so – allocating the item to the plenary of the General Assembly – every year the Assembly has adopted by consensus a comprehensive, self-standing resolution on the culture of peace. The General Assembly, through its annual substantive resolutions, has highlighted the priority it attaches to the full and effective implementation of these visionary decisions which are universally applicable and are sought after by the vast majority of all peoples in every nation.

The essence of the culture of peace is found in its twin features of self-transformation and global solidarity. These two elements – individual and global, individual to global – constitute the core of the culture of peace. Everybody can talk about and create the culture of peace because it lives in our communities and in each of us. We do not have to become peace studies experts or street protesters to make a difference. We just have to leave our own mark on this world as peaceful and non-violent individuals.

The terminology has shifted in a subtle but meaningful way, from 'a' culture of peace to 'the' culture of peace. During the negotiations, 'a' remained, as there was no agreed document yet to be replaced by 'the'. When consensus was reached on the whole document, there was unwillingness on the part of some foot-draggers to change to 'the', possibly with the intention to deny the definitive stamp of approval to the concept of the culture of peace. Because of our eagerness to seal the deal on the agreed document through a decision of the General Assembly on the last day of the 53rd session, the expression 'a' remained in the title and the text. This change in article is an elevation from the general to the specific, conveying that there is only one definition, one narrative of the culture of peace. The distinction being that there should be one well-articulated globally accepted culture of peace, without any reservations or objections, for the United Nations to promote.

The international community owns it collectively. Of course, it can be adjusted to various national contexts but overall it is a shared vision.

In addition to this important shift in understanding, we have seen a rise in engagement on the culture of peace. Civil society has done the most to advance the cause. To energize civil society activism, the Global Movement for The Culture of Peace (GMCoP) was founded in 2011 in New York as a coalition of NGOs for the culture of peace and is now at the forefront of advocacy for the implementation of the UN decisions on the culture of peace. Individuals, as the core of civil society, have also done a lot, especially as educators at all levels. I have great pleasure teaching 'The Culture of Peace' as a learning cluster course at Soka University of America regularly since 2009. I also taught a course on the same subject at the City University of New York's Lehman College. The culture of peace as a term is being referenced in more and more political and civil society statements and discourses. The culture of peace did not have a high profile in 1999, and it still does not have a level of acceptance and recognition which all well-meaning and peace-loving people of the world expect. But things are picking up. It always takes time. Think of the Universal Declaration of Human Rights adopted 70 years ago is yet to become truly universal. The media has not championed the culture of peace much, but in view of continuing acts of violence and strife, there is increasing media focus on issues of peace and non-violence and on the need for moderation and dialogue.

The slowest actors have been the governments. Politicians have not found the culture of peace to be politically useful for them; principally, I believe, because political leaders seek short-term results while the culture of peace delivers slower but more lasting change. This is surely because the results of politicians' efforts to promote the culture of peace would only come much later, when their terms of office of four or five years were over. There is little short-term political impetus for them to find there to get elected or re-elected.

The UN system must do much more. The culture of peace has not permeated the UN senior management and senior leadership as strongly and effectively as we envisioned in 1999. Many in the UN system at all levels sadly view the Declaration and Programme of Action on a Culture of Peace as 'one of those documents that can lie there', without having the comprehension that it is one of the more forward-looking and potentially real change-evoking documents of the entire UN system. The Charter of the United Nations is one, the Universal Declaration of Human Rights is another, and there are all those great conventions and treaties. But the culture of peace declaration and programme has the potential to break through all sorts of barriers and boundaries, as is needed so much today. The UN should be smart enough to understand the intrinsic value of this time-tested concept.

That said, it is exciting to note that the culture of peace and non-violence as well as global citizenship were included among the subjects which needed greater attention in the learning process as part of a target for the Sustainable Development Goal (SDG)-4 on education. Also encouraging is to find that there are a number of educational institutions that have taken the initiative to put global citizenship at the core of their activities. The World Summit of Educators, which convened in 2016 at the Soka University of America (SUA), is one such initiative worthy of attention, and the recommendations that emerged from that summit should be internalized by many such institutions of learning. SUA again took the lead in 2014 by launching an annual event, called 'Dialogue on the Culture of Peace and Non-Violence', held every year on the UN-proclaimed International Day of Non-Violence on 2 October. That date is very significant because it is the birthday of Mahatma Gandhi, the apostle of non-violence; therefore the UN chose that day to spread the message of non-violence. In 2019, the world would respectfully celebrate the 150th birth anniversary of the Mahatma. Also in 2019, the SUA Dialogue would commemorate both that anniversary as well as the 20th anniversary of the culture of peace concept as adopted by UN. Another significance of the date is that on that day the co-author of this dialogue, Dr Ikeda, set foot in the Western world to bring his message of peace and non-violence to many other people of the globe. Another welcome initiative that took place at SUA in 2017 was the formation of an activity club called 'Students Movement for the Culture of Peace' (SMCP) as an example of student-led activism for promoting the culture of peace among them and in the community through, inter alia, organizing annual symposia.

Also, we find that more and more governments represented at the UN are advocating for the culture of peace. They are beginning to find the culture of peace of increasing significance than before, at least in terms of their UN roles (though at the national level they may not be doing much). The annual consideration of the agenda item on 'Culture of Peace' in the Plenary of the General Assembly results in the consensus adoption of the resolution on the follow-up of the implementation of the Declaration and Programme of Action. Since the first one in 2012 convened by General Assembly's visionary President Nassir Abdulaziz Al-Nasser, the subsequent Presidents of the General Assembly have convened annually the UN High Level Forum on The Culture of Peace. The sixth annual Forum in September 2017 focused on the theme 'Sowing the Seeds of the Culture of Peace: Early Childhood Development is the Beginning' and attracted high-profile attention from the UN community. The latest High Level Forum on 5 September 2018 focused on the theme 'The Culture of Peace: A Credible Pathway to Sustaining Peace'. Out of the seven Forums, in four, Nobel Peace Laureates Leymah Gbowee of Liberia, Ouided Bouchamaoui of Tunisia, Betty Williams of Ireland and Rigoberta Menchu-Tum of Guatemala shared their thoughts on the culture of peace as keynote speakers. My good and respected friend Federico Mayor Zaragoza, during whose tenure as the UNESCO Director-General the concept germinated, has been attending the Forum since 2012 to energize and encourage us all.

The international community enthusiastically welcomed the adoption by the UN General Assembly of a resolution on 12 December 2018 to observe on 13 September 2019 the 20th anniversary of the unanimous adoption of the Declaration and Programme of Action on Culture of Peace in 'an appropriate and befitting manner'. Japanese daily *Seikyo Shimbun* has planned year-long coverage of the 20th anniversary of the culture of peace. I would particularly commend the Soka Gakkai Women's Peace Committee for this brilliant initiative to bring the message of the culture of peace to the people of Japan. Well-meaning people of the world are proud that SGI under its President Daisaku Ikeda has been a truly devoted partner in the building of the culture of peace as espoused by the United Nations.

Recognizing the need for continual support to further strengthen the global movement to promote the Culture of Peace, as envisaged by the United Nations, particularly in the current global context, the day-long General Assembly High Level Forum is intended to coincide with the anniversary date of the adoption of this landmark, pioneering and norm-setting resolution containing the declaration and programme of action popularly referred to by its number as 53/243. The Forum is an open public opportunity for the UN Member States, UN system entities, civil society including NGOs, media, private sector, and all others interested, to have an exchange of ideas and suggestions on the ways to build and promote the culture of peace and to highlight emerging trends that impact on the implementation process.

Transforming the Individual

The culture of peace, its conceptual elaboration and activism necessitated by it does not need to limit itself to the traditional role in the context of peace studies or peace issues. There is a subtle difference between peace as generally understood and the culture of peace. Generally when people refer to 'peace', they expect action to be taken by others – apparently so-called decision-makers; when we say 'culture of peace', one envisages one's own commitment to act. Simply put, the Culture of Peace as a concept, as a motivation, means that every one of us needs to consciously make peace and non-violence a part of our daily existence. It should rather be seen as opening up opportunities at every level of human activity. In other words, everybody can contribute to create the culture of peace because it lives in our own communities and in each of us. It is about our own contribution, having been born as human beings, to the world. Each one of us can make a difference in that process. Peace cannot be imposed from outside; it must be realized from within.

As my work took me to the farthest corners of the world, I have seen firsthand similar interest in communities for building sustainable peace. I have seen time and again how people – even the humblest and the weakest – have contributed to building the culture of peace in their personal lives, in their families, in their communities and in their countries. And that ultimately is contributing to the global movement for the culture of peace. I am always inspired by the human spirit and its resilience and capacity to overcome all adversity.

As I say time and again, 'Peace does not mean just to stop wars, but also to stop oppression, injustice and neglect'. The United Nations focus on promoting 'international peace' – peace among nations – was being taken as the absence of war between states. To see peace as the opposite of war is fallacious. Absence of war or absence of active violence is not peace. It may bring cessation of hostilities, but it is obviously not peace in its totality – for sure it is not sustainable peace.

The preamble of the UNESCO Constitution expressed this brilliantly when it declared that 'a peace based exclusively upon the political and economic arrangements of governments would not be a peace which could secure the unanimous, lasting and sincere support of the peoples of the world, and ... the peace must therefore be founded, if it is not to fail, upon the intellectual and moral solidarity of mankind'. A positive peace, a sustainable peace is needed that does not allow for the outbreak of war, that abolishes war forever as an available option for humanity. Paraphrasing a statement by the great anthropologist Margaret Mead, one can say 'the same species that invented war is capable of inventing peace'.

We should not isolate peace as something separate or distant. We should know how to relate to one another without being aggressive, without being violent, without being disrespectful, without neglect, without prejudice. It is important to realize that the absence of peace

takes away the opportunities that we need to better ourselves, to prepare ourselves, to empower ourselves to face the challenges of our lives,
individually and collectively. It is also a positive, dynamic participatory
process wherein 'dialogue is encouraged and conflicts are solved in a
spirit of mutual understanding and cooperation'.

Each and every individual is important to the transformation
required to secure the culture of peace in our world. Each person must
be convinced that nonviolent, cooperative action is possible. If a person
succeeds in resolving a conflict in a nonviolent manner at any point in
time, then this individual has made a big contribution to the world, for
this singular act has succeeded in transferring the spirit of non-violence
and cooperation to another individual. When repeated, such a spirit
will grow exponentially; a practice that will become easier each time
the choice is made to resolve a conflict nonviolently. It is a good that
belongs to each one of us – one that can be transferred to and shared
with others.

On 16 December 1998, at a Security Council meeting on the
maintenance of peace and security and post-conflict peace-building, I
asserted that

> International peace and security can be best strengthened,
> not by actions of States alone, but by men and women
> through the inculcation of the Culture of Peace and non-
> violence in every human being and every sphere of activity
> … The objective of the culture of peace is the empowerment
> of people. It contributes effectively to the overcoming of
> authoritarian structures and also exploitation, through demo-
> cratic participation. It works against poverty and inequality
> and promotes development. It celebrates diversity, advances
> understanding and tolerance and reduces inequality between
> women and men.

Seeds of peace exist in all of us. They must be nurtured, cared for, and
promoted by us all to flourish and flower. We need to always look for

opportunities to promote this transformative potential of humanity, which begins with the transformative potential of individuals. It cannot be left solely to the governments, the United Nations, or to anyone or anything, other than ourselves. Federico Mayor has articulated it boldly, declaring that

> a universal renunciation of violence requires the commitment of the whole of society. These are not matters of government but matters of State; not only matters for the authorities, but for society in its entirety, including civilian, military, and religious bodies. The mobilization which is urgently needed to effect the transition ... from a culture of war to a culture of peace demands co-operation from everyone. In order to change, the world needs everyone.

At the 2018 UN high level forum, I compared this process to pixel-like arrangements in which many very small dots come together to make a total picture – the same way each one of us, like the pixel-dots, has an indispensable role in creating the culture of peace.

When we see what is happening around us, we realize the urgent need for promoting the culture of peace – peace through dialogue, peace through non-violence. The culture of peace begins with each one of us – unless we are ready to integrate peace and non-violence as part of our daily existence, we cannot expect our communities, our nations, our planet to be peaceful. We should be prepared and confident in resolving the challenges of our lives in a non-aggressive manner. This individual dimension is the core message of the culture of peace, more so in recent years, and can create the collective action for peace which the United Nations has been aiming to achieve for more than the seven decades of its existence.

More Attention on Children

In the culture of peace movement, we are focusing more attention on children as this contributes in a major way to the sustainable and long-lasting impact on our societies. A person's tendency toward either violent aggressiveness or non-violence begins to take shape as early as age four or five. That is why the culture of peace movement is focused increasingly on children. UNICEF has taken the lead by integrating many elements of the culture of peace into its work, particularly through the Early Childhood Peace Consortium (ECPC) formed in 2013.

I was invited to speak about the culture of peace and children at a 2013 brainstorming forum with mostly neuroscientists and peace activists in Frankfurt, Germany. In the Foreword of the book that came out of the Forum's deliberations titled *Pathways to Peace: The Transformative Power of Children and Families*, I wrote:

> Early childhood provides a unique opportunity to address issues that would contribute to transform the culture of war to the culture of peace. . . . The events that a child experiences early in life, the education that this child receives, and the community activities and socio-cultural mindset in which a child is immersed all contribute to how values, attitudes, traditions, modes of behaviour, and ways of life develop.

Indeed, early childhood is the most significant window of opportunity for us to eradicate violence and foster the culture of peace in the world. I believe that early childhood affords a unique opportunity for us to sow the seeds of transition from the culture of violence to the culture of peace. The events that a child experiences early in life, the education that this child receives, and the community activities and socio-cultural mindset in which a child is immersed all contribute to how values, attitudes, traditions, modes of behaviour, and ways of life develop. We need to make good use of this opportunity to instill the rudiments that each individual needs to become an agent of peace and non-violence from an early life. As said earlier, the theme of the UN's sixth high level forum very appropriately focused on the connection between the culture of peace and early childhood development.

Women's Rights in Jeopardy

A stark and inexplicable reality of today's world is that patriarchy and misogyny continue to thrive as scourges that pull us all back from our aspiration to live in a world of equality, peace and justice. Unless we confront those vicious and obstinate negative forces with all our energy, determination and persistence, we will never make any real headway with the 2030 Agenda for Sustainable Development, more so as SDG-5 included women's equality and empowerment as a self-standing goal by itself. Gender equality has huge positive effects on food security, extremism, health, education, and, in fact, on all global concerns.

One soul-stirring inspiration that I have experienced from my work for the culture of peace is that we should never forget that when women – half of world's seven plus billion people – are marginalized, there is no chance for our world to get sustainable peace in the real sense. It is my strong belief that unless women are engaged in advancing the culture of peace at equal levels at all times with men, sustainable peace will continue to elude us. Women bring a new breadth, quality and balance of vision to a common effort of moving away from the cult of war towards the culture of peace. Women's equality makes our planet safe and secure.

We should remember the UN's pioneering role in this context. The Charter of the United Nations is the first international agreement affirming the principle of equality between women and men, crafted in 1945. We have the Convention on the Elimination of all Forms of Discrimination Against Women of 1979 and the Beijing Declaration and Platform for Action adopted in 1995. The UN programme of action on the culture of peace includes equality between women and men as a top priority among its eight action areas. And we have UN Security Council Resolution 1325 (2000) on 'women and peace and security'.

UNSCR 1325 is very close to my intellectual existence and my very small contribution to a better world for each one of us. To trace back nineteen years ago, on International Women's Day in 2000, as the President of the Security Council, following extensive stonewalling, I was able to issue an agreed statement that formally brought to global attention the role and contribution of women towards the prevention of conflict and building of peace.

Adoption of the mother resolution 1325, followed by seven other Security Council resolutions for its follow-up and implementation, reaffirmed that when women participate in peace negotiations and in the crafting of a peace agreement, they have the broader and long-term interests of society in mind.

We recall that in choosing the three women laureates for the 2011 Nobel Peace Prize, the citation referred to 1325, saying that 'It underlined the need for women to become participants on an equal footing with men in peace processes and in peace work in general.' The Nobel Committee further asserted that 'We cannot achieve democracy and lasting peace in the world unless women obtain the same opportunities as men to influence developments at all levels of society.' 1325 is the only UN resolution so specifically noted in the citation of the Nobel Prize.

This dialogue has focused also on this landmark resolution. Dr Ikeda has always been a most ardent champion of women's equality and empowerment and has been a strong supporter of Resolution 1325, as this dialogue evidences.

On the occasion of the resolution's 15th anniversary in 2015, the Secretary-General commissioned a Global Study on the Implementation of 1325, which was put together by the 17-member UN High Level Advisory Group for the Global Study of which I was a member. 'Preventing Conflict, Transforming Justice, Securing The Peace', as the report was titled, found that the change in the nature of conflict has women 'constantly living in a state of insecurity and ambivalence', and emphasized that for women in particular, peace is more than an absence of violence, and security is not limited to containing physical violence. We believe that there is a lot of merit in the recommended actions based on the future course charted in that global study.

In that context, it is embarrassing to note that as we are heading towards the 20th anniversary of the adoption of 1325 in 2020, a mere 81 out of 193 UN Member States have prepared their respective National Action Plans (NAP) for implementation of 1325 and its related resolutions as called for by the Security Council.

Despite all these encouraging developments, we see around the world an organized and determined rollback of women's gains. We see new and virulent attacks on their equality and empowerment. As Foreign Minister Margot Wallström of Sweden, architect of the world's first feminist foreign policy, put it, 'No society is immune from back-lashes, especially not in relation to gender. There is a continuous need for vigilance and for continuously pushing for women's and girls' full enjoyment of human rights.'

As an example, the elation of women following the fall of repressive regimes in the Middle East during the Arab Spring in the early 2010s turned out to be premature. A targeted and brutal pushback against women is happening throughout the Middle East, with activist women finding themselves with no pockets of support. Those countries are failing to recognize how, in countless ways, women hold the key to a stable, peaceful and prosperous Middle East for all.

Gender inequality is an established, proven and undisputed reality – it is all-pervasive. It is a real threat to human progress! Reiterating this reality, UN Secretary-General António Guterres, who took office in January 2017, said very succinctly that 'The truth is that north and south, east and west – and I'm not speaking about any society, culture or country in particular – everywhere, we still have a male-dominated culture.' Therefore, the role of men is extremely crucial to reverse the current pushback. In this context, the recent launch of the initiative for 'Mobilizing Men as Partners for Women, Peace and Security', with which I am closely associated, is significantly purposeful.

I join my humble voice to Foreign Minister Wallström's assertion that 'Feminism is a component of a modern view on global politics, not an idealistic departure from it. It is about smart policy which includes whole populations, uses all potential and leaves no one behind.' Real, full, all-encompassing gender equality is good for everybody and is long overdue to the equal half of humanity.

I am proud to be a feminist. All of us need to be. That is how we make our planet a better place to live for all. We should always remember that without peace, development is impossible, and without development, peace is not achievable, but without women, neither peace nor development is conceivable.

Terrorism and Extremism

This has never been more urgent with the rise in recent years of horrifying new manifestations of terrorism. In confronting this scourge, I return again to the ideas I exchanged with Dr Ikeda during our dialogue. My concern is always the security of the common people. Any terrorist act will have many innocent victims, including children, which is totally unacceptable. It disrupts the regular, normal flow of life in any society. The global effort to contain those entities that threaten humanity should not be a military one. This is because military efforts, as history – including recent history – has shown, will never work against terrorism. In the end, we just wind up paying more – and also suffering more. We even become the unwitting victims of our own propaganda, inspiring yet more terrorism. Now, we often speak of 'violent extremism', but any extremism, even extremism of thought, is violent. Talking too much about 'violent extremism' thus dilutes the peace dimension. People start to mistakenly think that extremism is acceptable if it is 'non-violent extremism', but this is exactly why we are stuck where we are. As we repeatedly noted in this dialogue, no attempts to resolve these challenges will work in the long run unless we also change our mindsets. This is where the value of the culture of peace comes in: transforming individuals and their mindsets.

A related issue is social media and the media in general. All terrorist entities are finding it useful to get global attention on social media and again in the media in general. We are inadvertently giving the terrorists wide-ranging attention, including for recruitment. Yes, the internet is a hallmark of human progress in terms of interconnectivity, but it is also home to countless hate sites. The fact so many young people are being drawn into those hate groups poses a major challenge for the culture of peace.

No attempts to resolve these challenges will work in the long run unless we also change our mindsets, our hearts. This is where the value of the culture of peace comes in. It is the best avenue for us to pursue given the current fragile state of our world. We should reach out to people, especially young people, with a spirit of openness. It should be clear in our conviction that violence never achieves any goal for peace; for that matter anything worthwhile in life. My point is that the culture of peace cannot be the culture of peace unless it is inclusive. The culture of peace is the culture of empathy, respect, compassion and solidarity.

As Dr Ikeda puts it so well in this dialogue, 'We must break this cycle of hatred and violence, and build, through dialogue, a world in which peace and harmonious coexistence prevail. To accomplish this, world leaders must return to the fundamental point – the dignity of life – and work together in unity.'

Human Right to Peace

Years of hard and passionate struggle by civil society, which has been actively advocating for a UN Declaration on the Human Right to Peace since the 50th anniversary of the Universal Declaration on Human Rights in 1998, failed in 2016 to secure a positive outcome. Our efforts to incorporate in the UN Culture of Peace resolution in 1999 a recognition of this right as the most significant of all third generation solidarity rights was not successful, in view of the strong objections of some Member States – mainly industrialized countries. In 2010, the Barcelona Declaration on the Human Right to Peace was adopted by consensus by the International Drafting Committee, comprising ten independent experts: two from each of the five geographic regions of the UN. I had the honour to be one of them and to be the chair of that Committee. The UN Human Rights Council (HRC) Advisory Committee submitted a draft UN declaration on the right to peace and appointed an Open-ended Intergovernmental Working Group on the Right to Peace in 2012. Strong opposition of the industrialized countries resulted in the adoption of a much-diluted version of the original Advisory Committee proposal by vote in the Human Rights Council in 2016 and finally that action was repeated in the UN General Assembly the same year during its 71st session in New York. An essential and exalted right such as the Human Right to Peace does not deserve to be recognized by a divided vote among the membership of the United Nations. Change of this unfortunate reality should be on the future global agenda.

A Clarion Call for Constant, Continuing Endeavour

The challenges to peace continue to mutate. In our dialogue, Dr Ikeda shared with me that 'securing a victorious future requires nations, societies, and individuals to courageously rise to the challenges of the present and to move steadily forward'. With that ever-valid inspiration, I am always encouraged. The future keeps moving, and so must the culture of peace, which ultimately requires each one of us to make our own unique contribution in making our world better than what we inherited.

The culture of peace ultimately talks about transforming the individual, which naturally takes time. The whole essence of the culture of peace is its message of self-transformation and its message of inclusiveness, of global solidarity, of the oneness of humanity. Unless we address our efforts toward the individual while remaining fully inclusive, the global opportunities for making the culture of peace a reality will continue to elude humanity. Without the culture of peace growing deeper roots in our mindsets, the global aspiration for sustainable peace will unfortunately remain stalled.

Notes

1. Bangladesh Beginnings

1. According to Nippon.com ('Japanese Publishing in Free Fall', www.nippon.com/en/features/h00092/, accessed 17 May 2016), this decline includes the ability to read and write Japanese characters (*kanji*) and the growing lack of focus on reading literature. Technology, in particular, is 'gobbling up more and more of the leisure time that the Japanese had formerly devoted to reading books and magazines'. Accompanying this is the phenomenon of 'character amnesia', forgetting how to write using characters. It is considered a significant issue in China and Japan. (See 'Character Amnesia', https://en.wikipedia.org/wiki/Character_amnesia, accessed 20 May 2016).

2. In a 2006 interview, Under-Secretary-General Chowdhury described his commitment as High Representative for the United Nations Office for Least Developed Countries (fall 2006 *World & I*, pp. 48–9; http://unohrlls.org/UserFiles/File/Interviews/World_and_I_Fall2006.pdf, accessed 20 May 2016).

3. Mr Chowdhury served as president of the UNICEF Executive Board in 2000.

4. The United Nations Convention on the Rights of the Child is a human rights treaty setting out the civil, political, economic,

social, health and cultural rights of children (intended for people under age 18). The UN General Assembly adopted the Convention on 20 November 1989, and it came into force on 2 September 1990. As of 2013, 193 countries are party to it.

Article 31 reads:

1. States Parties recognize the right of the child to rest and leisure, to engage in play and recreational activities appropriate to the age of the child and to participate freely in cultural life and the arts.

2. States Parties shall respect and promote the right of the child to participate fully in cultural and artistic life and shall encourage the provision of appropriate and equal opportunities for cultural, artistic, recreational and leisure activity.

5. Arnold Toynbee and Daisaku Ikeda, *Choose Life: A Dialogue* (London: I.B.Tauris, 2007) p. 293.

6. In 1905, after this poem was set to music, it became the national anthem of Bangladesh.

7. Soka schools: Beginning with the Soka Junior and Senior High Schools established by Daisaku Ikeda in Kodaira, Tokyo, in 1968, the Soka schools system today includes kindergartens, elementary schools, junior and senior high schools, a university in Japan, and a university in Aliso Viejo, California. Kindergartens have also been established in Hong Kong, Singapore, Malaysia, South Korea and Brazil. The educational system is based on the pedagogy of founding Soka Gakkai president and educator Tsunesaburo Makiguchi, who believed that the focus of education should be the lifelong happiness of the learner. Makiguchi was concerned with the development of the unique personality of each child, and he emphasized the importance of leading a socially contributive life.

8. 'National Anthem', National Encyclopedia of Bangladesh (http://en.banglapedia.org/index.php?title=National_Anthem, accessed 22 May 2016).

2. The Struggle for Independence

1. For the UN Declaration on a Culture of Peace, see http://www.un-documents.net/a53r243a.htm, accessed 23 May 2016. For the UN Programme of Action on a Culture of Peace, see http://www.un-documents.net/a53r243b.htm, accessed 23 May 2016.

2. The SGI-USA Culture of Peace Resource Centers – located in New York, Santa Monica, Chicago, Washington, DC, Honolulu and San Francisco – offer the Culture of Peace Distinguished Speaker Series to engage people in a dialogue on the values, attitudes, and behaviours that reject violence and inspire creative energy for peace (for more information, see http://www.sgi-usa.org/cop-resource-center/cop_lecture_schedule/). Lecturers in this series focus on one or more of the eight action areas defined by the 1999 UN Declaration and Programme of Action on a Culture of Peace: (1) Fostering the culture of peace through education, (2) Promoting sustainable economic and social development, (3) Promoting respect for all human rights, (4) Ensuring equality between women and men, (5) Fostering democratic participation, (6) Advancing understanding, tolerance and solidarity, (7) Supporting participatory communication and the free flow of information and knowledge, and (8) Promoting international peace and security. As of 2016, three volumes of *Voices for the Culture of Peace* provide collections of these lectures (Santa Monica, CA: Culture of Peace Press).

3. In 1971, the Bangladesh Liberation War led to the independence of Bangladesh from Pakistan.

4. Nichiren, *The Writings of Nichiren Daishonin,* vol. II (Tokyo: Soka Gakkai, 2006), p. 637.

5. The Dominion of Pakistan was created by the partition of India in 1947 and comprised several ethnic and linguistic groups. Bengali-speaking people in East Bengal (eventually Bangladesh) made up 44 million of Pakistan's 69 million people. In 1948, after Urdu was proclaimed to be Pakistan's sole national language, the

Bengali Language Movement was begun to advocate recognition of the Bengali language as an additional official language. The movement reached its climax on 21 February 1952, when police killed student demonstrators at the University of Dhaka. In 1956, the Pakistan government recognized the Bengali language as an official language. In 1999, UNESCO declared 21 February as International Mother Language Day, in tribute to the Language Movement and the ethno-linguistic rights of all people. See 'Bangladesh: Bengali Language Movement' (https://www.mthol yoke.edu/~mahbo22d/classweb/bengali_language_movement/ celebrating%20ekushey%20february.html, accessed 5 June 2016).

6. 'Celebrating Ekushey February: Language Martyrs Day', Mount Holyoke College (https://www.mtholyoke.edu/~mahbo22d/class web/bengali_language_movement/celebrating%20ekushey%20 february.html, accessed 2 June 2016).

7. International Mother Language Day was proclaimed by the General Conference of UNESCO in November 1999 (30C/62). On 16 May 2009, the United Nations General Assembly in its resolution A/RES/61/266 called upon Member States 'to promote the preservation and protection of all languages used by peoples of the world'. By the same resolution, the General Assembly proclaimed 2008 as the International Year of Languages, to promote unity in diversity and international understanding, through multilingualism and multiculturalism.

8. Sheikh Mujibur Rahman (1920–75) was Bangladesh's first prime minister (1972–75) and later its president (1975). He and most of his family were killed in a coup d'état seven months after his January 1975 inauguration as president. (See *Encyclopaedia Britannica*, http://www.britannica.com/biography/Mujibur-Rahman, accessed 20 May 2016).

9. 'Shadhinota Tumi' (Freedom, You), trans. Syed M. Islam (https:// mukto-mona.com/Articles/smi/shamsur_rahman.htm; http://www. poemsabout.com/poet/shamsur-rahman/, accessed 1 June 2016).

10. Ibid.

3. Rabindranath Tagore, Poet of Humanity

1. Translated from Japanese. Rabindranath Tagore, *Tagoru Chosaku-shu* (Collected Works of Tagore), trans. Tatsuo Morimoto (Tokyo: Daisanbunmei-sha, 1981), vol. 1, p. 590.

2. Rabindranath Tagore, *Gitanjali: Song Offerings*, intr. William Butler Yeats (New York: Macmillan Company, 1916), pp. 27–8.

3. Ibid., p. 27.

4. 'Padma', trans. Kumad Biswas, http://www.boloji.com/index.cfm?md=Content&sd=Poem&PoemID=8961#sthash.FTOE3BVb.dpuf, accessed 6 July 2016.

5. Henry Wadsworth Longfellow, *Outre-mer: Or, A Pilgrimage to the Old World by an American,* vol. II (New York: Harper & Brothers, 1835), p. 209.

6. Tagore, *Gitanjali*, pp. 64–5.

7. William Wordsworth, *The Compete Poetical Works of William Wordsworth,* ed. Henry Reed (Philadelphia: Heys & Zell, 1854), p. 666.

8. Ibid.

9. Rabindranath Tagore, *Tagore for You* (Kolkata: Visva-Bharati, 1966), p. 133.

10. Daisaku Ikeda, *Songs from My Heart,* trans. Burton Watson (New York: Weatherhill, Inc., 1997), p. 110.

11. S. Radhakrishnan, *Rabindranath Tagore: A Centenary Volume 1861–1961* (Delhi, India: Sahitya Akademi, 1992), p. 94.

12. Rabindranath Tagore, *Glimpses of Bengal: Selected from the Letters of Sir Rabindranath Tagore, 1885 to 1895* (London: Macmillan & Company, Ltd, 1921), p. 49.

13. Krishna Kripalani, *Tagore: A Life* (New Delhi: Orient Longman, 1961, 1971), p. 91.

4. Education of the Whole Person

1. Kumkum Bhattacharya, *Rabindranath Tagore: Adventure of Ideas and Innovative Practices in Education* (New York: Springer Science & Business Media, 29 Nov 2013), p. 64.

2. *Rabindranath Tagore: An Anthology*, ed. Krishna Dutta and Andrew Robinson (New York: St Martin's Press, 1997), p. 68.

3. Daisaku Ikeda. 2001. 'Daisaku Ikeda Up Close.' Videocassette. Tokyo: Owners Promotion, Inc.

4. Rabindranath Tagore, *The English Writings of Rabindranath Tagore*, vol. 3: A Miscellany, ed. Sisir Kumar Das (New Delhi: Sahitya Akademi, 1996), p. 908.

5. Daisaku Ikeda, 'A New Humanism for the Coming Century', *Living Buddhism* (Santa Monica, CA: SGI-USA, January 1998), p. 8.

6. Tsunesaburo Makiguchi, *A Geography of Human Life*, trans. Dayle Bethel (San Francisco, CA.: Caddo Gap Press, 2002).

7. *Tagore and the World*, ed. Chinmohan Sehanavis (Kolkata: Mukand Publishers, 1961), p. 38.

8. See *Seikyo Shimbun,* 31 May 1992.

9. See Kathleen M. O'Connell, *Rabindranath Tagore: The Poet as Educator* (Kolkata: Visva-Bharati, 2002).

10. Tagore, *The English Writings,* vol. 3, p. 64.

11. Rabindranath Tagore, *Towards Universal Man* (Bombay: Asian Publishing House, 1962), p. 79.

12. Translated from Japanese. Rabindranath Tagore, *Tagoru chosakushu* (Collected Works of Tagore), vol. 7 (Tokyo: Daisan Bunmei-sha, 1986), pp. 467–8.

13. Rabindranath Tagore, *The Religion of Man* (London: Unwin Paperbooks, 1988), p. 105.

14. *Vinaya,* Mahavagga, VIII, 26, 3, vol. I, p. 302.

15. R. K. Prabhu, *This was Bapu: One hundred and fifty anecdotes relating to Mahatma Gandhi* (Ahmedabad, India: Navajivan Publishing House, 1954), p. 12.

16. Swaraj movement for Indian independence – the Purna Swaraj declaration, or Declaration of the Independence of India, was promulgated by the Indian National Congress on 26 January 1930, resolving the Congress and Indian nationalists to fight for Purna Swaraj, or *complete self-rule* independent of the British

Empire. (Literally in Sanskrit, *purna*, 'complete', *swa*, 'self', *raj*, 'rule', thus 'complete self-rule'.)

17. Rabindranath Tagore, *Towards Universal Man*, p. 234.

18. For decades following the establishment of the Soka Gakkai (1930), it wholeheartedly supported the Nichiren Shoshu priesthood, building hundreds of temples and restoring the head temple. The crux of the priesthood's motives, however, lay in its view that priests are necessary intermediaries between lay believers and the teachings of Nichiren Buddhism. The priests sought to make veneration and obedience to themselves the keys to a practitioner's faith. They taught, for example, that the high priest is absolute; without unquestioningly following the high priest, practitioners cannot attain enlightenment. In contrast, the Soka Gakkai bases itself directly on the spirit and intent of Nichiren as set forth in his writings.

19. Mohandas Gandhi, *All Men Are Brothers* (New York: Continuum Publishing Co., 1980, 2011), p. 91.

20. Ibid., p. 65.

21. Quoted in Daisaku Ikeda, 'Laying the Foundations for Victory One Hundred Years Ahead', in *Embracing Compassion: A Revolution in Leadership*, vol. 1 (Santa Monica, CA: World Tribune Press, 2009), p. 50.

22. See Daisaku Ikeda, 'Mahayana Buddhism and Twenty-First-Century Civilisation', in *A New Humanism: The University Addresses of Daisaku Ikeda* (London: I.B.Tauris & Co. Ltd, 2010), pp. 165–75.

23. John Dewey, *A Common Faith* (New Haven and London: Yale University Press, 1934), p. 47.

5. *Children's Rights*

1. The exhibition has been shown from 2006 to 2015 in 205 venues in Japan and drawn 1.2 million visitors.

2. The exhibition *Treasuring the Future: Children's Rights and Realities* first opened in June 1996 at the SGI-USA New York Culture

Center. It was developed to commemorate the fiftieth anniversary of UNICEF.

3. Ralph Waldo Emerson, *Lectures and Biographical Sketches, The Complete Works*, vol. x, intr. Edward Waldo Emerson (Boston and New York: Houghton Mifflin Company, 1883, 1904), pp. 153–4.

4. 'SGI Exhibit Opens at UN Headquarters', *SGI Newsletter* No. 5895 (12 February 2004). For more information on the Universal Declaration of Rights for Children (promoted by the World Centers of Compassion for Children), go to http://www.centers ofcompassion.org/universal-declaration-of-rights-for-children. php, accessed 10 September 2013.

5. In March 2002, Ambassador Chowdhury was appointed by UN Secretary-General Kofi Annan (demise in August 2018) as the first Under-Secretary-General and High Representative for the Least Developed Countries, Landlocked Developing Countries and Small Island Developing States, in the UN General Assembly created new office (UN-OHRLLS) for the most vulnerable countries of the world. He served till 2007.

6. United Nations Note No. 5847 (4 Feb. 2004), '"Culture of Peace" Exhibit, Highlighting Contributions of Both Ordinary and Renowned Peace-Builders, to Open on 4 February' (http://www. un.org/press/en/2004/note5847.doc.htm, accessed 1 June 2016).

7. Personal communication.

8. Child Soldiers International (a coalition to stop the use of child soldiers), http://www.child-soldiers.org/global_report_reader. php?id=97, accessed 6 January 2016.

9. Julie A. Mertus and Nancy Flowers, *A Handbook on Women's Human Rights* (New York: Routledge, 2016), p. 99.

10. In 2010, according to a UN report submitted to the Security Council, children were involved in warfare in 22 countries.

11. From the Office of the UN High Commissioner for Human Rights, http://www.ohchr.org/EN/ProfessionalInterest/Pages/ OPACCRC.aspx, accessed 11 September 2013.

12. International Labour Organization, http://www.ilo.org/dyn/

normlex/en/f?p=NORMLEXPUB:12100:0::NO::P12100_ILO_
CODE:C182, accessed 9 September 2013.

13. Red Hand Day is a 'worldwide initiative to stop the use of child
soldiers'. The organization's signature activity occurs each year
on 12 February, when children and young people create red
handprints on paper, which are collected and presented to decision-makers to draw attention to the continuing human rights
tragedy of child soldiers. For more information, see http://www.red
handday.org/index.php?id=4&L=0.

14. Nichiren, *The Writings of Nichiren Daishonin,* vol. I (Tokyo: Soka
Gakkai, 1999), p. 1045.

15. Child Soldiers International (a coalition to stop the use of child
soldiers), http://www.child-soldiers.org/global_report_reader.
php?id=97, accessed 6 January 2016.

16. Dhammapada-avadana Sutra in *The Scriptural Text: Verses of the Doctrine, with Parables*, trans. Charles Willemen (Moraga, CA: Numata
Center for Buddhist Translation and Research, 1999), p. 26.

17. See Dale Kunkel, 'The Effects of Television Violence on Children',
presented during a hearing before the US Senate Committee on
Commerce, Science, and Transportation, 26 June 2007 (http://
www.apa.org/about/gr/pi/advocacy/2008/kunkel-tv.aspx, accessed
6 January 2016).

6. A Constant Renewal of Strength

1. Tagore, *Gitanjali,* pp. 54–5.
2. Daisaku Ikeda, 'Directing the Spiritual Current of Humanity
toward the Rejection of Violence', *SGI Newsletter*, No. 2852
(Tokyo: Soka Gakkai International, 4 July 1996), pp. 2–3.
3. Since January 2011, the number is 48.
4. *See* UNICEF press release, 'Children Out of Sight, Out of Mind,
Out of Reach', 14 December 2005 (http://www.unicef.org/
sowc06/press/release.php, accessed 5 January 2016).
5. Daisaku Ikeda, *Youth and the Writings of Nichiren Daishonin* (Santa
Monica, CA: World Tribune Press, 2012), p. 146.

6. Statement by Ambassador Anwarul K. Chowdhury, permanent representative of Bangladesh to the United Nations at the 51st session of the UN General Assembly, 17 October 1996.

7. Joseph Rotblat and Daisaku Ikeda, *A Quest for Global Peace: Rotblat and Ikeda on War, Ethics and the Nuclear Threat* (London: I.B.Tauris & Co. Ltd, 2007).

8. Janusz Korczak, *Jak kochac dzieci* (How to Love a Child) Part I: Warsaw, 1919; Part II: Warsaw, 1920. English translation in *Selected Works of Janusz Korczak*, ed. Martin Wollins, trans. Jerzy Backrach (Springfield, VA: Department of Agriculture, 1967).

9. Ibid., p. 240.

10. Ibid., p. 254.

11. Translated from Japanese. *Tsunesaburo Makiguchi zenshu* (Complete Works of Tsunesaburo Makiguchi) (Tokyo: Daisanbunmei-sha, 1983), vol. 6, p. 14.

12. Quoted in Alan B. Krueger, *What Makes a Terrorist: Economics and the Roots of Terrorism* (Princeton, NJ: Princeton University Press, 2008), p. 2.

13. In this case, the treaty is first signed by individual states, indicating the state's preliminary endorsement. While signing does not commit a state to ratification, it does oblige the state to refrain from acts that would defeat or undermine the treaty's objectives. Ratification comes when the appropriate ruling organ of the country's parliament, senate, crown, head of state or government formally agrees to be a party to the treaty and to be legally bound by its terms. The provisions of the treaty determine the date on which the treaty enters into force, typically at a specified time following its ratification by a fixed number of states. For example, the Convention on the Rights of the Child entered into force on 2 September 1990, 30 days after 20 states had ratified it.

14. Japan's Okayama Medical Center was certified as the first baby-friendly hospital (BFH) in the developed world in 1991. Since then, the Japan Breastfeeding Association has received a mandate from WHO/UNICEF to certify Japanese BFHs. See 'Japanese

trends in breastfeeding rate in baby-friendly hospitals between 2007 and 2010', http://www.ncbi.nlm.nih.gov/pmc/articles/PMC4225712/, accessed 20 May 2016.

15. Now USA is the only country which has not become a party of the Convention on the Rights of the Child after Somalia ratified.

16. Tagore, *Towards Universal Man*, p. 323.

17. A new and third Optional Protocol of the Convention on the Rights of the Child on a Communications Procedure was adopted by the United Nations' General Assembly on 19 December 2011 and entered into force on 14 April 2014.

18. Hazel Henderson, Daisaku Ikeda, *Planetary Citizenship: Your Values, Beliefs and Actions Can Shape a Sustainable World* (Santa Monica, CA: Middleway Press, 2004).

19. Ibid., p. 138.

20. Convention on the Rights of the Child, http://www2.ohchr.org/english/law/crc.htm, accessed 1 June 2016.

21. Declaration of the Rights of the Child (1959), http://www.cirp.org/library/ethics/UN-declaration/, accessed 2 June 2016.

7. An Effective United Nations

1. Nichiren, *The Writings of Nichiren Daishonin*, vol. I, p. 279.

2. BRICS is the acronym for an association of five major emerging national economies: Brazil, Russia, India, China and South Africa. With the possible exception of Russia, the BRICS members are all developing or newly industrialized countries. They are all distinguished by their large, fast-growing economies and significant influence on regional and global affairs.

3. According to the United Nations, the Least Developed Countries represent the poorest and weakest segment of the international community. They comprise more than 880 million people (about 12 per cent of world population), but account for less than 2 per cent of world GDP and about 1 per cent of global trade in goods. The UN General Assembly officially established the category of

LDCs in 1971. The current list of LDCs includes 48 countries (the newest member being South Sudan); 34 in Africa, 13 in Asia and the Pacific and 1 in Latin America. See http://unohrlls.org/about-ldcs/, accessed 1 June 2016.

4. Starting in 1983, Daisaku Ikeda began composing peace proposals and sending them annually to the United Nations on 26 January, SGI Day, the anniversary of the 1975 founding of the Soka Gakkai International. These proposals offer perspectives on critical issues facing humanity, suggesting solutions and responses grounded in Buddhist humanism. They also put forth specific agendas to strengthen the United Nations, including avenues for the involvement of civil society.

5. Nichiren, *The Writings of Nichiren Daishonin,* vol. I, p. 24.

6. Inter Press Service: 'World Needs a Global Culture of Human Rights' (28 Mar. 2008), http://www.daisakuikeda.org/sub/resources/interview/interview2/200803-ips-interview.html, accessed 2 June 2016.

7. Ibid.

8. The Congress of Humanity

1. As of 2016, Ikeda Center publications have been used in more than 900 courses at more than 275 colleges and universities.

2. On 20 February 2014, the United Nations Alliance of Civilizations sponsored a book launching at the UN Headquarters for *A Forum for Peace,* the compilation of excerpts from President Ikeda's peace proposals submitted to the United Nations annually since 1983. Nobel Peace laureate Betty Williams offered the keynote address. Ambassador Nassir Abdulaziz Al-Nasser, High Representative for the Alliance of Civilizations, also spoke (See http://www.unaoc.org/2014/02/remarks-by-he-nassir-abdulaziz-al-nasser-the-un-high-representative-for-the-alliance-of-civilizations-at-the-book-launch-and-discussion-of-global-citizenship-the-future-of-the-united-nations/, accessed 3 June 2016), as

did former UN Under-Secretary-General Chowdhury (7 March 2014, World Tribune, p. 1).

3. Ambassador Anwarul Chowdhury, 2006. Vision Statement at the international conference on Transforming the United Nations: Human Development, Regional Conflicts, and Global Governance in a Post-Westphalian World, sponsored by Toda Institute for Global Peace and Policy Research, 4–5 February, in Los Angeles, USA.

4. See Daisaku Ikeda, 'Fulfilling the Mission: Empowering the UN to Live Up to the World's Expectations', in *A Forum for Peace*, ed. Olivier Urbain (London: I.B.Tauris & Co Ltd, 2014), pp. 3–143.

5. Joseph Rotblat and Daisaku Ikeda, *A Quest for Global Peace: Rotblat and Ikeda on War, Ethics, and the Nuclear Threat* (London: I.B.Tauris, 2007), p. 110.

6. See *Gandhi on Non-Violence: Selected Texts from Mohandas K. Gandhi's Non-Violence in Peace and War*, ed. Thomas Merton (New York: New Directions, 1964), p. 24.

9. *To Protect the Vulnerable*

1. New York, 24 October 2008 – Secretary-General's opening remarks to the press on the Chief Executive Board's Response to the Global Financial Crisis, http://www.un.org/apps/sg/sgstats. asp?nid=3497, accessed 6 November 2008.

2. See International Monetary Fund, *Global Monitoring Report 2010: The MDGs after the Crisis*, p. 13 (https://www.imf.org/external/ pubs/ft/gmr/2010/eng/gmr.pdf, accessed 8 January 2016).

3. Stand Up and Take Action is an annual global event encouraged by the UN Millennium Campaign and the Global Call to Action against Poverty. It is one response to the Millennium Declaration signed by 189 Member States in October 2002. Participation is held regionally and may include concerts, marches, public gatherings of banging spoons on metal plates, church bells ringing simultaneously throughout a nation, or

local musicians performing in innovative locations. The UN Millennium Campaign encourages participants to record the events and report their results to the campaign. It started in October 2006, with more than 23.5 million people in 80 countries.

4. As of 2011, the Least Developed Countries numbered 48, with 33 in Africa, and had a population of 880 million.

5. The eight Millennium Development Goals were established in 2000, with a target date of 2015. The goals included: 1) Eradicate extreme poverty and hunger; 2) Achieve universal primary education; 3) Promote gender equality and empower women; 4) Reduce child mortality; 5) Improve maternal health; 6) Combat HIV/ADS, malaria, and other diseases; 7) Ensure environmental sustainability; and 8) Develop a global partnership for development. The final report of the MDG Gap Task Force ('Taking Stock of the Global Partnership for Development') is available at http://www.un.org/millenniumgoals/pdf/MDG_Gap_2015_E_web.pdf. By 2015, world leaders launched the 2030 Agenda for Sustainable Development in 2016 to continue the momentum of the original MDGs. The new agenda calls on countries to achieve 17 Sustainable Development Goals in the following 15 years.

6. Daisaku Ikeda's 2008 peace proposal to the United Nations is titled 'Humanizing Religion, Creating Peace.' See ed. Urbain, *A Forum for Peace*.

7. M. S. Swaminathan and Daisaku Ikeda, *Revolutions: to Green the Environment, to Grow the Human Heart* (Chennai: East West Books [Madras] Pvt., 2005), p. 53.

8. 12 March 2006, *Seikyo Shimbun* (Tokyo: Soka Gakkai, 2006). *Seikyo Shimbun* is the daily Japanese-language publication of the Soka Gakkai.

9. *The Lotus Sutra and Its Opening and Closing Sutras*, trans. Burton Watson (Tokyo: Soka Gakkai, 2009), p. 232.

10. Ralph Waldo Emerson, 'Power', in *Essays and Lectures*, ed. Joel Porte (New York: The Library of America, 1983), p. 982.

11. *Human Security Now* (New York: Commission on Human Security, 2003), p. 134.
12. Rabindranath Tagore, *The English Writings of Rabindranath Tagore*, vol. 2: Poems, intr. Mohit K. Ray (New Delhi: Atlantic, 2007), p. 432.

10. Redefining Development

1. See United Nations Development Programme, Human Development Report 2007/2008: Fighting Climate Change: Human Solidarity In a Divided World (New York: UNDP, 2007), http://hdr.undp.org/sites/default/files/reports/268/hdr_20072008_en_complete.pdf.
2. Nichiren, *The Writings of Nichiren Daishonin*, vol. II, p. 850.
3. See United Nations Development Programme, *Human Development Report 2007/2008: Fighting Climate Change: Human Solidarity In a Divided World* (New York: UNDP, 2007), http://hdr.undp.org/sites/default/files/reports/268/hdr_20072008_en_complete.pdf, accessed 10 June 2016.
4. Ibid.
5. Ibid., p. 72.
6. Daisaku Ikeda, *Soka Education: For the Happiness of the Individual* (Santa Monica, CA: Middleway Press, 2010), p. 36.
7. Mahbub ul Haq, *Reflections on Human Development* (New York: Oxford University Press, 1995), p. 116.
8. Ibid., p. 39.
9. The *Human Development Report* is an independent, annual publication commissioned by the United Nations Development Programme. It was initiated in 1990 by Pakistani economist Mahbub ul Haq and Indian Nobel laureate Amartya Sen. Its goal is to place people at the centre of the development process in terms of economic debate, policy and advocacy.
10. See Daisaku Ikeda, 'Fulfilling the Mission: Empowering the UN to Live Up to the World's Expectations' (August 2006 peace proposal) in ed. Urbain, *A Forum for Peace*, pp. 3–143.

11. The Uncarved Block: In 1952, the UN Meditation Room opened at the UN Headquarters as a permanent sanctuary for prayer and meditation. In 1956, Dag Hammarskjold undertook the complete redesign of the room. When it reopened, a six-and-a-half-ton triangular block of crystalline iron ore from a Swedish mine dominated the room. The polished top is lit by a single beam of light from a hidden source in the ceiling. Hammarskjold wrote: 'In a room of this kind in a house of this character we could not use any kind of symbols with which man has been used to link his religious feelings ... What we had at the back of our minds was something which is said, I believe, in one of Buddha's scripts – that the significance of the vessel is not the shell but the void ... We had to create a room of stillness with perhaps one or two very simple symbols, light and light striking on stone. ... That is the only symbol in the room – a meeting of the light of the sky and the earth.' Dag Hammarskjöld, *Markings,* trans. Leif Sjoberg and W. H. Auden (New York: Alfred A. Knopf, 1964, 2003), p. 159.

12. 'Attacking Poverty: Opportunity, Empowerment, and Security', World Development Report 2000/2001, http://siteresources.worldbank.org/INTPOVERTY/Resources/WDR/overview.pdf, accessed 31 October 2008.

13. Amartya Sen, *Development as Freedom* (New York: Oxford University Press, 1999), p. 53.

14. Amartya Sen authored a book by this title, published by Oxford University Press in 1999.

15. The Non-Aligned Movement refers to a group of states that are neither aligned with or against any power bloc. The organization was founded in Belgrade in 1961 and, as of 2012, includes 120 members.

16. They met in Tokyo on 19 December 1993.

17. Rabindranath Tagore, *The English Writings of Rabindranath Tagore,* vol. 4, Poems, Plays, Essays, ed. Nityapriya Ghosh (New Delhi: Sahitya Akademi, 2007), pp. 100–101.

11. No Peace Without Women

1. Rabindranath Tagore, *The English Writings of Rabindranath Tagore,* vol. 4, Essays, ed. Mohit Kumar Ray (New Delhi: Atlantic Publishers & Dist., 2007), p. 433.
2. *The Sutta-Nipata,* trans. H. Saddhatissa (London: Curzon Press Ltd., 1998), p. 16.
3. Henderson and Ikeda, *Planetary Citizenship,* p. 134.
4. Swaminathan and Ikeda, *Revolutions,* p. 95.
5. Elise Boulding and Daisaku Ikeda, *Into Full Flower: Making Peace Cultures Happen* (Boston: Dialogue Path Press, 2010), p. 68.
6. *The Lion's Roar of Queen Shrimala: a Buddhist Scripture on the Tathagatagarbha Theory,* ed. Alex Wayman, trans. Alex Wayman and Hideko Wayman (New York: Columbia University Press, 1974), p. 65.
7. Mahatma Gandhi, *All Men are Brothers: Autobiographical Reflections,* ed. Krishna Kripalani (New York: Continuum International Publishing Group, 1980), p. 146.
8. From the 8 March 2000, statement issued on behalf of the UN Security Council: https://www.un.org/events/women/press.htm, accessed 4 September 2013.
9. UN Security Council Resolution 1325: Adopted on 31 October 2000: http://daccess-dds-ny.un.org/doc/UNDOC/GEN/N00/720/18/PDF/N0072018.pdf?OpenElement, accessed 10 September 2013.
10. 'Security Council Resolution on Women and Peace and Security.' *Disarmament Policy* Volume 52 (2000). The Acronym Institute for Disarmament Diplomacy. 28 March 2011. See 'Stronger Decision-making Role for Women in Peace Processes Is Called for In Day-Long UN Security Council Debate', SC6937, http://www.un.org/press/en/2000/sc6937.doc.htm, accessed 22 June 2016.
11. *Integration of the Human Rights of Women and the Gender Perspective: Violence against Women* (New York: United Nations Commission on Human Rights, 2003), p. 9.

12. They met in 1996. Daisaku Ikeda, 'Mrs Karen Olsen de Figueres – Mother of Costa Rica's Former President', *SGI Newsletter*, No. 4589 (Tokyo: Soka Gakkai International, 22 March 2001), p. 8.

13. Ann M. Veneman held the position from 2005 to 2010, and Thoraya Ahmed Obaid from 2000 to 2010.

14. Wilton Park is an international forum for strategic discussion initiated by Winston Churchill. It organizes more than 50 events a year in the United Kingdom and elsewhere, bringing together leading representatives from the worlds of politics, diplomacy, academia, business, civil society, the military and the media to focus on issues of international security, prosperity and justice.

15. See *Human Rights Tribune*, http://www.infosud.org/Post-War-Peace-Building-Still-a,424, accessed 25 September 2013.

16. In July 2010, the United Nations General Assembly created UN Women, the United Nations Entity for Gender Equality and the Empowerment of Women. For more information, see http://www.unwomen.org.

17. Henderson and Ikeda, *Planetary Citizenship*, p. 138.

18. Read Ambassador Chowdhury's elaboration of and commitment to feminism in the Epilogue.

19. A 'Peace Fair' commemorating the tenth anniversary of Resolution 1325 and co-sponsored by several organizations, including the Global Network of Women Peacebuilders and the International Civil Society Action Network, was held from 25–29 October 2010, at the UN Plaza. At the gathering, Ambassador Chowdhury declared that 1325 is a 'common heritage of humanity'. (See http://www.peacewomen.org/content/peace-fair-com memorating-10th-anniversary-united-nations-security-council-resolution-1325).

12. *The Road to Hope*

1. Statement at the graduation ceremony of Soka University, 'Culture of Peace: Beacon of Hope for the New Millennium'.

(See http://www.unohrlls.org/en/orphan/447/, accessed 10 June 2016).

2. Boulding and Ikeda, *Into Full Flower*, p. 7.

3. Kaneko Ikeda, *Kaneko's Story: A Conversation with Kaneko Ikeda* (Santa Monica, CA: World Tribune Press, 2008), p. 98.

4. Daisaku Ikeda, *The New Human Revolution*, vol. 20 (Santa Monica, CA: World Tribune Press, 2010), p. 36.

5. Nichiren, *The Writings of Nichiren Daishonin*, vol. I, p. 319.

6. 11 September 1998, The New Human Revolution, p. 8.

7. In 2014, Ambassador and Mrs Chowdhury were blessed with a fifth grandchild and fourth granddaughter by their youngest son and his wife.

13. *The School of Life*

1. Daisaku Ikeda, 'Fulfilling the Mission: Empowering the UN to Live Up to the World's Expectations', in *A Forum for Peace*, p. 22, the first time he calls for 'a UN decade of action by the world's people for nuclear abolition'.

2. Statement by Ambassador Anwarul K. Chowdhury titled 'Culture of Peace: Beacon of Hope for the new Millennium' (Tokyo, 19 March 2003). See http://unohrlls.org/meetings-conferen ces-and-special-events/statement-at-the-ceremony-of-the-soka-university-culture-of-peace-beacon-of-hope-for-the-new-millen nium/, accessed 15 June 2016.

3. In the Soka Gakkai, the Women's Peace Committee and other groups have steadily worked to plant in society the culture of peace. As of printing, the exhibition *Women and the Culture of Peace* has been seen by 970,000 people in 29 cities throughout Japan, and another exhibition, *Children and the Culture of Peace*, by 880,000 people in 128 cities. In addition, 200,000 people have participated in peace-culture forums held in more than 300 locales. In May 2010, in connection with the NPT (Treaty on the Non-Proliferation of Nuclear Weapons) Review Conference, SGI

youth representatives presented to the United Nations a petition signed by 2,270,000 people calling for the abolition of nuclear weapons.

4. Curriculum at Soka University of America is conducted through learning clusters. Since 2008, students in Ambassador Chowdhury's learning cluster on 'The Culture of Peace' have studied the historical background and conceptual context of the culture of peace and its evolution within the United Nations. There is significant focus on the role of individuals in advancing the culture of peace, especially that of young people and that of women. Students have also studied the elements of forgiveness, dialogue and reconciliation.

5. Rabindranath Tagore, 'Unconquered' in *The Herald of Spring: poems from Mohua,* trans. Aurobindo Bose (London: John Murray, 1957), p. 33.

6. Nichiren, *The Writings of Nichiren Daishonin,* vol. I, p. 471.

7. Gandhi, *All Men Are Brothers,* p. 168.

8. Mohandas Gandhi, Richard Attenborough & Johanna McGeary, *The Words of Gandhi* (New York: Newmarket Press, 2008), p. 45.

9. Nichiren, *The Writings of Nichiren Daishonin,* vol. II, p. 844.

10. Ibid., p. 86.

14. Opening the Book of the World

1. Tsunesaburo Makiguchi, *Education for Creative Living: Ideas and Proposals of Tsunesaburo Makiguchi,* trans. Alfred Birnbaum; ed. Dayle M. Bethel (Ames, Iowa: Iowa State University Press, 1989), p. 10.

2. Cora Weiss, 'Inventing Peace' (see http://www.opendemocracy. net/faith-iraqwarphiloshophy/article_1799.jsp; accessed 30 September 2013).

3. Victory Over Violence first launched in 1999. In 2009, the movement was reinvigorated with a redesigned website and several events in Hawaii, starting with a lecture at Punahou

School on the culture of peace by Dr Lawrence Carter, dean of the Martin Luther King Jr. International Chapel at Morehouse College. The VOV mission statement reads: 'To inspire people, especially young people to identify and counteract the root causes of violence in their lives, homes, schools, and local communities through awareness, introspection, individual empowerment and a creative commitment to dialogue and action.' For more information, see www.vov.com.

4. The Soka Education Conference, an annual student-driven conference, is intended to explore the values and ideas of Soka education. Each year, the Soka Education Student Research Project at Soka University of America invites a wide spectrum of people, from SUA students, alumni and faculty to community members, to share their studies, experiences, and applications of Soka education pedagogy and humanistic education in traditional and non-traditional spheres. (For more information, see http://www.soka.edu/student_life/student-activities/soka-education-student-research-project/soka-education-confer ence-.aspx.)

5. A fifth grandchild is added. See Note 7 of Chapter Twelve.

6. *The Collected Works of Mahatma Gandhi,* vol. 48 (New Delhi: The Director Publications Division Ministry of Information & Broadcasting Government of India, 1971), p. 240.

7. 'It Doesn't Have to be That Way: Interview with Betty Reardon.' *SGI Quarterly: A Buddhist Forum for Peace, Culture and Education.* April 2008. 1 April 2011.

8. Tagore, *The English Writings,* vol. 3, p. 523.

Index